AF352667

To Fix a National Character

To Fix a National Character

*The United States in the
First Barbary War, 1800–1805*

ABIGAIL G. MULLEN

Johns Hopkins University Press

Baltimore

Printed in the United States of America on acid-free paper

2   4   6   8   9   7   5   3   1

Johns Hopkins University Press
2715 North Charles Street
Baltimore, Maryland 21218
www.press.jhu.edu

Library of Congress Cataloging-in-Publication Data

Names: Mullen, Abigail G., author.
Title: To fix a national character : the United States in the First
Barbary War, 1801–1805 / Abigail G. Mullen.
Description: Baltimore : Johns Hopkins University Press, 2024. | Includes
bibliographical references.
Identifiers: LCCN 2023049729 | ISBN 9781421449265 (hardcover) |
ISBN 9781421449272 (ebook)
Subjects: LCSH: United States—History—Tripolitan War, 1801–1805. |
United States—Foreign relations—1783–1815. | United States—Foreign relations—
Africa, North. | Africa, North—Foreign relations—United States.
Classification: LCC E335 .M88 2024 | DDC 973.4/7—dc23/eng/20240206
LC record available at https://lccn.loc.gov/2023049729

A catalog record for this book is available from the British Library.

*Special discounts are available for bulk purchases of this book. For more information,
please contact Special Sales at specialsales@jh.edu.*

For Lincoln, who believes in me

CONTENTS

I finished the dissertation that became this book in April 2017. While writing the dissertation, and in the more than six years since then, I've accrued debts to a lot of people who helped to shepherd this book into existence. Some of those people I've never met and likely never will—the many, many people who have worked to digitize and make publicly available many primary source collections at the Library of Congress, the National Archives, the University of Virginia, the American Naval Records Society, and more. Without the digitization of these multiple thousands of pages of navy, consular, and personal records, this book wouldn't exist. A few people digitized things just for me—for example, the librarians at the Houghton Library at Harvard (though I didn't end up citing any of the papers they digitized for me). I want to acknowledge in particular Kate Hanson Plass at the Longfellow House National Historic Site, who digitized Henry Wadsworth's magnificent and poignant letterbook and journal for me.

Many scholars have read pieces of this work and provided commentary. I am grateful to my dissertation committee, Bill Fowler, Heather Streets-Salter, and Ben Schmidt, who not only helped to bring the dissertation to fruition but have checked in on the progress of the book as well. Christopher McKee, whose work has long been my gold standard for early American naval writing, provided comments on the manuscript at various stages and offered helpful advice on how to structure the book, as well as sending me to new collections of source materials. Fred Leiner, another historian whose work I have admired for a long time, likewise encouraged me to think about some of my arguments in a different way. The scholars who participated in the Microhistory and the USA in the World symposium at UCL in May 2023, though they didn't read any of the book itself, provided comments on a related piece that have made this book stronger as well. And various audiences at conferences have heard small pieces of my arguments throughout the past several years and provided valuable feedback.

I have been fortunate to have colleagues at several institutions who provided feedback and encouragement throughout the writing of this book. I am grateful for the community of graduate students at Northeastern University and for my colleagues at George Mason University, especially at the Roy Rosenzweig Center for History and New Media. Though most of my work at GMU did not relate to this book, I'm truly grateful for my team on the Tropy project, who took almost all of my self-interested suggestions for making the software more usable for my own research, and for my R2 Studios podcast teams, who helped me to refine my skills in narrative writing for *Consolation Prize*, which is certainly the intellectual child of this book.

I am especially grateful to my colleagues at the United States Naval Academy. I arrived at USNA ready to hit *send* on the revisions to the book. I'm grateful to my chair, Tom McCarthy, and associate chair, BJ Armstrong, for convincing me to slow down. It's beyond dispute that the book is better for having had another year to develop. In addition to giving me time to make it better, my colleagues also gave me valuable feedback on parts or all of the manuscript. I'm grateful to all who provided comments on the two works-in-progress sessions I participated in. Ernie Tucker always took time to answer my questions about Turkish words, customs, and geography, and he helped me on numerous occasions to choose the proper terms for Turkish officials and documents (any mistakes that are still in the book are of course my own fault). Claude Berube and Sondra Duplantis at the USNA Museum let me look at amazing sources like the logbook of the USS *Constitution* and Stephen Decatur's charts of the Mediterranean. BJ Armstrong helped me decipher handwriting and wrestle with strategy conundrums. Ryan Mewett read every word of the manuscript.

I'm also grateful for those who have contributed to making the book a reality in its present form. In particular, I'm thankful for Laura Davulis at Johns Hopkins University Press, who has believed in the project from the beginning. I'm also grateful to Nat Case, who made the maps.

Some debts are personal rather than professional. My family and friends have supported me through significant personal and professional challenges. Many have asked about the progress of the book and encouraged me to keep at it. I'm especially grateful for my friend Deborah Bitzer, who has given me a huge amount of emotional support for the past ten years.

My husband, Lincoln, a historian, not only gave me his expert historical skills but also encouraged me when I felt like this was a hopeless project and affirmed me when I felt like maybe I was saying something worth saying. He has been a true partner in every sense of the word and my biggest supporter. Likewise, my children, who often demanded my attention when I was trying to work, nevertheless have evinced an unfailing interest in what I do and an unwavering certainty that I'm good at it. They've read parts of the book out loud to me, listened to me read silly stories from my sources, demanded to know more about the characters in this tale, and a dozen other things that have made the process of writing the book better. I couldn't have done this without Lincoln, Maggie, and Paul, nor would I have wanted to.

Most of the sources referenced in this book are published somewhere, either in edited volumes, document collections, or online. Some of these documents I looked at in person in a physical archive; some I never did. But it's important for books like mine to be transparent about the possibility of doing research that doesn't require long trips to faraway archives—in fact, almost every document I looked at in a physical archive I later found digitized. So when I use a source that I found in multiple places, I have chosen to cite the online collections such as *Founders Online* instead of the manuscripts in the National Archives, in part because I accessed the source online at some point and in part to make the trail of my research easier to follow if you choose to do so. The bulk of the sources in this book come from the excellent six-volume document collection created under the supervision of Captain Dudley W. Knox in the late 1930s and early 1940s. This collection is very nearly comprehensive for documents of relevance for the First Barbary War. But even this collection I accessed virtually, through the digitized copy provided by the American Naval Records Society.

As more and more primary and secondary sources appear online, it is important that we acknowledge the labor that goes into the digitization of those materials by citing the location of these sources properly, and it is also important that we acknowledge the ways in which we actually do our work.

When I have quoted from sources that I found in manuscript, I have tried to be faithful to the punctuation and spelling as I saw it (many of the published and digitized works have been cleaned up for legibility). In most cases, I have chosen in the body text to use the more modern spellings of names in cases where the historical actors were divided on which to use (e.g., "Livorno" instead of "Leghorn"). For names that have been transliterated from a non-Latin alphabet, such as the names of almost all the North African officials, I have tried to rely on good sense and the advice of those who know Arabic better than I in order to render their names into something both recognizable to readers of Arabic but also not too far from how the Americans referred to them (e.g., I have retained the spelling of "Hamet," because that is almost invariably how the Americans refer to Hamet Karamanli, but I have chosen the spelling "Yusuf" rather than "Joseph" or "Jusuf" for Hamet's brother, whose name appears in all of these forms in the American correspondence).

To Fix a National Character

Introduction

On the campus of the United States Naval Academy stands a monument—the oldest military monument in the United States, erected in 1806—with six names on it: Somers, Caldwell, Decatur, Wadsworth, Dorsey, Israel. As one side of the monument recounts, these six men were killed in "the different attacks that were made on the city of Tripoli in the Year of our Lord 1804." The monument provides little additional information about them or about the war that brought the navy to the city of Tripoli in 1804.[1] Perhaps the most telling line inscribed on the monument is this: "commerce laments their fall." From the perspective of the officers who commissioned this monument to honor their fallen comrades, the attacks on Tripoli were an effort to allow the United States to trade freely in the Mediterranean. But commercial freedom was just one part of a much bigger project for the United States: full integration into the community of nations that traversed the sea.

This book is the story of that war, the First Barbary War, fought from 1801 to 1805. I use this term advisedly, rather than the First Tripolitan War or the War against Tripoli, because it truly was a war that encompassed all four Barbary states. Simply by behaving toward the United States as they behaved toward the older nations of Europe, these states helped establish the US Navy and American diplomatic relations with nations all over Europe and North Africa. Sometimes American historians talk about the First Barbary War as a conflict that primarily involves the protagonist United States versus the antagonist Tripoli, and the rest of the world is just a series of bit players. But in reality, the United States and Tripoli were only a tiny part of a system that encompassed centuries-old fights between European continental powers and as well as centuries-old economic structures.

On July 4, 1776, when the United States officially declared its independence, American merchants suffered a critical blow: they could no longer count on the protection of the British Royal Navy. Not only might American merchant vessels face attack by the British themselves, but they were now vulnerable to any other country or group at odds with the United States. After 1783, when the Peace of Paris was signed, the merchant ships of the United States were truly unprotected.

In the years after the American Revolution, the list of nations at odds with the United States was substantial. Great Britain and France headed the list, though for different reasons. Great Britain, though it lost the American Revolution, sometimes did not behave as though the United States was a sovereign nation. The Royal Navy needed men to crew its vessels for war with France in the 1790s, and its leadership thought nothing of stopping American ships to take off British subjects (or erstwhile British subjects).[2] In addition, border disputes in the western United States and American suspicions that the British were manipulating Indigenous people against the Americans led to tensions between Great Britain and the United States. The United States also alienated its closest ally, France. After the French Revolution in 1789, the United States refused to honor the agreements signed with France during the American Revolution, preferring to remain neutral in the French revolutionary conflicts. In response, the French began capturing American ships in the Caribbean, eventually leading to the Quasi-War with France from 1798 to 1800.

But one group occupied an outsized place in the fears of the American maritime community: the Barbary states. They were a group of loosely affiliated states on the coast of North Africa. Three of them—Algiers, Tunis, and Tripoli—owed nominal allegiance to the Ottoman Empire. One, Morocco, was an independent sultanate. These four states had practiced a system of privateering, sometimes characterized as piracy by observers at the time and historians since, for hundreds of years. They demanded payment, both annual and unscheduled, from all the nations who traded in the Mediterranean, in exchange for leaving those nations' commercial ships alone. The treaties that determined the amount of the payments were renegotiated frequently as the Barbary rulers changed the terms. The annuities did not function simply as bribes or tribute. Rather, they took the form of both money and naval stores, so in reality, all the nations that had treaties with the Barbary states were subsidizing their attacks on other nations.

In 1784 Morocco captured an American ship, the first American casualty to the Barbary system; however, Morocco seemed to want friendship with the United States. This capture was a not-so-subtle attempt to get the attention of the US government, and once the United States sent a negotiator to create a treaty of amity, the Moroccan government released the ship and its crew.[3] In 1785, unconvinced that a standing navy upheld the principles of the new republic, the US government sold off the last ship of the Continental Navy. That same year, Algerian corsairs (essentially privateers) captured two American ships, the *Maria* and the *Dauphin*. The captives from these two vessels remained in captivity for more than ten years, joined periodically by prisoners from new captures. Over the next fifteen years, Algiers formed the largest American concern, the other three states of only secondary importance. Initially, United States officials believed that the Barbary threat in the Mediterranean was significant—in fact, in 1790 Thomas Jefferson believed that American trade in the Mediterranean had come to a complete standstill because of the fear of Barbary capture.[4] This was not quite true—there were certainly still Americans in the Mediterranean. But it's impossible to estimate what trade might have been like in a different world. Between 1785, when the *Maria* and *Dauphin* were taken, and 1815, at the conclusion of the Second Barbary War, the four Barbary states captured a total of 35 American vessels. Algiers alone was responsible for 22 of those captures. Around 700 sailors were captured.[5]

The threat of capture was terrifying enough for the newly unprotected American merchants and crews in the 1780s and 1790s. During the 1790s, the French captured hundreds of American ships before and during the Quasi-War, and the British captured dozens. Though historians do not have a clear picture of the trade volume in the Mediterranean, 35 ships seems like a very small number to be concerned with in comparison to hundreds. But capture by a Barbary vessel was especially terrible, because unlike a French or British capture, sailors would not simply be given their parole or be put into prison—they would be enslaved and forced to work for the Barbary ruler until they could be redeemed. So while the threat of capture by an Algerian, Tripolitan, Tunisian, or Moroccan vessel was significantly lower than the threat of British or French capture, it inspired a great deal more fear. These fears were stoked by the publication of captivity narratives and other forms of literary output that painted the Barbary states as places of unredeemable ferocity and cruelty, where the differences between white-skinned Europeans or Americans and brown-skinned Muslim North Africans led to even greater suffering. These kinds of tales had circulated in North America and Europe since at least the beginning of the eighteenth century.[6]

Thus, when Congress took up the question of rebuilding a navy in the 1790s, the Barbary states were at the forefront of consideration. Merchants could not defend themselves easily, but with a navy, quashing the Barbary problem seemed almost simple. The Naval Armament Act of 1794 authorized the construction of six frigates—four of 44 guns and two of 36 guns. These frigates seemed like more than enough firepower to bring the Barbary states to heel. In fact, the act explicitly tied the construction program to the trouble with Algiers. If peace in the Mediterranean were restored, the program could be stopped.[7]

Meanwhile, American diplomats made forays to the Barbary states to try to negotiate treaties the old-fashioned way—by paying money. When the United States entered into the Barbary system of tribute or annuities, it was joining a centuries-long practice. Nearly every nation in the Mediterranean had treaties with the Barbary states. But it was not because the Barbary states were invincible, but rather because they served a useful purpose. For instance, the British had long paid the annuities demanded, not because they were unable to mount a naval defense but because it was politically expedient to give the Barbary states the chance to focus on other targets, such as their centuries-old foes, the French, or, more likely, the smaller European powers such as the Italian states or the states of Scandinavia. And to them (and the Barbary states), the United States was one of those smaller powers.

The Americans' first order of business was redeeming the captives in Algiers, who assisted in negotiations while they were still captive. In particular, two of the captives played a leading role: Richard O'Brien and James Leander Cathcart. The redemption of captives led to the establishment of commercial treaties with each of the Barbary states. Morocco had signed a treaty first, in 1784. Algiers came to terms in 1795, Tripoli in 1796, and Tunis in 1797. Taking into account the treaties eventually signed with each of the four Barbary states, the United States paid out about $1.25 million, which was equivalent to one-fifth of one year's federal budget.[8] By 1797 the United States had sent back the former captives O'Brien and Cathcart as consular representatives. O'Brien went to Algiers as consul general, and Cathcart went to Tripoli. Indian fighter William Eaton was appointed consul to Tunis. Congress appointed James Simpson, a British merchant already serving as US consul in Gibraltar, to the post of consul in Tangier.

But the peaces created in these initial treaties were very fragile. The consuls were responsible for fulfilling the terms of the treaties, an especially challenging task since the United States did not produce the promised annuities with the speed that the Barbary rulers expected. Meanwhile, the brand-new US Navy went to the Caribbean to fight the French instead of sailing for the Mediterranean. The attention of the US government was divided, and the battle for even having a navy was by no means over.[9] It was clear by 1800, though, that the navy needed to go to the Mediterranean to fend off whatever threats might exist.

When the bashaw of Tripoli declared war on the United States in May 1801, the US Navy was already on its way.

The United States was entering the Mediterranean at a time when the region was in turmoil. The French Revolutionary Wars spilled over into the fight against Napoleon Bonaparte, and most nations of Europe were caught up in the conflagration. In some ways, this moment was advantageous for the United States—some thought the Europeans were too busy fighting each other to spend much time harassing the Americans. But in other ways, it was singularly unfortunate: if the antagonism was less pronounced, so too was the European willingness to help the Americans as they fought against the Barbary states. Though the Americans who came to deal with the Barbary problem saw their own conflict as primary and worthy of European focus, in reality this small conflict between a new nation and a tributary nation to the Ottoman Empire was nothing more than a sideshow.

In these conditions, the United States had two main goals. The primary goal was to enter into the Mediterranean community. Though the Americans did not often articulate community entrance as an explicit outcome, they spoke about the war in ways that made the unstated assumption clear, and the actions of the navy often betrayed that community relations were more important than victory over Tripoli. Trade in the Mediterranean was critical to being accepted in the international rhythms of commerce and politics that centered on Europe.[10] Representation in that community indicated that the United States was a fully accepted sovereign nation. So treaties with the Barbary states were, in some ways, a rite of passage—recognition by the Barbary states that the United States was worth having a treaty with. The reverse is also true. The United States wanted to be part of the coalition that pitted European Christians against the Barbary other. Forming treaties with the Barbary states was only a necessary stepping stone to entrance into the European community. But all of the negotiations could theoretically be accomplished without fighting.

Working against this goal was a deep-seated belief by many of the Americans in the fight that the United States was superior to the nations of Europe and North Africa. It offended many American officials that the Barbary states treated the young nation as a lesser power, on the level of Sweden or Naples, rather than Britain or France. The honor of the republic was bound up in being more concerned with fairness, equality, and freedom than the mercantilist nations. Americans viewed the British, in particular, as venal and opportunistic, as they chose to pay off lawbreakers or pirates rather than eradicate them. In 1786 George Washington wrote to the Marquis de Lafayette, "In such an enlightened, in such a liberal age, how is it possible the great maritime powers of Europe should submit to pay an annual tribute to the little piratical States of Barbary.

Would to Heaven we had a navy able to reform those enimies to mankind, or crush them into nonexistence."[11] The United States wanted to take a more forceful stand against the Barbary states than the great powers to prove that not only were they members of the European community, but that they actually shared the top of the food chain as a major power. Despite all the evidence that the United States was in fact a minor power, the Americans persisted in believing they should be treated differently. In order to improve its standing, the United States had to fight.

The Americans struggled to hold these two ideas simultaneously—they wanted more than anything for the United States to be viewed as an established nation with strong international ties, but they often refused to work within the cultural and customary systems that constructed those very ties. Gains in one area were often erased or circumscribed by miscues in others, depending on how much individual actors weighed the value of difference versus the value of commonality. But the goal was always the same: as William Eaton wrote to James Madison in 1802, "It is not only then in Barbary that we are about to fix a national character—it is in the world!"[12]

Because its leaders prioritized entrance into the Mediterranean community, the United States sometimes floundered at its second goal: the defeat of Tripoli. By the time war broke out, many of the naval officers and diplomats in the region, as well as the government back in the United States, seemed to think that the defeat of Tripoli would require little to no effort. At the beginning, they thought that merely showing up off the coast of Tripoli would be sufficient to bring the bashaw—the ruler of Tripoli—to terms. When the bashaw did not capitulate as expected, new strategies had to be put in place, but for nearly the whole war, American naval officers seemed to believe that the United States could easily defeat Tripoli if the weather was better, or if the Tripolitans played fair, or if the supply ships would only arrive faster. Even if all of these things were true, it is equally true that the United States never viewed the bashaw, or for that matter, any of his peers in the other Barbary states, as worthy opponents who could fight on the level of the United States.

The problem with these goals was that the United States could not really achieve them alone. Ironically, in order to prove superiority over the European powers, and achieve victory over Tripoli, the United States was absolutely dependent on those very same European powers, and it could defeat Tripoli only if it kept the peace with the other Barbary states. When the US Navy arrived in the Mediterranean, it found itself in a situation that it had rarely faced before or since. The ports of the United States—Baltimore, New York, Philadelphia, Boston, and others—where the naval yards built and supplied American naval vessels were more than 3,500 miles away. The United States owned no naval bases in the Mediterranean, or indeed anywhere in the world. In order to even stay in the Mediterranean, the navy was at the mercy of its international connections. Commodores had to hone their negotiating skills in order to get the navy into bases like Gibraltar and Malta, and these personal connections became much more important than any high-level diplomatic wrangling by the heads of state.

The lack of bases meant that a great deal of the commodores' time was spent finding places where the US naval vessels could get supplies, repairs, or medical attention. For instance, Gibraltar, the gateway to the Mediterranean, was the logical first stop for American vessels. The British owned that town. The navy had to cultivate good relations with British officials both civilian and naval in order to use the base there. And in some instances, keeping the peace with the British meant accepting injustices that might otherwise have been intolerable, as well as facing the threat of impressment.

The consuls, who had fewer supply needs, were just as dependent on other nations. They needed the consuls of other nations to advocate for them in the courts of the Barbary states or even to speak on their behalf. They needed help in understanding the customary practices that would allow them to gain audiences with the Barbary rulers in the first place.

These are just a few examples of how the United States' goals butted up against its capabilities in the Mediterranean. This book charts the course of the war, from the sending of the first American ship in 1800 to just after the signing of the treaty with Tripoli in 1805, focusing on how the navy and the American consuls and diplomatic agents in the Mediterranean tried to manage these conflicting goals, and also how the realities of the job impacted which goal they were attempting to meet at any given time.

It is important to note what this book is not. First, it is not a book primarily about Thomas Jefferson or his naval policies. Much ink has been spilled already about whether or not Jefferson was pro-navy, but in the day-to-day operations of the Americans in the Mediterranean, it mattered little either way.[13] The philosophy of the officers and consuls in the war area mattered much more than the opinions of the president, for they were the ones who had to act in accordance with their understanding of American principles, and they had little recourse to ask anyone back in the United States for immediate help. As such, this book does not address the history of the war in Washington, DC.

This book also deals only cursorily with all the negotiations that brought the United States to the brink of war with one or more of the Barbary states previous to 1800. Relations with the Barbary states did not have to be bad—Morocco had been the first nation in the world to recognize the sovereignty of the United States during the American Revolution. Things seemed like they were starting well. But when the United States tried to enter the Barbary system, it soon became clear that the Americans lacked both the capital and the diplomatic skill to easily manage their place in that system. Many other historians have written about the struggle to negotiate the treaties, so this book will not focus on that facet of this story.[14]

This book is also not, strictly speaking, an operational naval history. For one thing, there were very few significant naval operations during the war. Instead, the focus is on how the navy interacted with all the others in the Mediterranean. I spend a lot of time discussing all the things that the navy did that were not operational, because in those mundane interactions with others lie the seeds of collaboration, or at least acceptance. And really, the navy and the consular service are co-protagonists of this story—their antagonistic but symbiotic relationship forms the basis for almost all command decisions by both groups. There is no good collective noun for "the navy and the consuls," however, so when I use the term "the Americans," I usually mean the consuls and the naval officers as a unit.

This book is, at its heart, about how specific Americans acted as the representatives of the US government, and how none of them was completely sure what it meant to do so. Each individual officer or consul had his own beliefs about how the war should go, and because of the dispersion of people and resources across the Mediterranean, he often acted on those beliefs without permission or even consultation. The everyday interactions of the navy and consuls went farther to establishing real relationships and developing a shared culture among themselves than any high-level treaty negotiations or official orders. I treat these interactions, mundane though they may be, as just as worthy of notice as the more flashy parts of the war. Moreover, even though not one of these people held a tremendous amount of power by himself, each of them is consequential because he was the first or only to do the things he was doing. Just as George Washington set precedents for the presidency simply by being the president, so many of these men set precedents just by being in the Mediterranean, and their actions helped the other countries of the world form some of their early opinions about Americans and how the United States was going to do business.

Because everything about this situation was so new for the Americans, they had no frame of reference to predict what actions would be consequential and what wouldn't. They were often wrong about which events would change their destiny, but their concerns about those events are no less important for the fact that they proved inconsequential.[15] Often hampered by bad information or no information at all, they acted in ways that they could not see all the ramifications of. Sometimes they made choices that turned out to be foolish or ill-conceived, but sometimes they chose actions that should never have worked and yet somehow did.

To tell this story, I have drawn as much as possible from the recollections of people who served in the Mediterranean, rather than the people who observed from a distance. Several of the commodores left significant correspondence, but we also have the writings of more junior officers whose observations about their surroundings tell us a lot about daily life in the Mediterranean for those who were not in charge. And the consuls wrote an astonishing number of reports to the secretary of state and letters to correspondents all over the Atlantic and Mediterranean. In particular, William Eaton and James Leander Cathcart left a near-comprehensive record of their views about the war, though they emphasize less their day-to-day lives. Though there are fewer non-American observers who wrote extensively about the war, the foreign consuls in Tripoli carried on correspondence with many Americans, and their views are reflected here as well.

Even considering the fairly large volume of sources we have for the history of this war, there are parts of this story that feel incredible—like we're missing key details that would explain why people acted the way they did, and how their actions (or inactions) affected everyone else. For the most part, we have only the American side of this tale, through the eyes of people whose experience was limited and whose prejudices ran deep. We have to take the word of observers who were known to be duplicitous and self-serving, men who would lie to anyone if it improved their situations. We have to try to follow the paths of people who moved around all the time, sometimes seemingly without object (and in fact I've sometimes left out some of the movements because they add little to the narrative). We have to try to trace multiple storylines that all occur simultaneously and sometimes contradict each other.

But from all the chaos of the sources emerges a story that is both compelling and frustrating. Those young men whose names are on the Tripoli monument died without knowing whether the United States would succeed at integrating into the Mediterranean community and defeating Tripoli. When the monument was built in 1806, the officers who commissioned it still may not have known. Despite the peace with Tripoli in 1805, the United States was still paying tribute to Algiers, Tunis, and Morocco. The frigate navy, which had seemed like it was well on its way to permanent status, would be downsized to accommodate Jefferson's gunboat-heavy force focused on defense of the American coast rather than on power projection in the world.[16] The British were still impressing American sailors—if anything, relations were devolving with Britain. On the surface, it seemed like little had changed. But the United States had established a permanent consular presence in many areas of the Mediterranean, including the Barbary states. The navy's young officers had gotten some experience in fighting a war. Though it may have seemed like little progress had been made, the United States had at least not diminished its status in the eyes of the world. And the experiences of this war would set up the United States for the War of 1812 and the subsequent Second Barbary War, which would fully establish the United States as a sovereign nation in the European community.

CHAPTER ONE

A Carrier for a Pirate

Is it not somewhat humiliating that the first United States ship of war which ever entered the Mediterranean should be pressed into the service of a pirate?

—William Eaton, November 10, 1800

To Algiers

The frigate *George Washington* was not the kind of naval vessel the American consuls hoped the government would send to the Mediterranean. Almost since the moment each consul had arrived, he had sent repeated missives to the State Department and whoever else would listen, begging for a show of force in the Mediterranean to check the perceived overweening greed of the Barbary rulers. Two frigates, six frigates, ten ships, the number did not really matter; the only thing that mattered was a demonstration that the United States would not take insults lying down. The government did not necessarily oppose the idea of sending a few ships, but the undeclared naval war with France took up all its time and energy, and no ships could be spared except the *George Washington*, not one of the navy's best or most powerful.[1] And the *George Washington*, which arrived in the Mediterranean in late summer 1800, came not to fight but to pay tribute to Algiers.

The *George Washington* had entered an ecosystem that was at once volatile and stable. The Mediterranean was made up of several parts, but the key divisions for the United States were the European northern half and the North African southwestern half, sometimes called the Maghrib. The United States had little dealings with the other southern areas of the Mediterranean, such as Egypt. The Americans found the North Africans capricious and venal, but the southern

Mediterranean was at least as stable politically as the northern part, at least at the opening of the nineteenth century.[2]

Despite their relative stability, politically speaking, the Barbary states operated outside of what the United States recognized as legitimate legal practice, because of their commitment to corsairing. The corsair economy looked to the United States (and others) like piracy, but the bounds on corsairs were every bit as rigid and comprehensive as the bounds placed on American privateers during the American Revolution. This asymmetric style of warfare highlights the relative place of the Barbary states in the Mediterranean—they seemed like significant actors (and they were), but they were operating from a place of weakness.

The Mediterranean was traversed by a number of states with significant stakes in the area. There were the big ones—the European empires. The middling ones included the Ottomans, the Barbary states, and the Italian states. The small ones were the United States and other nations that had no land in the Mediterranean but engaged in seaborne trade there. The Barbary states occupied an unusual place within this system, exerting significant sea power in the region without either vibrant maritime trade or navies. At some points in the seventeenth and eighteenth centuries, Algiers could almost be called a seapower, according to historian Andrew Lambert's definition—a weak democratic state whose governmental and cultural focus was on the sea.[3] One historian has argued that almost all of the Mediterranean region was made up of weak states that struggled to maintain any control outside a tightly circumscribed urban area.[4] This was certainly true for the Barbary states, but it was also true for most of the European states, whose autonomy was constantly in flux in the early nineteenth century.

The Barbary system of treaties and tribute had been in place for more than two centuries by the time the United States entered it. In the seventeenth century, European states acknowledged the Barbary states as separate from the Ottoman Empire by making treaties directly with them rather than merely making treaties with the Ottomans that covered the actions of the Barbary states, though the Barbary states were still dependencies of (and tributary to) the Ottoman Empire when the United States arrived. The Europeans used their treaties with the Barbary states to establish customs and even legal precedents for the practice of using private ships for state-sanctioned violence.[5] So when the United States began to negotiate, it was entering a well-regulated and tightly bounded system of laws and customs, but it did not acknowledge that fact.

On the flip side, it was true that the Barbary rulers liked to renegotiate treaties or make extra demands that were accompanied by threats that the treaty would be broken if the demands were not met. In the eighteenth century, the heyday of Barbary diplomacy, 51 treaties were negotiated between the Barbary states and the Europeans who traded in the Mediterranean. In total, from the seventeenth through nineteenth centuries, there were 93, including the ones signed by the United States.[6] At least 11 countries signed treaties with the Barbary states over that time, a signal that, for everyone who traded in the Mediterranean, Barbary treaties were simply the most efficient way of doing business.

But the Barbary states were by no means the most powerful states in the Mediterranean—they never had been, and by the nineteenth century they were decidedly peripheral. On its voyage to Algiers, the *George Washington* encountered a number of British warships, a signal of how power had shifted. When the first US commercial ship arrived in the Mediterranean in the 1780s, the French were the dominant power in the region, particularly in terms of their relationship to the Barbary states.[7] By the time the US Navy arrived in the form of the *George Washington*, though, France's naval power had been broken, and smaller powers had begun to assert their own maritime trade in the region.[8] The Americans noted the activity of the British in the area when the *George Washington* was chased by the 74-gun HMS *Dragon*, though the two ships passed a cordial conversation once they were within speaking distance.[9]

When the *George Washington* sailed from Delaware in August 1800 under the command of William Bainbridge, it carried two passports, three legislative documents, 100 rounds of cannon shot, 130 men, 477 bags of coffee, and 3,585 pipe staves, plus a large number of other stores. Most of the cargo was intended for the dey of Algiers, as part of the United States' tribute payment. The dey had specifically requested the coffee, in addition to sugar, pepper, nankeens, pickled salmon, and a wide variety of other things. The *George Washington* brought only some of the requested stores; perhaps Secretary of State John Marshall hoped that Bobba Mustapha would accept some substitutions (such as pickled herring instead of the pickled salmon).[10]

The United States had spent a lot of time and money on Algiers. The initial treaty settlement in 1795, which included the ransom of the captives that Algiers had taken over the previous 10 years, amounted to nearly one-sixth of the federal budget—about $1 million.[11] The United States had also agreed to provide ships for Algiers, which would make the Algerian fleet of corsairs much stronger (American-built ships were known to be well-made). Ultimately, the United States made five ships for Algiers: a brig, the *Hassan Bashaw*; three schooners, the *Hamdullah*, the *Skjoldebrand*, and the *Lelah Eisha*; and a 36-gun frigate, the *Crescent*.[12] Ironically, the masters who delivered two of these ships to Algiers would end up serving in the US Navy, in part because of their experiences in the Mediterranean.[13]

Though many on both sides of the Atlantic objected to the Americans' buildup of the Algerian fleet, Richard O'Brien, the US consul general in Algiers, argued that these actions were more than just the capitulation of a weak state— at a time when most Europeans were seeking the destruction of the Algerian fleet, the United States was glad to help augment it so that it could go after their mutual enemy, the French, whom he called "the robbers & persecutors of the Musselmen & of the Neutral Nations." Since the United States was at peace with Algiers, these new ships could focus on the French privateers who had been harassing American shipping, which would then "have less obstructions in this quarter."[14] In making this argument, O'Brien was (knowingly or unknowingly) placing the Barbary states in exactly the same position as many European nations had done previously: a foil to larger imperial conflicts.

The *George Washington* was the second tribute ship to go to Algiers in 1800. In January, the United States had sent the civilian vessel *Sophia* with the first cargo since 1798, but the stores that the *Sophia* had brought were, in the words of O'Brien, "no more than the wing of a Lark to a hungry man." O'Brien lamented continually how little the United States had done to honor its treaty obligations to Algiers. In his usual style laden with seafaring metaphors, he wrote, "You might as well think of sending ships down the Delaware without anchors or Cables as to send consuls to Barbary without making good your stipulations & sending money to preserve your affairs."[15] The problem was that no one seemed to be keeping careful track of the money or the stipulations—the payments in goods—that the United States was sending.

In fact, neither the State Department nor the Navy Department knew exactly what the *George Washington* was supposed to take to Algiers. The secretary of the navy wrote in July while the ship was preparing to sail, "It is absolutely impossible to understand from the Documents to be found at this place [Philadelphia], the whole of the Algerine subject," averring that the State Department would know more.[16] But the secretary of state wrote to Richard O'Brien on July 29, "I find it difficult from the papers in this department to ascertain the precise state of our accounts with the Barbary powers." By the time Secretary Marshall wrote these words, the *Sophia* had already returned from its trip to Algiers, so it is surprising that the State Department still did not know what was left to be sent. Marshall must have known that whatever the *George Washington* carried, it would not be enough. He asked O'Brien, and his counterparts in Tunis and Tripoli, William Eaton and James Leander Cathcart, to draw up specific lists of what remained to be delivered to the Barbary states. He also wished that the United States could simply make its payment in specie rather than in goods, which would streamline the process in the United States as well as make it easier to pay on time.[17]

Nevertheless, Israel Whelen, the purveyor of public supplies for the United States, perhaps going off a list O'Brien had sent in 1799, managed to fill the *George Washington*'s hold with naval stores and manufactured goods from thirty-nine different Philadelphia merchants. The invoices included everything from planks of various kinds of woods—over 44,000 feet in length altogether—to linen napkins and bags of peppers and "Havannah sugar," acquired from all over the United States, Europe, and the Caribbean.[18]

When the *George Washington* arrived in Algiers on September 17, 1800, the crew found a delightful reception—"Light winds & Fair weather great plenty of fine fruit such as Grapes, Green Figs, Oranges, Almonds, pomegranates & Prickly Pears," recorded the ship's log. Algiers was known for its orchards, vineyards, and gardens, in addition to its sheep, goats, camels, and Barbary horses.[19] Not all Americans had found the city of Algiers delightful. Despite the abundance of produce, Joel Barlow, O'Brien's predecessor, had found the city "the most detestable place one can imagine." He complained of the dark alleys of the medina, the haphazard architecture, the strange furniture, and above all, the rudeness of the inhabitants of the city.[20] Bainbridge castigated "the weakness of their garrisons, and the effeminacy of their people."[21]

It took around two weeks for the crew to discharge all the stores the ship had brought. Though the frigate was a 36-gun warship, its crew and warmaking apparatus had been greatly reduced in order to fit all the materials brought for Algiers—it carried 90 fewer men than its complement, and a total of 100 rounds of shot (barely enough to mount any kind of attack). Instead, it carried yards and yards of calicos and other fabrics, those aforementioned bags of coffee, penknives and pipe staves, barley sugar, and other cargo that filled up its 624 tons. Even though the ship had essentially taken on the character of the merchantman it was before being brought into the navy, the materials it carried were not enough to meet the Americans' obligations. Before the *George Washington* arrived, Richard O'Brien wrote that the United States was two years in arrears for its payment to Algiers. After all the cargo had been unloaded, he estimated that it counted for only six months, leaving the United States still 18 months behind.[22]

Given the huge amount of stores the *George Washington* brought, it seems surprising that all of these goods only credited the United States with six months of payment. A clue lies in a letter from Samuel Hodgdon to Israel Whelen. He wrote, "Captain Smith [the master of the *Sophia*] is afraid the Dey will rage when he sees a Frigate loaded with goods arrive to pay the debts due the Jews—and only a small Brig is forwarded to discharge his demands."[23] The dey of Algiers was not the only power in Algiers to whom the United States owed an obligation. In order to keep the dey from declaring war earlier, O'Brien had had to borrow over $110,000 from the House of Bacri and Busnach, a Jewish banking house with influence in both the political and civil spheres of Algiers society.[24] The *Sophia* had carried some goods to the Bacris on her first voyage in 1799, but not enough, it seems.[25] Secretary Marshall explicitly noted in January 1800 that as the *Sophia* was already full for its next voyage to Algiers, "every just claim, every stipulation" for the Bacris "will be provided for by the shipment in the Spring," on the *George Washington*.[26] It seems more than likely that many of the stores on the *George Washington* were not intended for the dey at all, but for the Bacris.

In fact, the United States was struggling to keep up with its obligations to all of the Barbary states. "Our Barbary affairs . . . have been much neglected," O'Brien lamented. The naval stores bound for Tunis were, just like those sent to Algiers, woefully incomplete. The bashaw of Tripoli was trying to renegotiate the treaty by demanding annual payments like the United States made to Algiers and Tunis.[27] But the US government had chosen to treat Algiers as the key to Barbary peace. In fact, the treaties with both Tunis and Tripoli invoked Algiers as a guarantor of the peace. The US government assumed that if Algiers could be placated, the other states would fall in line as well.[28] This assumption would come back to haunt the United States.

The demands of the other two Ottoman regencies were only escalating. The bey of Tunis had seen the ships the United States had built for Algiers and naturally wanted one for himself. The argument for providing a ship was not as compelling on either side as the argument for Algiers—Tunis did not depend so heavily on corsairing as Algiers did, so it did not need a ship with the same urgency. Tunis also had a strong relationship with France, so the United States had no expectation that France would be the target of any ramped-up attacks. Besides all that, the United States had chosen to prioritize Algiers, so there was not enough money to build a ship for Tunis. Consul William Eaton stood firm against the bey's demands, but privately he railed against American cowardice in the face of Barbary demands, expostulating that no one would look at the United States of 1800 and recognize the scrappy rebels who "braved the resentment of Great Britain" a mere twenty years previous.[29]

In Tripoli, the bashaw was demanding a present in order to keep the peace. He too had enviously noted the ships built for Algiers, and Tripoli's treaty with the United States did not even include an annuity such as the cargos that the *Hero* and the *Anna Maria* brought to Tunis in 1800. The tensions ratcheted up in September when a Tripolitan cruiser took an American ship. Though the bashaw insisted that the rais (captain) who had captured the American ship had done it without his authorization, he was nevertheless perfectly willing to use the American ship as a bargaining tool to extract annual presents, or at least periodic presents. Consul James Leander Cathcart insisted that the existing treaty did not allow for such gifts, but the bashaw went away from their meeting displeased.[30]

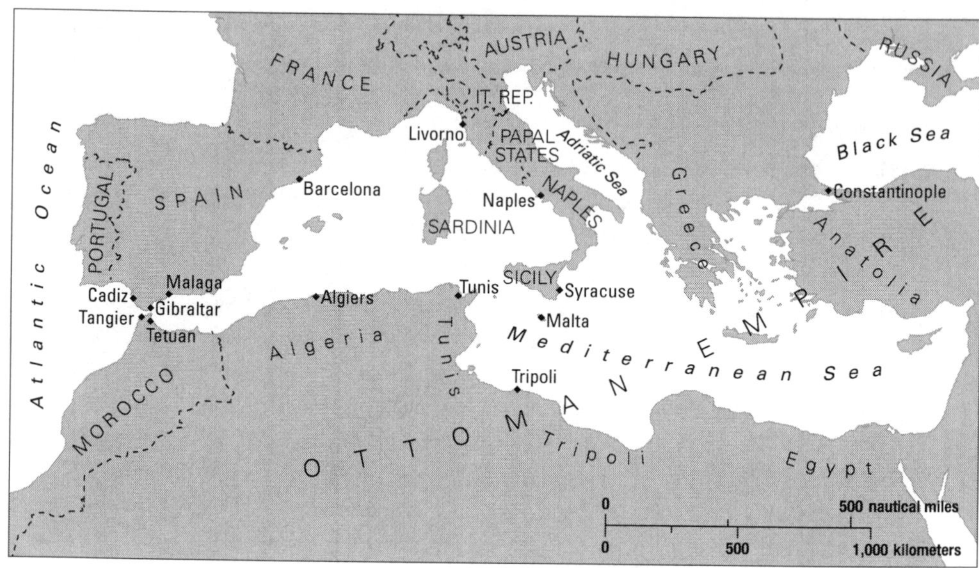

Figure 1.1 Barbary states and Mediterranean region, ca. 1800. Map by Nat Case.

With little recourse internally, Cathcart wrote to Richard O'Brien in the faint hope that he would be able to induce the dey to intervene on the Americans' behalf. However, Cathcart strongly disliked O'Brien and even accused him of working against the United States on numerous occasions, so his "hope that he will act in such a manner as will promote the honor and interest of our country" seemed a faint hope indeed. To be fair, Cathcart's beefs with O'Brien were only a little about his professional work and mostly about Cathcart's intense jealousy of O'Brien's success.[31]

To Constantinople

Captain William Bainbridge soon learned that he would have to do more than just deliver some payments to the dey. Richard O'Brien broke the bad news a few days after Bainbridge arrived: the dey was commandeering the frigate as a cargo vessel to take his own tribute to the Ottoman Porte in Constantinople.

The Americans bristled at this imposition, but there was little they could do—all the circumstances were stacked against them. To start with, even after the cargo from the *George Washington* and *Sophia*, the United States was significantly behind on its payment to Algiers, so they could not appeal to the dey's sense of fair play or ask him to take pity on them. There was no hope of a forceful refusal, either. Against 15 Algerian ships (including the 5 built in America), 60 gun and mortar boats, and at least 12,000 janissaries within the well-fortified walls of the city, the Americans would be crushed before even beginning a fight.[32] The shore batteries that lined the entire harbor meant that the frigate also could not just slip away.

Despite days of remonstrating with the dey and his ministers, O'Brien made no headway. He and Bainbridge argued that the ship had no orders to sail anywhere but Algiers, and that the dey was taking a huge risk by sending his cargo on the ship of a minor and unknown power that might incur the ire of other powers in the region. It must have pained O'Brien grievously to argue that a US naval vessel might be unable to protect itself against powers such as Naples or Portugal, but he argued that because the *George Washington* had no orders to attack such powers, the dey's cargo was vulnerable. None of these arguments accomplished anything.[33] Upon hearing about O'Brien's failed efforts, Bainbridge despaired, "The event of this day makes me ponder on the words INDEPENDANT UNITED STATES."[34]

Several days into the negotiations, O'Brien saw a way out of this conundrum. The British consul, John Falcon, had asked Admiral Lord Keith for a ship to carry the Algerian tribute to the Ottoman Porte.[35] If the ship arrived, the dey could send his tribute on that British vessel instead of an American one. Perhaps the British were less protective of their national identity, or they saw this kind of mission as routine—the dey argued to O'Brien that "other nations had rendered Algiers the like favours"—but in any case, if a British ship could be found, then the British might be able to help the Americans maintain their honor and integrity as an independent nation.[36]

On October 3 a 24-gun British warship arrived in Algiers, with explicit orders from Lord Keith to carry the Algerian ambassador and tribute to Constantinople. But the dey had turned against the British, and on October 4 he told O'Brien that he had rejected the British offer and the Americans "had no alternative but to do him this favour." O'Brien later told the secretary of state that the British ship was too small, a much more plausible reason for its rejection than simply the dey's caprice against the United States.[37] But the dey was not done belittling American independence. His minister informed O'Brien that the *George Washington* must sail to Constantinople flying the Algerian flag. Despite his fury at this order, O'Brien had to admit that he had seen Spanish and French vessels do the same as they left Algiers and came into Constantinople, as a way to signal the purpose of the mission—and that while underway, the ships flew whatever flag they pleased.[38]

At every turn, Bainbridge and O'Brien felt the honor of the United States violated. Bainbridge wrote to the secretary of the navy, "Had we 10 or 12 frigates and sloops in those seas, I am well convinced in my own mind that we should not experience those mortifying degradations that must be cutting to every American who possesses an independent spirit."[39] But they did not have frigates or sloops, only one stripped-down converted merchantman, which had to be altered even further to fit the tribute. The log from October 11 noted that the crew were "employed fitting our Decks for the Wild Beasts." On October 12 the crew worked on creating partitions for the new passengers.[40]

These new modifications were necessary because of the specific cargo the *George Washington* would carry to Constantinople. Exactly what made up the cargo is a matter of uncertainty. In a letter written by a US officer on board, the list included 20 gentlemen (probably the retinue of the Algerian ambassador), 100 "Negro Turks," 60 Turkish women (the reason for the building of partitions, no doubt), and the wild beasts: 2 tigers, 2 lions, 4 horses, and 200 sheep. Then there were the jewels and money, which the officer did not have a clear accounting of.[41] O'Brien's accounting is even more outlandish—possibly his standard practice when reporting outrages to the State Department. He claimed the ambassador's suit numbered 100, with an additional 100 women and children, and his accounting of the menagerie included 4 horses, 150 sheep, 25 cattle, 4 lions, 4 tigers, 4 antelope, and 12 parrots. The money and jewels amounted to almost $1 million.[42] Yet another account listed ostriches in the menagerie.[43]

The *George Washington* set sail from Algiers on October 20, "to save the peace of the US with Algiers," Richard O'Brien told James Madison, the new secretary of state. Nevertheless, if something should happen to the frigate, O'Brien feared that the dey would recoup the worth of the lost cargo by capturing American commercial vessels. He pleaded with Secretary Madison to send six fast frigates to the Mediterranean, hoping that the United States had come to an agreement with France that would allow them to redirect the small navy to the Mediterranean. O'Brien and Bainbridge both believed that agreeing to this errand for the dey was unavoidable and in fact went far to maintaining the peace. They were likely right—and furthermore, if it was really true that the dey often used European vessels to carry tribute, then they could have even seen this errand as a way to further ingratiate themselves into Mediterranean customary practices, establishing the United States as a part of the community. Algiers had served this purpose for the United States before, when the signing of the peace treaty with Algiers brought the United States into the financial structures of Europe that helped establish it as independent (and financially viable).[44]

Though William Eaton was furious at Bainbridge and O'Brien for subjecting to this indignity, he nevertheless found a way to spin the story to his advantage in a conflict with the bey of Tunis. The bey asked Eaton to volunteer an American vessel to take some goods to Marseilles, and when Eaton quoted a price for the charter, the bey threatened to take what he wanted by force, just like the dey of Algiers had coerced the *George Washington* to do his bidding by

force. Eaton lied that the bey had entirely misconstrued the situation—the frigate had only stopped in Algiers on its way to Constantinople, where the Americans were working to establish commercial and diplomatic relations. It was just
convenient that the Algerian minister also needed to go to Constantinople, and
the dey wished to "have assisted the project by sending some one of his distin-
guished officers of government to introduce the American messenger" to the
Ottoman court. Despite the fact that every detail of this story was a lie, the bey
backed down from his demands.[45]

The *George Washington* arrived in Constantinople on November 11, 1800. Bainbridge reported that the first officers that greeted them had never heard of the
United States before—though even if these particular officers had not heard of
the United States, the sultan almost certainly had. It took about six days to un-
load the ship, but the frigate had to stay until the Algerian ambassador, its
passenger, had spoken to the sultan, who was away and would not return for
three weeks.[46]

Though Bainbridge found this delay irritating, he used his time to establish connections with the other foreigners in Constantinople, particularly the
British ambassador, Lord Elgin, and the Danish ambassador, Baron de Huslech.
Both gentlemen offered the Americans assistance if it were needed. In fact, it
was the Americans who were able to assist the British. The *George Washington*
took on board firmans from the Ottoman sultan demanding the release of
British captives in Algiers; Bainbridge would deliver these papers back to the
dey.[47] Bainbridge wrote, "I shall endeavour to make the flag of the U.S. appear
as respectable as my present situation can admit" while also gathering as much
information as he could on the Ottomans and their court.[48] Doing this service
for Lord Elgin was one way Bainbridge could make the US flag respectable, at
least in the eyes of the British. Finally, on December 30, 1800, the *George
Washington* left Constantinople.

Though contemporary commentators and historians since have considered
the *George Washington*'s voyage to Constantinople a singularly degrading episode in American foreign affairs, the Americans perhaps had this reaction
because of their unrealistic expectations of life in the Mediterranean. After the
fact, many explanations for the actions of Bainbridge and O'Brien other than
the simplest one—the Americans were left with no choice—emerged from various corners. William Eaton was convinced that it was a scheme of the Bacris,
though his virulent antisemitism made him see Jewish perfidy in every shadow.[49]
There was also a rumor that Bainbridge had been involved somehow. President
Jefferson wrote about it to Secretary of State Madison, "I have received information through a single hand from one of Bainbridge's lieutenants, that Bainbridge
himself connived at the pretended impressment of the George Washington, &

perhaps recieved a douceur."[50] Neither of these explanations seems particularly likely, though the Bacris did hold political power in Algiers, so they were perhaps consulted in the decision to use the *George Washington*. But from their perspective, it was no different whether the Americans or the British carried the tribute.

Though the American consuls and diplomats in the area knew how the Barbary system worked, they seemed overwrought at the idea that the United States was just another nation to the Barbary states—not special, not unique, and certainly not immune to the unstated rules of the region. Their grudging acquiescence to the Barbary treaties, combined with the lassitude with which they fulfilled their treaty obligations, did more to harm their reputation than simply ponying up until they were truly ready to take on the Barbary system with force. One could argue that the fact that the *George Washington* was not able to bring enough tribute to satisfy the agreed-upon demands of the Algerian dey was just as much a blow to national honor as taking Algiers' tribute to Constantinople, a practice which, if not common, was at least not unheard of. But never once did any American suggest that the honor of the United States was impinged by its inability to pay its debts, only by its inability to break free of its obligations.

CHAPTER TWO

Squadron of Observation

If the United States will have a free commerce in this sea they must defend it: There is no alternative.

—William Eaton to Secretary of State
James Madison, April 10, 1801

On December 24, 1800, Richard O'Brien wrote to William Kirkpatrick, his counterpart at Malaga, "We should immediately have a fleet of Corsairs in this Sea, to keep the evil minded in awe, & to make us Something respected, if not we shall share the fate of the Deans [Danes] at Tunis, of the Swedes at Tripolia, & of many at Algiers, war will be the result of detention & neglect."[1] The fate of Denmark and Sweden that O'Brien decried was not only the captivity of their citizens, though that was certainly part of it. It was also the loss of honor for the governments who chose to pay off the Barbary states instead of fighting back. O'Brien feared that if the US government did not send some kind of aggressive force to the Mediterranean—not like the *George Washington*—the United States might be classified and treated like one of those "lesser" powers of Europe; war might also break out.

If the United States sent an aggressive force, it would enter into a complex web of relationships and histories that its consuls and navy had little knowledge of or appreciation for. O'Brien knew some about how the Mediterranean worked, but his limited perspective gave the Americans only a little of the information they needed in order to succeed in a space where they had no bases and few real friends. The commodore of any naval force the United States sent would have to learn how to manage the logistics of keeping a squadron in a faraway place, how to act as both military leader and diplomat not just with the Barbary states but with the Europeans as well, how to maintain relationships with representatives of the Department of State, and how to use his resources in the most efficient and most honorable way within the American conceptions of those ideas. If he succeeded, he could help the United States to become a full member of the Mediterranean community and end the Barbary extortion. But the secretary of the navy could not foresee all of the choices a commodore might have to make, or the most effective formation of a squadron, based only on the experiences the navy had already had.

At the beginning of 1801 most of the navy was occupied fighting against France in the Caribbean. The convention of Mortefontaine ending the undeclared naval war between the two nations had been agreed upon in September 1800, but word reached Washington only in January 1801, and the order to withdraw took even longer to reach the Caribbean, the location of most of the fleet. French privateers continued to capture American vessels throughout the Atlantic region for many months after the official end of hostilities. On the other side of the Atlantic, in the Mediterranean, the bashaw of Tripoli was agitating for war, and the other Barbary states had only fragile peace treaties with the United States. Since the US Navy had been authorized in the first place in 1794 to take care of the Barbary problem, many Americans called for an expedition to the Mediterranean in order to tamp down the greediness of the Barbary states. But so far the only naval vessel to enter the Mediterranean had been the *George Washington.*

The United States had signed a treaty with Tripoli in 1796. In it, the United States agreed to give the bashaw $12,000 in Spanish dollars and a number of naval stores in exchange for protection from the Tripolitan corsairs. The treaty specifically stated that there would be no annual presents required. But in 1800 the bashaw, Yusuf Karamanli, decided to renegotiate the treaty. He informed James Leander Cathcart that he expected additional presents from the American government—and a personal response from the American president to his letter of demand—within six months, or he would declare war. In January 1801 the situation devolved even further, when Sweden's consul negotiated a treaty with Tripoli that Cathcart viewed as "degrading, humiliating, and dishonorable": $250,000 to ransom Swedish captives and establish a peace, and $20,000 per year in perpetuity. Cathcart knew that Karamanli saw Sweden and the United States as similar in wealth and prestige, so he informed the secretary of state that the Americans should expect similar demands from the bashaw.[2]

Cathcart was right about the demands. In February 1801 Karamanli demanded $225,000 up front, plus $20,000 per year, as the price of keeping the peace.[3] Rather than advising the American government to agree to such demands, Cathcart urged the immediate departure of all American vessels. Richard O'Brien requested that all British naval vessels and privateers in the

Mediterranean help spread the word to American commercial vessels about the impending war with Tripoli.[4]

Despite these circulars, Cathcart knew that it would take weeks, even months, for word of any new demands from the bashaw to reach the United States, but Karamanli might not wait that long to begin taking American ships. So he tried to leverage his international connections to find some protection for American merchants in the region. Up to this point, the Swedes had been at least sympathetic to American problems, if not officially allied against the Barbary states.[5] Since Sweden had a treaty with Tripoli now, Cathcart could no longer lean on Swedish support, so he looked to the United States' other potential ally in the Mediterranean, Denmark. He hoped that the Danish force near Tunis would be able to sufficiently intimidate, or at least distract, the bashaw in order to give the United States a little breathing room.[6]

Cathcart had become increasingly frustrated at what he perceived as a lack of interest from the State Department about the dire situation in Tripoli, and he suspected active obstruction from Richard O'Brien in Algiers. But even if O'Brien were working in the United States' best interest, Cathcart believed that the bashaw would make his demands in a way that made them impossible to fulfill. Diplomacy would not work in this instance. The only way the United States could avoid a humiliating treaty was to send "a sufficient force into the mediterranean with the greatest dispatch."[7]

The Navy in the Mediterranean

The choice to send a squadron lay in the hands of acting secretary of the navy Samuel Smith. Benjamin Stoddert, the first secretary of the navy, had retired in 1800 before the new president, Thomas Jefferson, could appoint a permanent replacement. Henry Dearborn had been appointed acting secretary, and Samuel Smith had initially functioned like his chief of staff while also holding a seat in the US House of Representatives. Eventually Smith himself was appointed acting secretary.[8] Smith's first task was determining what to do about the Barbary states. If he decided to send a squadron to the Mediterranean, he might be starting down a path that would take a long time to come to fruition. Smith was not even sure he wanted the secretary job (and he did not end up staying secretary very much longer).[9] But he agreed with Cathcart and many other Americans in the Mediterranean that the mere presence of an American squadron would sufficiently cow the Barbary rulers into tempering their demands. So he gave the order to fit out a squadron.

As ships began to prepare for the cruise in Hampton Roads, Virginia, rumors began to circulate that the squadron's destination was Algiers, and that Thomas Truxtun, the most senior officer in the navy, would be the commodore of this squadron. These rumors were partially true, but the secretary did not want the squadron's formation advertised. The objective was not a direct strike on Algiers but something considerably less direct. To help Secretary Smith, Attorney General Levi Lincoln planted a story in the *National Intelligencer* denying the rumors.[10]

Smith did offer the command of the squadron to Truxtun. On April 10, 1801, Smith wrote to Truxtun that "such a squadron Cruizing in view of the Barbary Powers will have a tendency to prevent them from seizing on our Commerce, whenever Passion or a desire of Plunder might Incite them thereto." Truxtun had already declared that he would not command a squadron whose goal was not decisive action against Algiers, so he declined the command.[11]

Public opinion was mixed about the squadron, whose activities became a very ill-kept secret indeed as it fitted out in Norfolk. Everyone agreed that the Barbary states should not be allowed to continue their depredations of American ships, but not everyone thought the squadron was going to work. Plenty of misinformation also circulated about the state of affairs with the Barbary states. Thomas Boylston Adams summed up the arguments, including several of the incorrect assumptions about the squadron, in a letter to his brother John Quincy Adams:

> The Dey of Algiers, we hear, has declared war against the U.S. and the whole den of thieves will probably be let out upon us, ere long. I think it doubtful whether any great effect will result from this armament, but we tolerate it for the sake of the small naval establishment retained by it in service. The Aurora-man [William Duane, the editor of the Philadelphia *Aurora*] disapproves the expedition & says the better way would be to renounce our Mediterranean trade, altogether. Tribute is abhorrent to his republican sensibility and his high notions of National independence; and as to force against these barbarians, he thinks the expence of the armament will exceed any benefit to be calculated from the object of it.[12]

When the small squadron was dispatched to the Mediterranean in June 1801, its commodore was Richard Dale. The squadron comprised four ships: three frigates (*President*, the flagship; *Philadelphia*; and *Essex*) and a schooner, *Enterprize*. Commodore Dale had experience in both naval war and commercial sailing. In the American Revolution, he had served in the Virginia state navy and then the British navy before being recruited by John Barry to serve as a midshipman in the Continental Navy. His service in the Continental Navy included a stint with the *Bonhomme Richard* during its battle with HMS *Serapis*; he finished the war as a privateer. After the war, Dale went to sea again as a commercial captain in the China trade. When the Naval Armament Act was passed in 1794, Dale received a captain's commission in the US Navy, but conflicts over seniority led him to decline many opportunities for service during the Quasi-

War with France. Eventually he returned to the navy to take command of this first Barbary squadron.[13]

The captain of Dale's flagship, James Barron, undoubtedly knew Dale quite well. He had also served in the Virginia state navy during the American Revolution, and he had also served under John Barry as both a lieutenant and a captain in the Quasi-War. James's older brother Samuel commanded another frigate in the Barbary squadron, the *Philadelphia*. Yet another veteran of the Virginia state navy, Samuel Barron had been in commercial service after the war until he was appointed a captain after the Naval Armament Act.[14]

The third frigate's captain was much younger than the other three, and the most junior on the entire seniority list. William Bainbridge had been only a child during the Revolution, the son of Loyalist parents. He received his US Navy lieutenant's commission during the Quasi-War. His first command was not a resounding success. When he tried to take on two French frigates single-handedly, his ship *Retaliation* became the first American naval vessel captured by the French.[15] Despite this humiliation, Bainbridge received a promotion to master commandant in 1799. He was given command of the *George Washington* in 1800 along with his captain's commission. The *George Washington's* voyage to the Mediterranean did not sit well with many people, including Bainbridge himself. Doubtless he hoped that this squadron's cruise would give him the opportunity to redeem himself from these several misfortunes.

Secretary Smith's orders for the squadron reveal the United States' priorities for this first cruise. Smith assumed that the squadron would not encounter much action. Instead, he saw the cruise as a training mission for the younger officers, anticipating a future when the Mediterranean would be an important strategic area. He ordered Dale to go first to Gibraltar, a common stopping place for all ships entering the Mediterranean. He was then to work his way down the North African coast, bringing dispatches to the consuls and presents to the rulers of each regency. Although the United States was at peace with all of the Barbary states as far as he knew, relations were tense and could erupt into war at any moment. If all of the Barbary states had declared war, Dale was to spread out his squadron to "protect our commerce & chastise their insolence." If Tripoli had declared war, Dale was to cruise off that coast and "lay your ships in such a position as effectually to prevent any of their Vessels from going in or out"—in other words, a blockade. President Jefferson made sure the bashaw of Tripoli knew that the squadron was coming, writing to him, "We mean to rest the safety of our commerce on the resources of our own strength and bravery."[16] However, Smith's orders hint that he hoped any conflict would already be resolved by the time Dale and his ships got there, since he surely could not have thought that a four-ship squadron would be able to fight three or four antagonists simultaneously.[17]

The squadron was meant to do more than just show the flag—though not much more. It was also going to the Mediterranean to protect American ships by convoying them as they navigated the sea. The squadron's presence was intended as both physical protection and morale boost. Smith noted in his orders to Dale that the squadron would "give confidence to our Merchants" as they sailed.[18] The consuls in the Mediterranean thought that merchants did need some confidence. O'Brien wrote, "On account of the Alarm of Tripoli our Commerce has Suffered a great Shock Many of our Vessels is Sheltered in the ports of Spain and is affraid to proceed."[19]

But the American government had larger concerns than only the Barbary states. With the United States having just come out of an undeclared naval war with France, Smith did not want to antagonize the larger Mediterranean community. Therefore, he ordered Dale to allow naval vessels of any nation except the Barbary states to search any merchant under the squadron's convoy if Dale could not "avoid it in a friendly way." The squadron's own vessels were not to be boarded or searched, nor was any person to be allowed to be taken off them. Smith encouraged Dale, "In all cases of clashing with the Vessels, Officers or Subjects of other Powers, we enjoin on you the most rigorous moderation, conformity to right & reason, & suppression of all passions, which might lead to the commitment of our Peace or our honor." This part of Dale's orders was not about the Barbary states, but rather about keeping the tenuous peace with Britain and France.[20]

The Consuls in the Mediterranean

Before the US Navy got to the Mediterranean, the only protection American sailors received from the government came through the consular service. Now the consuls had to learn how to work alongside the navy. Secretary of State James Madison wrote to the consuls of the Mediterranean to inform them that the squadron had been sent. Though he also seemed to think the squadron would see little fighting, he informed the consuls of its proposed activities and purposes, in order that, if asked, "you may be able by proper explanations, to prevent its being misunderstood." Madison referred to the possibility of trouble with the European powers, noting that the squadron's timing worked well because the United States was at peace with all of Europe.[21] In both naval and diplomatic affairs, keeping the peace with Europe came first. Nevertheless, Madison also recognized that he could not foresee all the ways in which the situation might change between the giving of orders and their receipt. Thus, he wrote to consuls Richard O'Brien and William Eaton, "In effecting this object, the means must be left in a great degree to your knowledge of the local and other circumstances, which cannot be understood at this distance."[22]

In the absence of more formal diplomatic officials such as ambassadors, consuls played a vital role in maintaining the international relations of the United States. According to the 1792 Act Concerning Consuls and Vice-Consuls, American consuls had several roles to play, primarily related to protecting American commercial interests. Serving as government representatives to American sailors and travelers in foreign ports, consuls adjudicated complaints and declarations from any seamen who felt wronged by a foreign person or government. They also settled financial affairs for American seamen. They reported back to the secretary of state about American commercial traffic through the ports they were stationed at. They settled disputes about property belonging to Americans who died in their port, as well as disputes about shipwrecks that American sailors had claim to.

Though the consuls were agents of the US government, they were expected to provide their own living, either through charging for some of their official services (such as document authentication) or through running their own commercial ventures. The one exception to this rule was the consuls appointed to the Barbary states. There, it was assumed that the volume of commercial traffic would be comparatively low and the diplomatic squabbles would be comparatively frequent. So each Barbary state had a consul who did receive a small salary from the United States.[23]

In these early days, American consuls did not have to be American. James Simpson, consul at Tangier, in Morocco, was not; he was a British merchant who had worked in several other capacities. He served first as the Russian consul and then the American consul at Gibraltar. Aside from his business acumen and his interest in helping the United States, "he has also a considerable correspondence in Barbary & knowledge of the affairs in that Country," wrote David Humphreys when he recommended Simpson for the Gibraltar post in 1794.[24] Simpson negotiated the renewal of the treaty between Morocco and the United States in 1795 while he was still consul at Gibraltar.[25] In 1796 he took the consular post in Tangier. Of the four Barbary consuls, Simpson was perhaps the most suited to consular duties.

The consuls for Algiers and Tripoli, Richard O'Brien and James Leander Cathcart, had a different sort of knowledge of the Barbary system. They had both been captured by Algerian cruisers in 1785 and had spent several years in captivity in Algiers. O'Brien, the captain of the *Dauphin*, had been the leader of the captive Americans. Despite his relative lack of education and polish, he was well-regarded by the Adams administration. After his release, he returned to Algiers in 1796 with an appointment of consul general, following on the heels of Joel Barlow, who had recently negotiated the peace. Cathcart's fortunes had been quite different from O'Brien's.[26] Cathcart was educated and spoke at least

Spanish and French.[27] Only 17 years old when he was captured in 1785, Cathcart rose over the next decade to be chief Christian clerk for the dey of Algiers. He spent a great deal of time in the court and learned about Algerian customs and culture. By 1796 he held such a prominent position that the dey allowed him to be part of his own ransom negotiations.[28] Though he never fared nearly as badly as some of his crewmates, he never forgot the indignities of captivity. In 1797 Cathcart was appointed to the Mediterranean in an official capacity: consul for Tripoli. He was accompanied by William Eaton, the new consul in Tunis. Eaton did not have any Barbary experience. He had been an officer in the army, where he had negotiated with the Creek people while serving in Georgia during the American Revolution.[29]

It was important that the four Barbary consuls work in concert, but personal conflict soon got in the way. Cathcart was not an easy person to work with under the best of circumstances, and he had developed a strong resentment toward O'Brien. After Cathcart propositioned his own wife's maid on the voyage from the United States, she took refuge in the consulate of Algiers and eventually married O'Brien. Cathcart took great umbrage at the ascension of his servant to be his social superior as the consul general's wife.[30] From that point on, relations between Cathcart and O'Brien devolved into bitter acrimony. Cathcart thought that O'Brien purposely sabotaged all of Cathcart's activities for the rest of the war.[31] His 1801 description of O'Brien and his communications are worth reading in full, including Cathcart's flagrant antisemitism:

> A man who has done nothing (this two years past) but write nonsense dictated by the perfidious Jews at Algiers, & who has not taken one step to enforce our treaty by that Regency since my arrival at Tripoli, the whole of his communications being a complicated chaos of contradiction misrepresentation ignorance & duplicity mixt together with rocks shoals anchors cables masts rigging & a thousand other absurdities which would puzzle Lawyer Lewis or any one else to understand; the only article in which he has been consistant is in demonstrating a desire of throwing the whole of our affairs both at Tunis & Tripoli into the hands of the pusillanimous jews as they are at Algiers & of writing unintelligible metaphors no more to the purpose than the proverbs of the inimitable Cervantes de Saavedras auxiliary Hero Sancho Panca were.[32]

Ironically, O'Brien had similar feelings about Cathcart's communication abilities. By 1801 he appears to have stopped reading Cathcart's dispatches because they were so long, frequent, and incoherent. With some justification, O'Brien thought that Cathcart was pompous and deceitful. He accused Cathcart of sexual misconduct with a local woman in 1787 and embezzling money from the dey in 1800.[33] Eaton was caught in the middle, though he tended to side with Cathcart against O'Brien. He wrote to the secretary of state, "I do not hesitate to allege that the most essential communications of Mr. OBrien relative to Barbary in General are gross misrepresentations calculated to bewilder and decieve rather than to instruct: and it is not uncharitable to believe that these misrepresentations are rather the effect of speculative views than of ignorance."[34] Setting aside their differences to work together proved almost impossible for the three men to do.

Contra Cathcart's beliefs, O'Brien did communicate with the secretary of state about the Tripoli affair and about his own struggles in Algiers ("I am heartily tired of this Country," he wrote). He reported that the dey of Algiers had written to Yusuf Karamanli in both January and April of 1801 advocating for the United States, though it is impossible to know exactly what that advocacy looked like. At the same time, O'Brien believed that the interference of Algiers would not be sufficient to keep Tripoli at bay, and he advocated for a naval force.[35]

War with Tripoli

When the squadron arrived in the Mediterranean in July 1801, the United States was no longer at peace. On May 14, 1801, Yusuf Karamanli had ordered the flagpole cut down at the American consulate in Tripoli, a signal that he had declared war. In response, on July 23, William Eaton distributed a circular announcing that Tripoli was officially under blockade. Eaton likely crafted this announcement of the blockade in conjunction with James Leander Cathcart, who had taken up residence at Livorno since fleeing Tripoli when the war was declared. Eaton did not consult Commodore Dale before sending the circular, so he could not have known what Dale's orders said—and Eaton did not have the authority to announce such a strategy without Dale's approval. Luckily, Eaton's ideas did align with those of Dale, who wrote to the secretary of the navy, "Should the United States Determin to carry on the War against Tripoli it will be highly necessary to keep it closly Blockaded."[36]

The close blockade would attempt to serve two purposes. Naval historian Andrew Lambert argues that blockades could take two forms. A *commercial blockade*, which was particularly effective against nations that relied on the sea to bring their food, prevented commercial civilian vessels from entering and exiting a particular harbor, keeping them from accessing needed supplies and trade routes. The commercial blockade affected the merchant traffic not only of the belligerent port but also of all its trade partners. Enforcing a commercial blockade was a calculated judgment that deprivation of the enemy was worth the irritation of friendly nations. A *military blockade* denied the navy of the blockaded country access to potential targets, by either keeping its ships within a particular area or capturing them out in the open ocean. The military blockade affected the government that relied on its warships for capital; the commercial blockade affected its people who needed food and goods to live.[37] The American squadron's strategy combined these two types of blockade.

Using only four ships, the US Navy had to come up with an operational plan to execute both the commercial and military blockades. O'Brien suggested that the frigates should be deployed in a cordon from Gibraltar to Port Mahon in Minorca, a distance of more than 570 nautical miles.[38] Since the United States did not have enough vessels to even consider such a strategy, it is not clear how O'Brien thought such an effort would work—certainly it would not be the blockade that Dale was instructed to execute. William Eaton, conversely, wanted a small concentrated force to not only blockade Tripoli but also bombard it. Commodore Dale chose a strategy that fell in between these two ideas. He planned to block commerce coming into and out of Tripoli and prevent Tripolitan cruisers from getting to their prey. The cruisers in Tripoli harbor were to be bottled up there. The cruisers that were out at sea were to be kept out of friendly ports so that they had nowhere to return plunder to or acquire supplies. This strategy was one that the American navy had implemented with a fair amount of success in the Caribbean during the Quasi-War.[39] The blockade of the port had potentially serious ramifications for the entire regency. According to Eaton, the region was dependent on Tunis for basic foodstuffs, and though Tripoli and Tunis adjoined each other on land, food traveled on the sea.[40] Restricting access to the port, then, might allow for leverage over the entire country.

Upon his arrival in Gibraltar in early July, Dale discovered that the Tripolitan threat extended well beyond Tripoli. He found the *Meshouda*, the flagship of Tripolitan admiral Murad Reis, and another Tripolitan warship at anchor in the harbor. Dale left Samuel Barron in the *Philadelphia* at Gibraltar to keep Murad penned up, an action that amounted to a military blockade of questionable legality at Gibraltar. The *Essex*, under William Bainbridge, had orders to cruise between Gibraltar and Tunis, primarily on convoy duty. Only Dale's *President* and the *Enterprize*, commanded by Lieutenant Andrew Sterett, sailed for Tripoli.[41]

The *President* and *Enterprize* arrived off Tripoli on July 25, 1801, just a few days after Eaton's declaration of the blockade. Dale cruised off Tripoli for about a month and a half before heading back to Gibraltar. After an initial cruise off Tripoli, the *Enterprize* cruised off Algiers before rejoining the *President* off Tripoli in late August, but Sterett headed back to Algiers early in September, so *Enterprize*'s total time at Tripoli was very short. The *Essex* took over for the *President* in September 1801, in company with the *Philadelphia*. The week that the *Essex* and the *Philadelphia* cruised together was the tightest the blockade ever got under Richard Dale.

After fighting French privateers in the Caribbean during the Quasi-War, some of the American naval officers viewed the cruise in the Mediterranean as a vacation. William Turner, surgeon on the frigate *Philadelphia*, speculated that the squadron would have time for some sightseeing in the Levant and Egypt, as the squadron would have "very little to do"; he wrote, "I sanguinely contemplate a great deal of Enjoyment on the Impending Expedition."[42] But this hope turned out to be illusory. Instead, many sailors found the Mediterranean deeply disorienting.

The shallow waters and intricate harbors of the Mediterranean were an ideal location for practicing the finer points of navigation, which was one of the original goals for the cruise. But the physical features of the sea made a blockade difficult. Lack of ships made the blockade porous, but even if the United States had sent enough frigates to adequately cover the area under blockade, the squadron still would not have been able to access all parts of the coast. During the winter it was not safe to anchor near Tripoli because the wind created such a heavy sea.[43] And the coastline of Tripoli was simply too shallow and dangerous for the deep-draft vessels of the American squadron. The areas near Tripoli harbor got as shallow as three feet, but the draft of the *President* was nearly 14 feet. Even the smaller *Enterprize*'s was 10 feet.[44]

The Mediterranean was a new experience for most of the sailors. To acclimate themselves mentally, the sailors related the conditions to the more familiar waters of the Atlantic. But far from feeling at home, their observations indicate a pervasive discomfort with their surroundings: they compared the Mediterranean to "the latitudes between the Island Bermuda & Cape Hatteras," notorious as the Graveyard of the Atlantic.[45] Neither Carolina nor the Mediterranean was comfortable space for these deep-draft naval vessels.

Dale faced an impossible task in blockading Tripoli with only one or two ships. In order to bolster the effectiveness of the blockade, he turned to his European counterparts. Luckily for Dale, the king of Sweden had refused to ratify the treaty that his consul had negotiated at the beginning of the year. Instead, he sent a squadron of naval vessels to do something similar to what the American navy was supposed to do.[46] The Swedes had been helping the United States even before there was a US Navy. The Swedish consul in Algiers had been instrumental in keeping American prisoners clothed and fed in captivity in Algiers in the 1790s.[47] The Swedish government had reached out in 1800 about joining forces against the Barbary states, but President John Adams had declined the offer on the grounds that acting warlike against the Barbary states might actually cause a war.[48] It is possible Dale did not even know about Adams's refusal to work with the Swedes, but circumstances were different now anyway.

Commodore Dale embraced the Swedes with open arms and formed an agreement with Baron Rudolf Cederström, admiral of the Swedish squadron, about how the two forces could work in concert. Dale's agreement received some pushback from Cathcart and Eaton, who advocated against it because they wanted to set an example for the Barbary states without assistance, proving the superiority of the United States. A joint operation would mean sharing the honor when the victory was won.[49] Nevertheless, the deal was struck. Primarily, the two squadrons agreed to convoy each other's merchant vessels. Though Admiral Cederström met with Dale several times to discuss strategy, Dale let the Swedes do most of the work on the blockade. He offered Cederström advice about attacking Tripoli directly, and promised his help, but he could do very little because his orders said nothing about bombarding the port.[50] Dale rarely had more than one American vessel available for patrol off Tripoli anyway. By May 1802 Alexander Murray, captain of the *Constellation*, asserted optimistically that the Americans did not need to worry about the blockade at all because the Swedes were there.[51]

Enforcing the blockade required more than just brute force; sometimes it also required some detective work. A passport was the traditional method of distinguishing whether a ship was authorized to be where it was, carrying what it was. Passports were designed as agreements between countries that were not at war, but that might have commerce with countries that were. They served varying purposes in the Mediterranean, including helping to establish international legal customs regarding identity and the bounds of maritime power.[52] In the seventeenth century, the French used passports to protect their trade monopolies, stipulating that only Moroccan vessels carrying French passports would be able to do business in French ports. Ships not carrying the French passport could be attacked by the French navy.[53] In the nineteenth century, ships carried passports, issued by their own home government, that indicated their nationality and therefore their protection under any peace treaties that were in effect.[54]

A ship was eligible for an American passport if it was owned by an American, whether it was built in the United States or not. This distinction was critical because the re-export trade boomed in European ports, where ships were easier to acquire. As secretary of state in 1793, Thomas Jefferson argued that American commerce should be given all the advantages possible. If passports were given only to American-built vessels, "we shall lose also a great proportion of the profits of navigation. The great harvest for these is when other nations are at war, and our flag neutral. But if we can augment our stock of shipping only by the slow process of building, the harvest will be over while we are only preparing instruments to reap it. The moment of breeding seamen will be lost for want of bottoms to embark them in." Jefferson was well aware that this more liberal categorization of American vessels might lead to abuse by unscrupulous captains, so he argued that ships should only be issued passports when they left American ports.[55] However, the consuls of the Mediterranean frequently granted passports as well.

Figure 2.1 This document, issued to the ship *Dean* in November 1804, is an example of a Mediterranean passport. The wavy cut at the top is visible. If the cut did not match the half issued to Barbary powers, the *Dean* might be at risk of capture. National Archives, NAID 81144011.

According to the treaties with the Barbary states, ships from the treaty nations had to carry passports in order to keep from being captured—a stipulation that gave the Barbary states significant power to shape the maritime environment of the Mediterranean.[56] Sometimes American ships traveling in the Mediterranean also had to get passports from various Mediterranean authorities, seemingly in addition to whatever American papers they carried.[57] To prevent forgery, the tops of the passports were cut off using a specific pattern. Barbary corsairs were given a copy of the top of the passport, which they matched to an American bottom of the passport when they stopped a ship. If the patterns matched, the passport was considered valid. If not, the passport was assumed to be a forgery. This system was not foolproof, however. Richard O'Brien complained in November 1801 that the passports being issued for Algiers were defective, as the bottoms issued to American vessels did not match the top that the corsairs at sea had. Though no Americans suffered as a result of this confusion, several other nations had lost ships and cargos because of similar discrepancies.[58]

Passports were also issued on a more ad hoc basis. American consuls and naval officers could issue passports to foreign ships for identification. For instance, Richard Dale issued passes to Tunisian ships so they could travel freely throughout the Mediterranean except to Tripoli. These passports were the only way the navy could discern whether a ship was friend or foe. Dale exhorted those vessels to keep their passes with them at all times, since he could not distinguish a Tunisian vessel from a Tripolitan on sight.[59] The ability to give or deny passports turned out to be a vital responsibility for the consuls in the Barbary states.[60]

Commodore Dale knew that the blockade was unmaintainable, so he could grant exceptions to the blockade without really compromising the mission. He gave some potentially hostile states a great deal of leeway about their interactions with Tripoli. He granted Tunisian ships a longer period of free trade with the Tripolitans before enforcing the blockade, purportedly because he wanted to make sure the notification had reached them all.[61] In July, despite the concessions Dale had already granted, Tunis was the first to ask for an exception for its wheat ships bound for Tripoli. Eaton refused their request.[62] Whether Eaton had the authority to make that decision is not at all clear, but he believed that his declaration of the blockade also gave him power to grant or deny exceptions. Soon after, the British chargé d'affaires at Tunis, Henry Clarke, wrote to William Eaton, asking whether Tripolitan ships supplying cattle to Malta would be permitted to deliver their cargoes. If not, he suggested, America's friends might be hurt more severely than their enemies.[63]

The general concern the British chargé expressed was indeed one possible ramification of the blockade strategy—the blockade might end up hurting other neutral or friendly nations more than its intended target. But Dale gave both nations the same answer: the blockade was agnostic about the vessels it applied to. No vessels of any kind would be allowed to pass. In November, he also asked Thomas Appleton, US consul at Livorno, to remind Greece, Ragusa, and the Ottoman Empire that Tripoli was under a blockade; four months after the blockade was declared, their ships were still trying to get into the port.[64]

During the first squadron's term, Dale could do little except cruise off Tripoli and convoy merchants from one end of the Mediterranean to the other. Though each ship had a specific task, all the ships were also to be on the lookout for Tripolitan corsairs, which they could take as prizes. With only three frigates and a schooner in the squadron, each ship had more than enough work to keep it busy. The *President* was meant to maintain the blockade of Tripoli along with the *Enterprize*, though the *President* did not end up spending much time on blockade at all.[65] However, blockade duty quickly depleted supplies that then had to be replenished. When Commodore Dale sent the *Enterprize* to Malta for water, he issued Lt. Sterett a new set of orders that seemed to back off from his general orders to capture Tripolitan corsairs. Dale ordered Sterett not to chase any ships out of his way, and only to recapture American vessels that may have been taken prize. Rather than escort any recaptures to another port, Sterett was to take the recapture to Malta if he was on his way, and to bring it to Tripoli if he was on his way back. If Sterett did encounter a corsair on the way to Malta, he was to dismast it, dismantle its guns, and leave it to its own devices. If he found one on the way back, he could take it as a prize and bring it to Tripoli— if he thought the risk to his own crew and ship was low enough.[66]

Sterett did encounter a corsair. On August 1, 1801, while flying British colors on the way to Malta, the 12-gun *Enterprize* sighted a ship. When Sterett asked what the ship was doing, its commander replied that it was out "to cruise after the Americans." Upon hearing this reply, Sterett hauled down the British colors and raised the American flag, firing muskets into the 14-gun *Tripoli*. The *Tripoli* fired a partial broadside in return. The fight lasted about three hours, during which time the Tripolitans attempted to board the *Enterprize* three times. Each time the crew and marines repulsed them. The *Tripoli*'s captain also tried a strategy that most sailors considered dishonorable: striking his colors and then resuming the fight. The third time the *Tripoli* struck, Sterett disregarded the surrender and ordered the vessel to be sunk. Eventually the *Tripoli*'s crew "cried for mercy," and Sterett ordered their officers to come on board the *Enterprize*. He refused to board the *Tripoli* with his own officers, lest this cry for mercy be yet another trick.

After lying about the destruction of their boat, the Tripolitans eventually came over to the *Enterprize* and revealed the extent of the devastation Sterett and his crew had wreaked. Twenty of the 80 crewmen had been killed, with 30 more

Figure 2.2 A depiction of the battle between the *Enterprize* and the *Tripoli*, with the notation "Captain Sterrett, paying tribute to TRIPOLI, August 1801." Naval History and Heritage Command, NH 56076.

wounded. The captain and first lieutenant had been wounded, and the second lieutenant and surgeon killed. The *Tripoli* itself suffered so much damage that it was almost unable to be sailed, "having received 18 shot between wind and water." By contrast, the *Enterprize* had suffered almost no structural damage, and none of the crew were injured at all.[67] Since the surgeon of the *Tripoli* had been killed, Sterett ordered the *Enterprize*'s surgeon to patch up the wounded. The ship he ordered dismantled entirely. Because the first priority of his orders was getting to Malta for water as quickly as possible, he could not spare the time or manpower to take the *Tripoli* as a prize. So he let the *Tripoli* go, but not before he cut down its masts and threw all its guns overboard.[68]

In practical terms, this victory meant little, but it purportedly demoralized the Tripolitans so much that all the sailors who were to man other corsair vessels deserted them instead (at least according to the American reports).[69] On the American side, it helped to throw popular opinion even more strongly behind the use of force against the Barbary states. A letter from President Jefferson to Sterett, published in newspapers throughout the country, highlighted the victory: "In proving to [Tripoli] that our past condescensions were from a love of peace, not a dread of them, you have deserved well of our country."[70] This letter to Sterett was also meant for the American people. In explaining why the navy had not been sent before now, Jefferson justified the decision to send it at all.

Jefferson also made this argument in front of Congress in his first annual message, where he described the bravery of Sterett and his crew and lauded their American virtue. He argued that his inability to order the navy to take aggressive action, "without the sanction of Congress, to go beyond the line of defense," had been the reason that Sterett had merely dismasted the *Tripoli* rather than capture it. He then asked Congress to authorize any subsequent squadrons to take more aggressive action against the Barbary states, an appeal that Congress listened to.[71] However, Jefferson's interpretation of the battle between the *Enterprize* and the *Tripoli* was based on a misunderstanding of Sterett's actions. It was not timidity that caused Dale to order Sterett to merely dismast the *Tripoli*. It was the urgent need for water on the Tripoli blockade that animated Dale's orders to do the bare minimum in order to incapacitate a vessel. Sterett could not afford the time required to properly turn the *Tripoli* into a prize and incarcerate her crew—he had to focus on getting water quickly or both the *Enterprize* and *President* would have to leave the blockade.

After such rousing success, James Leander Cathcart believed that the time was ripe for a favorable treaty. He wrote to Secretary Madison,

> Never was a more fortunate inst. for establishing a permanent Peace upon honorable terms, not one of our Citizens in Captivity, two of their Cruisers block'd up in Gibraltar, & their capital in a state of blockade, while our third Ship the Essex is employ'd to Convoy our defenseless Merchantmen. The very judicious arrangement of so small a force by our Comodore undoubtedly merits the greatest applause and commendation, & I should not be in the least surprized to hear in his next dispatch, that the whole force of Tripoli were either destroy'd, or in our power.[72]

Cathcart's optimism about a quick settlement came to nothing. Just days before the victory over the *Tripoli*, Richard Dale had written to the bashaw that he had no treaty-making powers, and the battle had not changed that fact.[73] Dale was trapped in diplomatic limbo, authorized to make neither offensive war nor peace. Instead, he went back to trying to maintain the blockade. In Europe, newspapers noted the lack of swift action. "The outrages committed by the States of Barbary on the American commerce still continue to excite a considerable degree of speculation; but it does not appear that any vigorous measures have been adopted to take vengeance for the injuries sustained," wrote one London newspaper.[74]

Dale had to turn to the consuls for help on many occasions; communications among the Americans in the Mediterranean proved a difficult task, but coordination was essential. For instance, he relied on Thomas Appleton to enforce the terms of the blockade with the Ottomans. On one occasion, consul William Kirkpatrick in Malaga received intelligence from US minister David

Humphreys in Madrid, which he in turn had received from the Spanish chargé d'affaires, about a scheme the Tripolitans were using to evade the blockade. Kirkpatrick then passed this intelligence on to Dale, who could change his strategy accordingly.[75] These nodes in the network of correspondence functioned as an indirect form of blockade enforcement. Though the consuls had no actual power to stop ships, they nevertheless wielded diplomatic power with those ships' governments and, perhaps more importantly, heard news from many sources. What physical force could not accomplish, sometimes good intelligence could.

The consuls were remarkably adept at discovering and reporting the ways that various ships and governments were trying to thwart the blockade. In a circular in September, Cathcart alerted the squadron and American merchants that Morocco was trying to smuggle wheat into Tripoli.[76] He also informed Dale that the Tripolitan ambassador was trying to slip out of Tripoli to Algiers, probably to influence Algiers against the Americans.[77] Richard O'Brien resorted to outright deception to avoid exposing the ineffectiveness of the squadron. The crews of the blockaded Tripolitan ships at Gibraltar intended to go overland to Oran and then charter a new vessel to become "an Enemy in the Rear" of the two American frigates nearer Tripoli. To discourage them from trying this scheme, O'Brien leaked a story that four more frigates would be arriving from America any day. He hoped that the crews would be intimidated by the threat of more force and abandon their plan. Apparently O'Brien's plan worked—the crews did go to Oran but left without a vessel.[78]

As the consular networks worked to ease tensions in the Mediterranean, Dale's connections came under strain. While he was in Port Mahon in November 1801, he heard a rumor that Tripolitan corsairs were being permitted to fit out there and were also flying British colors to avoid detection. He wrote to the governor of Minorca, Major-General Douglas Clephane, that he found this situation unacceptable. Dale argued that the governor would not wish to trespass on the good standing between Britain and the United States, since it was undoubtedly the king's wish to maintain good relations.[79] If polite entreaties were not enough to convince Clephane to cooperate, Dale also reminded him of the tenets of Jay's Treaty between Great Britain and the United States that forbade the use of British or American ports for the fitting out of privateers.[80] Dale gave the governor a chance to deny the rumor, but he also made it clear that the protection of the British flag would not help any privateers that had been using it fraudulently. Whether Tripolitan cruisers counted as privateers was a question left unexamined.[81]

Because the *President* was under quarantine when Dale sent Clephane the letter, he could not go on shore to discuss the matter with Clephane directly. Instead, Clephane sent his secretary out to the *President* to inform Dale that the governor was innocent of the charges laid against him. The secretary reported that there was a Tunisian xebec at Port Mahon, but Clephane promised not to let it leave until its captain had signed a bond that the vessel was not owned in Tripoli or going to Tripoli.[82]

Communications among the squadron also posed significant difficulties. Dale reported on August 18, 1801, that he had seen neither the *Essex* nor the *Philadelphia* since July 19.[83] One set of orders to Andrew Sterett indicates how little control Dale would have over Sterett once the *Enterprize* sailed away—his orders were couched in four different potential circumstances, all with different commands. Sterett was to proceed off Tripoli and cruise until Dale got there. If he met the *Philadelphia*, he was to tell Captain Barron to stay near Tripoli, unless he needed water, in which case he should go to Syracuse. If the *President* did not arrive at Tripoli after 10 or 12 days, Sterett was to return to Malta, and if Dale was not there either, to Gibraltar. He was also to investigate the port of Syracuse to see whether it was fit for resupply.[84]

To more senior officers, Dale gave even more leeway. His orders to Samuel Barron, whom he left at Gibraltar in the *Philadelphia*, indicated a trust in Barron's discernment: "After saying what I have, I leave it to your own, good Judgement, being on the spot you will be better able to judge how to act than it is possible for me to direct."[85] Dale's orders to Bainbridge were similar: "Should you find it necessary to deviate from the above orders you have my concent so to do alway's keeping in view the honor and Interest of your Country, and the good of the Service."[86] The flexibility of these orders assumed that the moral character of the officer would trump any concerns about geography or strategy; the good of the service and the honor of the country would be sufficient guidance.

The squadron received little to no direction from home. Though the commodores appealed to the president for authority when dealing with foreign powers, in reality he was just as distant and shadowy to the US Navy as he was to the bashaw of Tripoli. In December 1801 Dale complained to minister Robert Livingston in Paris that he had received no instructions at all from the federal government for the entire time he had been in the Mediterranean.[87] Far from being a strong centralized show of force, the ships of the squadron often had to act completely independently of each other and their home government.

The strategy for the squadron was straightforward, but the logistics of the plan proved complicated. Enforcing the blockade involved more than cruising off Tripoli for long stretches of time. The Americans had to work closely with their European counterparts to keep their ships in the Mediterranean. In order to help the squadron pay for any supplies or repairs in foreign ports, the secretary of the navy lodged a sum of money with a European commercial house, De-Butts and Purviance, and asked it to place letters of credit with a few ports that he thought the navy might use. He identified Naples, Palermo, and Syracuse as likely ports, though none of these ports would be frequented by the navy for several years, if at all.

The US government preferred to provision the squadron by sending store ships from America, but this supply system had many limitations. The journey of one of the first store ships highlights several of the difficulties. The *American Packet*, dispatched from New York to Gibraltar on August 14, 1801, was captured by Spanish privateers and brought to Algeciras on October 5. Napoleon had railroaded the Spanish into fighting for France, and now he was using Spain's maritime forces in a blockade of Gibraltar, in lieu of the decimated French navy.[88] The *American Packet* was one of several American vessels that fell into the Spanish snare. The Americans thus found themselves on the wrong end of a commercial blockade, and they made the same protests that others would levy against the American squadron's blockade of Tripoli.

Before the *American Packet* arrived, Dale had written to the governor of San Roque in Spain notifying him of its imminent appearance. Dale thought that notification would be sufficient to protect the ship from the Spanish privateers, but it was not. He grumbled to David Humphreys, the American minister at Madrid, that the blockade was a farce, carried out not by ships from the Spanish navy but by privateers. "It is very strange to me, that the King of Spain suffers such nefarious conduct to be carried on under his Flag," he wrote. Dale thought that the use of privateers gave too much power to the governors of the Spanish ports, who were both the owners of the privateers and the judges of their prize cases.[89] One of the merchant captains who had been taken by the Spanish privateers also levied a charge of corruption against them. Writing to his banking house to ask for money, John Gibson lamented, "Every officer under this corrupt Government is open to bribery, and have no doubt but a few thousand dollars would be the most solid argument we could advance in our defense."[90]

In order to get his supplies, Commodore Dale had to petition the governor of San Roque to release the supply ship.[91] He requested simply that the governor would release the ship quickly, reminding him that he had notified the governor that it was coming and had promised that the ship contained only supplies for the squadron.[92] After the governor released the vessel, Dale discovered that the ship had, in fact, also carried cargo not intended for the use of the squadron, in direct opposition to Dale's guarantee to the governor. Dale was furious with the master of the *American Packet*, writing, "Such transactions might have a tendency to bring both me and my Country into disgrace in the Eyes of the people of this Country, particularly in the present Situation of things." When Dale finally got the supplies, he again had reason to be angry. There was no butter, cheese, molasses, or candles, and "the Bread that was sent is full of weevil."[93] The deficiencies of the supplies sent from the United States would be a refrain sounded again and again throughout the next four years.

At the time the *American Packet* was captured, Dale had already been waiting in Gibraltar for five days without enough provisions to go out on a cruise. It took Dale 10 more days, until October 16, to get possession of the ship. He waited a few more days at Algeciras for the other naval vessels who were supposed to put in for supplies from the *American Packet*. All told, it was not until the October 26 that Dale once again put to sea.[94] Though the case of the *American Packet* was extreme, the squadron spent a great deal of time waiting for supply ships.

The secretary of the navy sent a supply ship approximately every three months for the duration of the war. The contents of the cargo were roughly the same each time. No one got the dairy, molasses, or candles that Dale had hoped for. Instead, barrels of beef, pork, and flour were shipped along with quantities of bread, pease, and rice.[95] If the crews were to get fresh vegetables and fruit, which they needed to prevent scurvy, they would have to get them somewhere in the Mediterranean.

Good relations with European powers were especially important when the squadron needed to find these fresh supplies and get repairs. The US Navy tended to favor British ports for its supplies, even though its relations with and regard for the British were anything but solid. The ease of being able to freely communicate in English might be one reason for this tendency, as most of the officers probably did not speak any other languages. In July 1801 the British officially opened the ports of Malta, Minorca, and Gibraltar to American warships, according to Rufus King, the American minister in London.[96] Despite the agreement, that very month the governor of Gibraltar turned away Samuel Barron and the *Philadelphia*, which ended up getting water at Tetuan, across the straits in Morocco.[97] Perhaps the decision had not yet reached the governor. After that, the squadron was on good terms with the officials at Gibraltar; the officers there even promised to sell Dale supplies if the *American Packet* did not arrive.[98]

Malta was a better choice for supplies and water, geographically speaking, as it was much closer to Tripoli. But Malta proved a disappointment on many occasions. In August 1801, when the *Enterprize* made such haste to get water from Malta, Sterett ended up unable to get enough water to prevent the *President* from having to leave the blockade after all. Dale ended up at Malta himself, and while he was able to get water, he was not able to get other supplies.[99] After his experience in Malta, Dale recommended Syracuse to Samuel Barron, writing, "You may get every supply that you may want in the, Eating way, and that very cheap."[100] Syracuse became increasingly important for the American navy over the course of the war, but Malta remained the supply port of choice for most of the war.

Despite the difficulties with Spanish privateers, American warships got supplies on occasion from Spain. Morocco's Tangier and Tetuan were also possibilities for resupply.[101] Because of the wide dispersal of the squadron, it was paramount that its ships be able to get supplies from as many ports as possible. Finding ports and supplies for repairs was a slightly different matter. In some instances, repairs had to be done immediately, at whatever port was closest, no matter the relations with the port officials or their government. In other cases, more routine repairs could be put off until the vessel was going to an optimal location. As the war went on, the squadron pushed further and further into the Mediterranean, forging relationships with more and more ports where the ships could get supplies or repairs.

The navy also had to maintain relations with American civilians in the Mediterranean, specifically merchants and masters who were fearful of Barbary capture. There were ships aplenty that wished for protection. William Willis recorded, for instance, that 24 ships waited at Barcelona, "some of them with rich cargoes on board, but cannot go to sea for want of a Ship of war to protect them."[102] Aside from a blockade that was practically meaningless, the best way to protect Americans was to sail alongside them in convoy. Convoy duty was like sheep herding—the commercial vessels were the sheep and the naval vessels were the sheepdogs responsible for getting the sheep through to safe harbor. American convoys had sufficient force for only one naval vessel per run, and the number of commercial vessels in the convoy was also fairly small. On occasion, American naval convoys might also include commercial vessels from other nations such as Denmark or Sweden, if there were not too many American vessels. British and French convoys could contain hundreds of merchant ships, but American convoys usually had fewer than 30. Keeping even 30 ships together in the Mediterranean could be quite challenging. Commodore Dale complained, "It is Impossible to keep a number of Merchant ships togeather, in bad weather and long nights." Because of these difficulties, Dale considered ceasing convoys during the winter just as he would relinquish the blockade.[103]

The convoy system worked thus: a naval captain coming into a friendly port sent word ahead that he would be providing convoy to another port. Commercial vessels would wait for the naval vessel to arrive, or their captains might send word for the navy to wait for them. It could take days or weeks for the convoy to assemble. The secretary of the navy had instructed his captains to take under convoy as many ships as possible at one time, but the captains had to balance between waiting for a large convoy party and moving on to the next port where others might be also waiting for escort. Convoys did not span the entire length of the Mediterranean. Instead, particularly dangerous portions of the ocean would be convoy areas—at various times, the navy offered passage through the Adriatic Sea or the Straits of Gibraltar, for example.[104]

Naval commanders had to balance convoy duty with their other objectives in the Mediterranean. A small squadron meant few ships were available to provide convoy. As a result, commercial vessels sometimes had to wait quite a while for an available naval ship. Richard Dale summed up the problem for his squadron: "It is my wish and Intention to give protection to all American Vessels, Either bound up the Mediterranean or down, as much, as in my Power lays, but the Commanders must have patience, I have to observe to you there is only three Ships of War in those seas at present belonging to the United States, one of them must be kept in or about this place [Gibraltar], one off and about Tripoli so you see there is only one to go on the convoy Business."[105] Dale and the other commanders relied on the American consuls to both make commercial vessels aware of the convoy and also persuade them to wait till one was available. The consuls themselves strongly encouraged merchants to use the convoy system "on acct. of the Threatenings of Tripoli and The Snarling of Algiers, & murmurs of Tunis."[106]

Disease

All of the Americans in the Mediterranean faced a significant threat that complicated both logistics and operations: disease. In the First Barbary War, disease caused delays on both sides of the Atlantic and strained relationships between the United States and the nations in the Mediterranean. Disease also took a toll on the manpower of the navy, striking down both officers and common seamen. Nevertheless, perhaps because disease did not have any obvious catastrophic effects on the navy, historians have largely failed to consider disease as a factor relevant to naval operations during the Barbary Wars.[107]

Keeping sailors disease-free was no small task. Illnesses typically found on board ship, such as scurvy, were only part of the problem. Diseases contracted in port formed the other part. Some, such as syphilis, had easy explanations and were easily (though not desirably) preventable. Others, such as yellow fever or plague, wreaked havoc on both ship and shore. In wartime, ships and crews had to be in fighting condition at all times, and the navy's men simply were not in that condition much of the time. For example, after only a few months before Tripoli, Commodore Dale's *President* had to return to Malta because 152 of his men, out of around 400, were on the sick list.[108] Dale had intended to to keep the squadron near Tripoli for several more months, but when he left the blockade in September, the vessels that replaced the *President* remained there only a week before leaving for the winter.

On board ship, lack of manpower due to sickness had several detrimental effects. First, a ship without its full complement suffered loss of maneuverability. In the Mediterranean, where shifting seas and erratic weather caused frequent changes in sail, the absence of men meant that the ship was at greater risk of running aground or losing a mast in a sudden storm. For example, on board the *Essex*, "many of our people being sick, . . . the ship works heavy, for want of their assistance."[109] Second, fewer men available for the watch meant that those men had to stand watch more often, leading to a general fatigue among the crew. A more fatigued crew was even more susceptible to diseases.

Third, reduced manpower could mean a loss of the rigid discipline and structure that kept naval vessels functional. Common seamen were not the only ones to be attacked by disease. If officers were stricken, the command structure became confused and efficiency lapsed. In the case of the *Essex*, only a few days after Bainbridge noted the loss of efficiency in the crew, he reported that all of the officers on the ship were sick except one lieutenant and two midshipmen.[110] The structure of gun crews could also be damaged by disease. Gun crews were generally set, with the same people in them and the same officer as the leader of the crew, for long periods of time. But if sickness meant that some members of a gun crew were not available, then either the crews had to be rearranged or the affected gun crews had to be taken off duty.

On any given day, it was common to have at least a handful of men in sick quarters on a naval vessel. In a ship with a complement of 150 or more men, this small number was not too significant (as long as the sick person was not a high-ranking officer). But in 1801 several ships in the Mediterranean had more than 50 men on their sick lists at one or more points in their tour. During the same time the *Essex* was battling contagious disease, with 80 men on its sick list, the *President* also had nearly 100 men sick, and the *Philadelphia* had 70.[111] On Christmas Day, the *Philadelphia* put in to Malta with 50 men on its sick list, all suffering from pleurisy or scurvy. Though scurvy was relatively easy to cure, especially in the Mediterranean where fresh fruits and vegetables were readily available, it was also one of the more debilitating maladies suffered by seamen, depending on how advanced the cases were. Once his crew received the needed vitamins, Captain Samuel Barron had to simply wait for them to recover, a process that took more than two weeks.[112]

Despite the likelihood of large outbreaks on board ship, scurvy was not contagious. The contagious diseases had a much larger impact on both the health of the US Navy and its relations with people in the Mediterranean. One disease excited particular fear: yellow fever, a familiar but deadly contagion. Almost anyone who had ever sailed in the Caribbean had come into contact with it, and during the eighteenth and nineteenth centuries, the eastern coast of the United States was continually battling the fever. Philadelphia, the seat of the federal government, had experienced a particularly virulent epidemic of yellow fever in 1793, and during the time of the Mediterranean campaign, it struck again.[113]

In the nineteenth century, doctors had no effective treatment for yellow fever. It presented with high fever, muscle pain, and headache. After the initial fever dissipated, it sometimes returned with even worse symptoms—all the original symptoms plus hemorrhage and jaundice. Coughing up blackish-colored blood meant that the sufferer's organs were failing and he would soon die. There was no cure, and the typical remedies such as bleeding were ineffective.[114] The only benefit to getting yellow fever was that surviving the disease gave a person lifelong immunity.

Contagious diseases were particularly fearful for ship's crews, since close quarters made rapid spread almost a foregone conclusion. But contagious diseases also threatened cities, where many people lived in little space. This was certainly the case in the port cities of the Mediterranean, where the spread of yellow fever caused diplomatic concerns in the Mediterranean even before the US Navy arrived. David Humphreys expressed alarm to the secretary of state over potential contamination in 1799 when he received "a report circulated here a few days ago, that the yellow fever from the United States had been introduced at the Port of Gijon [Spain] with a Cargo of Codfish." If an American ship brought a deadly disease into a friendly port, there could be disastrous diplomatic and commercial consequences. It turned out that the report was false, but the American foreign service experienced some angst about the possibility.[115] Disease on the other side of the Atlantic also caused diplomatic problems. In 1800, for instance, President John Adams had to conciliate the bey of Tunis, Hamouda, about why the expected payments were not forthcoming. Adams averred that it was because epidemics in several large American cities had forced the relevant officials to flee into the countryside, thus halting all government activities.[116]

The other disease that affected American operations was one that no American sailor ever contracted during the war—its effects were felt in the structures created to combat it. The best-known and most-feared disease in the Mediterranean was the Levant plague, which could be either pneumonic plague, bubonic plague, or a combination. Outbreaks occurred frequently. Epidemics occurred in Egypt and Syria about every nine years, according to one historian. Benghazi, a city in Tripolitania relatively close to the capital city of Tripoli, was a locus of the plague because it was a crossroads for both sea and overland trade.[117] This disease was related to the feared Black Death that had swept Europe in previous centuries, though some doctors believed that the Levant plague was not able to survive the less temperate climates of northern Europe.[118]

The fear of contagion was especially great in the islands of the Mediterranean, where close quarters meant a quicker spread. City officials took correspondingly strict steps to guard against diseases. Port officials did not necessarily want to close their ports to any ship that might carry the plague contagion, but they also could not allow infected sailors free rein in their city. So they delayed potentially infected ships' entry into the inner harbor, a practice known as quarantine, until any active contagious disease had died out. The term *quarantine* implies "forty days," though by the early nineteenth century, maritime quarantines were usually much shorter.

One author described the treatment of the plague thus: "The soldier is the best physician, and the sword and bayonet, enforcing segregation of the diseased from the sound to be the surest treatment."[119] Because separation from the disease was considered the only sure way to keep from getting it, the Levant plague was the impetus for the introduction of quarantine regulations in almost every European port in the Mediterranean. For decades, the plague traveled by ship across the entire Mediterranean region, and epidemics killed thousands of people. Among medical experts in England in the early nineteenth century, considerable contention arose about how the plague spread—whether through physical contact or the air. This dispute led to major policy arguments in the British parliament about whether quarantine regulations were even effective. Despite the voices who argued against the regulations, quarantine against the plague was practiced for centuries. It was easy to identify "plague ships" and isolate them until the crews (and microorganisms) were no longer a threat, and one historian argues that the intermittent near-elimination of plague was a result of rigid quarantine practices.[120]

When quarantine was originally implemented in the British ports in the Mediterranean, it was specifically for isolating the Levant plague, but as yellow fever became more prevalent, the port authorities quarantined against that disease as well.[121] Officials from a port's board of health determined whether a vessel would be quarantined and for how long. Coming alongside the vessel, the health officer asked questions such as where the vessel had been, what other vessels it had communicated with, and how many sailors were sick. If the master's answers were satisfactory, the health officer granted the vessel *pratique*, or clearance to enter the port. If not, he ordered the yellow flag to be raised, signaling that the ship had been quarantined. Under quarantine, no sailors were allowed to leave ship, and no people were allowed to come on board. Captains could also be forced to remove their cargoes from the hold and either air them out or smoke them to remove any contagion clinging to them. All vessels, merchant and military, were subject to these regulations.[122]

The quarantine system of Europe, which came into its own during the 1790s, was one of the few things that bound the entire European community together.[123] Most European ports made quarantine mandatory for any ship that had even communicated with a ship from North Africa. Europeans feared the Barbary coast as the origin of the Levant plague (even though the Levant itself was considerably east of the Barbary states). The North African ports did not have corollary regulations against the European ports, which harbored just as much disease as North Africa. Maria Martin, a captive in Algiers, wrote that the citizens of Algiers did practice a type of sequestering, distancing themselves from foreigners in order to keep from catching disease.[124] But they did not regulate ships that entered the port of Algiers.

Perhaps no subject put greater strain on the Americans' friendly relations in the Mediterranean than quarantine. In an environment in which good relationships with neutral nations were vitally important, quarantine practices seemed to be the issue about which the navy groused the most, both to each other and to the quarantine officials. Though they often bridled at quarantine regulations, American naval vessels had to abide by other nations' laws, whether they wanted to or not, lest they risk an international diplomatic incident. Some naval officers bristled at what they perceived as irrational or inconsistent quarantine practices, seeing political undercurrents in an ostensibly medical regulation. They were very touchy about the honor of the American flag, which they often felt was being dishonored by unequal quarantine regulations.

On one occasion, Richard Dale lashed out at the commandant of the marine at Toulon, who he thought was unreasonably detaining American naval vessels (particularly his own). In addition to objecting to the capriciousness of the regulations, Dale objected when the health office at Toulon sent a "guard" on board the *President* to make sure that no one broke the quarantine. Dale promptly sent the guard back, writing, "Such a custom may be very necessary on Board of Merchant Vessels but will not be permitted on board of Ships of War Belonging to the United States, nor will it be, on Board the President, so long as I Have the honor to Command therefore I send him on shore." The *President* had not stopped at any of the Barbary ports—but it did have over 100 seamen on the sick list only 20 days previous. So it might not have been unreasonable suspicion on the commandant's part that made him insist that the *President* be quarantined.[125] The Toulon board of health returned the guard to the *President*, stating that the frigate would not get any supplies unless the guard remained.[126]

As winter fell, the American squadron gave up even the pretense of blockade. Sailors' enlistments were coming to an end, and the squadron's ships one by one were ordered home. The war with Tripoli was in stalemate, relations with the other Barbary states were fragile but holding, and despite the *Enterprize*'s victory, the Americans had generally demonstrated that they were only a lesser power in the Mediterranean community. But circumstances were ripe for change. A new squadron was being formed under a new commodore, Richard Valentine Morris. As Dale's squadron prepared for departure, the words of Richard O'Brien, uttered at the beginning of the cruise, rang even more true: "I Must repeat we want More frigates in This Sea."[127]

CHAPTER THREE

Quaker Meeting Houses

Circumstances may arise to induce a frequent change in your
position and we have a perfect confidence that you will provide
judiciously against every movement of the enemy.

—Secretary of the Navy to Richard Valentine Morris,
April 1, 1802

Hamstrung by ineffectual orders and needing serious repairs to his ship, Commodore Richard Dale spent the winter of 1801–1802 in Toulon. He used the time to select wine and other Mediterranean delicacies to take home to his wife.[1] Samuel Barron and the *Philadelphia* wintered in Malta, where they kept tabs on the Tripolitans. Barron surmised that the Tripolitans had also curtailed their activities due to the bad winter weather. Having heard nothing from the commodore, Barron wrote to former consul James Leander Cathcart, "I seem to be cut off from the rest of the world."[2]

Barron was not the only one cut off from the rest of the world. For most of the Americans in the Mediterranean, isolation and confusion reigned in the year 1802. Especially during the months between when Dale left and his successor, Richard Valentine Morris, arrived, the navy and the consuls struggled to find common ground with each other, with the European community, and in particular with the Barbary states with whom they were not at war. The fact that communications from home were slow and infrequent added an additional layer of complication. Because of threats from Morocco and Tunis, the Americans prioritized the Mediterranean community over Tripoli, though in a few instances Tripoli reasserted precedence. Even in these instances, the Americans called on their international connections to resolve the immediate problems, while doing little to move the entire campaign toward peace. In a year when two different squadrons sailed the Mediterranean, when Tripoli was taking American ships, and when the other three Barbary states were threatening escalation regularly, it was vital that the consuls and the navy work together toward the same goals. That is not what happened.

During the winter of 1801–1802, some of the American naval commanders worked to develop relationships with their European counterparts. For instance, Samuel Barron and his men found ways to entertain themselves by fraternizing with the men of the British fleet also wintering at Malta.[3] In contrast, Captain Daniel McNeill of the *Boston*, a latecomer to the squadron that had arrived in October 1801, was doing his best to antagonize the French and, seemingly, everyone else too. On numerous occasions, he chose to flout international custom and convention, as well as disobeying direct orders from his commanding officers. In January 1802 McNeill was in such a hurry to leave Toulon that he left port with some French officers and the purser of the *President* still on board. Commodore Dale was not pleased with McNeill's careless attitude, nor did the French officials at Toulon find his actions amusing. Dale reminded McNeill that being able to maintain a squadron in the Mediterranean meant "keeping up a good understanding with the Commanders of the Ships," both American and foreign, "that you have to act in conjunction with."[4]

In addition to carrying off foreign officers, McNeill violated a cardinal rule for interacting with foreign port officials: tell the truth to the health officer. When he arrived in Toulon after delivering a diplomat to L'Orient in France, he informed the quarantine officers that he had not touched anywhere in the Mediterranean before Toulon. In fact, the *Boston* had stopped at both Gibraltar and Malaga.[5] If McNeill had not entered any Mediterranean port, then the *Boston* would not require quarantine. But if he had, then the ship would be stuck in Toulon for several days, and possibly for as long as 25 days. Knowing this likelihood of quarantine, McNeill lied to the officials and thus evaded quarantine.[6] In July he did the same thing when he arrived in Naples from Malta, claiming he had come from Syracuse, "a place *I* never saw," Purser Charles Wadsworth recorded. McNeill probably told similar untruths at nearly every port he stopped at.[7] Commodore Dale was furious about this practice of deception. In his report to the secretary of the navy, he wrote, "Nothing should tempt a man to deviate from the truth in his report to a Health Office," but many American captains probably wished they were bold enough to lie their way out of quarantines.[8]

While the Americans became more accustomed to life in the Mediterranean, they began to project some of the prejudices that had circulated in both American and European society about the Barbary states. Perceptions of difference between White Americans and Arab "pirates," often connected to race and religion, had been embedded into cultural productions such as literature, illustrations, and music for several decades in the United States and in Europe for even longer, and these perceptions had worked their way into the navy as well.[9] Albert Gallatin, secretary of the treasury, called Morocco "a nation not within the pale of civilization," an opinion shared by Midshipman Ralph Izard. After visiting Tangier, Izard wrote, "It is [a] matter of astonishment to me that a people living so near a civilized nation as Spain should not imbibe some customs less barbarous than such as they have been accustomed to."[10] Even if Americans could grant the Barbary peoples a measure of civilization, they found them wanting in honor and justice. James Leander Cathcart wrote of the bashaw of Tripoli, "The Bashaw like Satan only flatters to deceive & is destitute of every honourable sentiment which dignifies the human heart."[11] The Algerians were no better. Lieutenant John Shaw called them "a people of no confidence or honor and ever ready to deceive there Nearest Friend."[12] The Tunisians were, of all the Barbary states, the most honorable, according to William Eaton, who offered the faint praise that the bey "seldom robs a man without first creating a pretext. He has some ideas of justice and not wholly destitute of a sense of shame."[13]

The Americans were none too impressed with European actions in response to the Barbary states either. Instead of upholding ideals of honor that the Barbary peoples lacked, the Europeans had allowed their selfishness and materialism to temper their actions, turning them more barbaric instead of bringing the Barbary states closer to civilization. "Why will the narrow & selfish policy of European Nations suffer those Piratical powers thus to usurp the dominion of this Sea?" Alexander Murray, captain of the *Constellation*, asked.[14] With these attitudes prevalent among the officer corps, it was no wonder that the Americans struggled to relate to their Mediterranean peers.

The New Squadron

Having spent the winter in Toulon, Dale and the *President* departed for the United States in February 1802. While he was in Toulon, Dale met with Admiral Cederström again, recommitting the squadron to the joint blockade and mutual convoy. He reminded Cederström, however, that he did not have the authority to join an assault on Tripoli. He hoped that the next squadron's commodore would have more aggressive orders. He also expected to meet the next squadron when he arrived at Gibraltar in mid-February.[15]

Ships in American squadrons neither came to nor went from the Mediterranean in concert with each other. Sometimes they traveled in small groups, but more often than not, a ship would depart for the Mediterranean when it finished fitting out in the United States, and leave the Mediterranean whenever it intersected with whatever diplomat or naval officer held its orders to return. Though the secretary of the navy envisioned that a new squadron would relieve Dale's squadron around the first of the year, the transfer of power from Richard Dale to the commodore of the new squadron was not so clean or timely. Ships from Dale's squadron stayed in the Mediterranean much longer than Dale himself, and ships from the new squadron arrived well before their commodore. Ultimately, Dale's squadron of three frigates and a schooner, supplemented in October 1801 by the frigate *Boston*, turned the Mediterranean over to the new squadron of five frigates and the schooner *Enterprize*, though not all the ships were in the Mediterranean at the exact same time.

The new squadron was expected to be ready to resume the blockade when the winter weather cleared. Dale believed that they were to leave the United States around January 1.[16] As of March 3, however, Thomas Truxtun, the captain chosen to relieve Dale as commodore, was still in Norfolk superintending the preparations of the *Chesapeake*, which was to be his flagship. He was not pleased with the state of the squadron. He told the new secretary of the navy, Robert Smith, "The officers destined for this ship are all young and very inexperienced and though in due time may be clever they are deficient at present and the task for me on the intended service would be too severe without some aid and I have had heretofore much trouble in organizing a squadron and at the same time attending all the duty in detail on board my own Ship." He told Smith that if he could not have a flag captain who would tend to the everyday duties of the ship, he would resign the service.[17]

The secretary refused the demand for a flag captain, and Truxtun resigned as he had said he would. In Truxtun's place, Smith appointed Richard Valentine Morris. Morris was directly beneath Truxtun in seniority and had fought alongside him during the Quasi-War in the Caribbean, from whence he had only recently returned.[18] He was not known for his bravery or skill, per se, but he was a part of a prominent New York family and the nephew of Founding Father Gouverneur Morris (who called him "Valentine"), so Morris perhaps had more political savvy, or at least clout, than his predecessor.[19]

The transfer of command from Dale to Morris proved complicated. Most of the American consuls and naval officers in the Mediterranean knew that Dale's tenure was up, but few knew who his replacement would be or when he would arrive. Many communications from the first few months of 1802 are addressed to "the commander of the U.S. squadron" rather than to an individual. The ships of the second squadron left the United States without rendezvousing with the other members of the squadron. Alexander Murray and the *Constellation* made it all the way to Malaga from the United States without knowing that the commodore of the squadron would be Richard Valentine Morris, and not Thomas Truxtun as previously announced.[20]

Planning a Coup

While the navy dithered, William Eaton was working on a different plan to end the war. This plan, concocted along with James Leander Cathcart, was intended to defeat the bashaw the old-fashioned way: a coup to replace Yusuf Karamanli with his older brother Hamet.[21] Yusuf had been the ruler of Tripoli for seven years. He had himself staged a coup, in which he killed one of his brothers and banished another, though he kept that brother's family as hostages.[22] The banished brother, Hamet Karamanli, formed the cornerstone of Eaton's plan. Eaton intended to overthrow Yusuf and set up Hamet, who had made many promises of support to the Americans if they would assist him.

Eaton met Hamet in Tunis to work out the details of the plan, but Eaton was not the only one paying attention to Hamet. Yusuf had caught wind of Eaton's plan and tried to stop it by offering Hamet the city of Derna, where Hamet had once ruled. Hamet found this offer appealing and almost accepted it.[23] When he asked Eaton in November 1801 for assurances that the Americans would back him as bashaw, Eaton gave him an unsatisfactory answer: "I recommended to him patience and silence; at the same time gave him leave to entertain the hope (may it not be illusive) that the next summers Operations would favor his views."[24] After this less-than-reassuring response, Hamet indicated that he might return to Derna, taking his chances that Yusuf would keep his word and give him the rule of the city.

Eaton tried to convince Hamet that Yusuf had no intentions other than to "cut his throat." He also refused to issue Hamet a passport to travel to Derna, informing him that if he tried to go to Tripoli he and his retinue would be seized and taken as prisoners to the United States. When Hamet suggested that he might retire to Malta instead, Eaton felt optimistic about Hamet's chances if he could just have a little more time to prepare: "He is assured of a revolution in his favor if he can be offered to his people with Sufficient show of force. . . . If [my plans] succeed it will be productive of incalculable advantages."[25] Eventually, Hamet did sail for Malta; Eaton wrote a circular asking any US Navy ships that encountered him to take care of him.[26]

Since Hamet was proving a skittish ally, Eaton believed he needed to keep an eye on him more closely. He left Tunis himself around the same time that Hamet left, on board a Danish warship.[27] But the consular network was also monitoring Hamet's movements. For example, Cathcart asked the US consul in Malta, Joseph Pulis, to inform him if Hamet ever seemed like he was planning to leave that port.[28]

Eaton did not think the consular network would be able to work quickly enough to keep Hamet from doing something rash, so he chartered an armed civilian vessel, the *Gloria* (Joseph Bounds, master) to carry dispatches to Malta for the squadron—in particular, for Daniel McNeill, captain of the *Boston*. If Bounds did not find McNeill at Malta, he was to search off Tripoli until he found him. The letter to McNeill informed him that Hamet and his entourage might be going to Derna instead of to Malta, in a ship flying Russian colors, and asked him to detain Hamet "that we may use him as an instrument of pacification at Tripoli." Eaton explained that he had engaged the *Gloria* because he needed an armed vessel to communicate with the navy, and that the vessel would be considered in public service until the next squadron arrived.[29] To Bounds, Eaton wrote that if he could not find and deliver this letter to McNeill, he should detain Hamet himself. Eaton told Bounds that the *Gloria* was eligible to get supplies from American naval agents or naval ships.[30]

The *Gloria* did find the *Boston*. McNeill authorized the *Gloria* to capture Tripolitan ships, congruent to Eaton's instructions (which did not include a provision for capturing Tripolitan ships), and to draw "one barrel of Beef & one of Pork" from naval stores.[31] Though Eaton had chartered vessels before to carry dispatches, the *Gloria* was the first civilian vessel authorized to become a combatant in the war. McNeill seems not to have questioned whether Eaton had the authority to make such a declaration, but then again, it was not clear that McNeill had the authority to confirm Eaton's authorization. But neither of them seems to have given the orders a second thought.

McNeill and Eaton were both working under outdated orders when they made these decisions about the *Gloria*. The relief squadron that sailed for the Mediterranean in 1802 had several new circumstances to account for. First, on February 6, 1802, in response to President Jefferson's plea in his annual message, Congress passed a resolution explicitly authorizing the navy to make captures of Tripolitan ships.[32] This resolution and the secretary of the navy's later clarifications changed the character of the mission, as they gave the navy the authorization to use force that Dale's squadron had needed. Second, relations with the other Barbary states had deteriorated to the point where a sustained naval presence might be required in Morocco, Tunis, or Algiers as well, if not more than one of them. So the commodore had to be even more careful in the "distribution of force." Third, the secretary of the navy confirmed the strategy the navy should employ: the blockade.[33] He did not, however, relieve the navy's responsibility to convoy merchant vessels through dangerous passages.

Despite this new, broader authorization for force, some in the navy still thought that the new squadron was ill-prepared for active campaigning. Before he even sailed to the Mediterranean, Alexander Murray complained to the secretary of the navy that the rations available to his men were inadequate and low in quality. Always comparing his own state to the British, he complained that the meat given to his ship was inferior to that of the British navy. He pointed out that these subpar rations jeopardized the health of his crew, many of whom (he said) ate better on board ship than they had on shore, and they needed good rations in order to rid themselves of whatever nutritional deficiencies they had been living with before signing on.[34]

Murray was able to leave the United States much earlier than Morris, but he still arrived in the Mediterranean well after Commodore Dale had returned to the United States. Because there was no commodore when Murray arrived, he took charge of the whole operation as the most senior officer, much to the chagrin of the diplomats and naval officers already present in the area.[35] During Murray's cruise in the Mediterranean, the *Constellation* faced a number of difficulties. Some were not unique to the ship or attributable to Murray. They were just vicissitudes of life on a navy ship on a faraway station. Before the ship even left the United States, three men died, two from smallpox and one from a cold.[36] The ship's log records four more deaths of unknown causes throughout 1802.[37] In September the *Constellation* spent around 10 days in Naples repairing a broken rudder pintle.[38] In November the ship sprung its foremast and foreyard on its way from Toulon to Gibraltar. Murray found Malaga a good place to get repairs, but he estimated the repairs would take a month.[39] While in Malaga, the ship's log records over 100 men on the sick list with violent colds.[40] Murray managed to overcome these difficulties and keep the *Constellation* off Tripoli for much of his tour during 1802. Other ships and captains would be less successful.

Some of the *Constellation*'s struggles could be linked directly to Murray, however. His leadership style garnered him few friends and supporters. Even though he was not a harsh disciplinarian, his ship was not a happy one. He had frequent disputes with his lieutenants, at least one so severe that he restricted Lieutenant Jacob Jones belowdecks until he apologized.[41] When the *Constellation*'s lieutenant, R.H.L. Lawson, killed the ship's captain of marines, James McKnight, in a duel, Murray was furious, but marine captain Daniel Carmick admitted that "Capt. Murray (being hard of hearing) had no idea of the Dissentions there were on board his ship."[42] His reputation spread beyond just his own ship. Charles Wadsworth of the *Boston* wrote in July that he was glad that Richard Valentine Morris had arrived, since he felt Morris would be able to bring the bashaw to terms, "notwithstanding what the old Woman Captn Murray has done."[43]

Murray also felt authorized to intervene in consular concerns. Somehow, he became aware of the *Gloria*, and Eaton's plans for Hamet Karamanli, within a few weeks of his arrival in April 1802. Unaware of McNeill's authorization—or unwilling to acknowledge McNeill's authority—he castigated Eaton for chartering the *Gloria*, writing on May 6 that he had dismissed the vessel from service because "as an Officer in the U. States service my Duty compels me to check all unwarrantable expences."[44] Murray also thought that the consuls had been crying wolf about the severity of the Tripolitan danger, noting that an entire squadron of Swedish frigates cruised off Tripoli.[45] Since the threat was not as dire as he expected, Murray disapproved of Eaton's entire plan for overthrowing the bashaw.

Eaton was furious at the lack of support he received from the navy. He felt that none of the American captains backed his plan (except perhaps McNeill), but Murray was particularly abrasive. He had rejected the plan "in an air of authority and reprimand which I should not expect from the highest departments of the government."[46] Eaton was incensed at the manner in which Murray had reacted. He did not "modestly express" his opinion, but simply denied the *Gloria* any naval stores and tried to take crew off the ship. Eaton also noted that almost no American ships had been off Tripoli for any length of time during the whole war. If the navy's leaders were not committed to the blockade, then they should not object when someone who wanted to win this war came up with a new plan to do just that. In contrast to the Americans, Eaton claimed, the Swedish both upheld the blockade and also (along with all non-American commanders in the Mediterranean) supported the coup.[47]

When Murray met Hamet in Malta in August, he seemingly had a change of heart. He wrote that restoring Hamet to the throne was *"certainly a desireable object, he is a mild, amiable man, & woud be perfectly friendly & Peaceable towards us,"* but he thought Commodore Morris would have to give the commands for the navy to assist. Most likely, Murray thought the plan was good but the leader, Eaton, was not.[48]

Because of the slow speed of communications in the Mediterranean, the feud between Murray and Eaton dragged on for several months. In August, Eaton was still complaining to the secretary of state, "Whatever may be Cap. Murray's opinion of my measures, he ought not to sacrifice the interest of service to individual resentments. Government may as well send out *quaker meeting-houses* to float about this sea as frigates with Murrays in command."[49] Other more junior officers also sided with Eaton against Murray, even if they disagreed with Eaton's overall plan.[50] Cathcart argued that Murray was ill-informed, unjust, and illiberal in his manner, but also that he was not even the senior officer of the squadron—that rank belonged to Daniel McNeill, who was the only officer who had a right to dismiss a vessel from service. (Cathcart was wrong about that; Murray was ahead of McNeill on the seniority list.) Cathcart also complained that Murray's actions blurred the lines between the Navy Department and the State Department. He wanted the president to make the distinction clear, so that the consuls, with years of experience in Barbary affairs, could not be blamed when they were overruled by the inexperienced and ignorant naval officers.[51]

This situation could have been resolved more quickly if the involved parties had corresponded with their commodore, but none of them knew *who* the new commodore was or *where* he was. It was impossible to discern who was in charge, and therefore difficult to develop a coherent strategy. These command fractures, which were birthed during Dale's tenure as commodore, grew to almost-disastrous proportions under Richard Valentine Morris.

In the first half of 1802, the depleted navy was in dire need of repairs and supplies, as the vessels still in the Mediterranean continued their duties of convoy and blockade, awaiting the arrival of their new commodore. When the *Boston* sprung its bowsprit off Tripoli in May, McNeill had to take the ship to Messina for repairs. Likewise, when the *Constellation* arrived in April, Murray went straight to Malaga to get two new anchors.[52] When he could not get them there, he had to go to Gibraltar and petition Lord Keith to acquire them.[53]

The New Commodore

Commodore Richard Valentine Morris arrived in Gibraltar on May 31, 1802. Morris seemed to believe that this cruise would not be too taxing, since he brought an entourage with him: his wife (whom Midshipman Henry Wadsworth referred to as "the Commodoress"), his son Gerard, and Mrs. Morris's maid Sal.[54] He was not the only man to bring family on the *Chesapeake*, and it seems probable that the presence of women and children kept him from being as aggressive toward belligerents as he might otherwise have been. At least one child was born on board ship: Melancthon Woolsey Low, son of James Low, captain of the forecastle. The baby was baptized in the berth of his godfather, Midshipman Melancthon Woolsey. Wadsworth records that there were at least four other women on board, and possibly more children as well. Mrs. Morris stayed on shore in friendly ports whenever possible; we do not know whether the other women did the same.[55]

When the *Chesapeake* arrived at Gibraltar, the ship had a rotten mainmast, which had sprung four days out from the United States. Instead of being able to strike at Tripoli during the favorable summer months, Morris and his crew were forced to remain in Gibraltar while their ship underwent critical repairs. Mrs. Morris resided on shore with an acquaintance.[56] Just like Murray, Morris depended on the goodwill of Lord Keith, with whom the Americans had made an agreement allowing them to get supplies and repairs at Gibraltar.[57] The officers of the *Chesapeake* spent a lot of time on shore, interacting with British officers and socialites in the town. Though the American officers got along well with their British counterparts, Midshipman Wadsworth noted acerbically in his journal on July 4 that the US squadron had saluted the king's birthday, but "now silently passes that anniversary of that day which gave birth to Independence

Figure 3.1 Midshipman Henry Wadsworth's unfinished sketch of the Rock of Gibraltar, from the frontispiece of his letterbook. Courtesy National Park Service, Longfellow House–Washington's Headquarters National Historic Site.

of the United States of America."[58] The British were not yet ready to acknowledge the Americans as equals.

But the British were the least of Morris's concerns. Upon his arrival at Gibraltar, Morris discovered that the conflicts with Morocco had become untenable. The conflict centered on the *Meshouda*, the Tripolitan warship that Dale had blockaded in the port over a year previous. Early in 1802 the emperor of Morocco, Mulay Sulayman, had requested that James Simpson, consul at Tangier, provide a passport for the *Meshouda* so that it could leave Gibraltar, as well as passports for some Moroccan ships that would carry wheat to Tripoli. Simpson had asked Dale his advice about the request, but Dale had deflected, saying that he could not make a determination without asking the president of the United States. At the very least, Dale suggested that the problem be left for his successor to untangle in conjunction with Admiral Cederström. When Simpson reported the delay due to command change, Sulayman relented, at least for the first few months of 1802. Though Simpson thought the emperor was overstepping his authority in intervening on Tripoli's behalf about the *Meshouda*, he could not justify going to the court of the emperor to make his case.

Simpson recognized the need to tread carefully with Sulayman. "With him it is not proper to speak all we think," he wrote. In order to plead his case, he relied instead on the advocacy of Peter Wyk, Swedish consul in Tangier, who "would use his utmost endeavours to convince Muley Soliman, of the impropriety of his takeing the part he has done in behalf of the Tripolines, in a War which they have so unjustly made against Sweden & the United States."[59]

Eventually, the emperor grew tired of waiting for the American reply. Simpson received word that Sulayman had declared war on the United States on June 19. Forced to leave Morocco on June 22, Simpson relocated from his home in Tangier to Gibraltar, where he could still keep tabs on the emperor's ships—though Tangier was not visible from across the Straits, observers in Gibraltar could have seen any ships that sailed into the Mediterranean from Tangier. He was surprised at the declaration of war, for though relations had been tense, he had received signs of friendship from some of the emperor's court, and he hardly thought denying a few passports for wheat ships was worth a full-scale war. He consulted with Commodore Morris, and together they determined to wait for the arrival of the *Adams*, due at Gibraltar any day. They hoped the *Adams* was carrying dispatches from the federal government with advice about what to do.[60] On June 30 the governor of Tangier invited Simpson to return to Tangier for six months in order to reopen negotiations. However, Simpson was reluctant to return without consulting first with the navy, so he was forced to send the *Enterprize* off to look for Morris, who had sailed with a convoy on July 1.[61] When Morris returned after a few days, the two men still believed they needed to wait for the *Adams*, which eventually arrived in late July.

Once Simpson had the orders he was hoping for, he met with the governor of Tangier and spokesperson for the court of the emperor, Abdashaman Hashash, who Simpson believed was responsible for the increase in aggression toward the United States. Through Hashash, Simpson begged the emperor to have patience with him and his government, since communications with the United States were painfully slow. He agreed to issue a passport for a Moroccan ship carrying wheat to Tunis. He also told the emperor that the president was sending him 100 gun carriages from the United States, as a sign of good relations between the two countries.[62]

On August 6, 1802, Simpson received a letter from the emperor's court reestablishing the previous terms of their agreement: annual, or possibly biennial, presents from the United States as a guarantor of peace. Secretary of State Mohamet ben Absalem Selawy, who wrote the letter, blamed the Americans for all the troubles, but said that the emperor forgave them and wanted relations restored.[63] Though peace was reestablished, there were a few minor negotiations yet outstanding. Simpson believed that the presence of the *Adams*, the

Chesapeake, and the *Enterprize* in Gibraltar had limited the emperor's antagonism, so he suggested that Morris leave a frigate off Gibraltar in order to monitor Moroccan warships.[64] Simpson's suggestion, combined with Morris's orders to keep the secretary of the navy informed of all movements by the emperor of Morocco, convinced Morris that he needed to stay near Morocco himself.[65]

While negotiations with Morocco continued, Tripoli was still at war with the United States. As the Americans had no direct entry into the court of Tripoli, they had to attempt to gain access through their international connections. The bashaw, according to William Eaton, wanted to use Tunis as a go-between, but Eaton did not trust the bey of Tunis to act fairly.[66] At the same time, Richard O'Brien sought to bring peace with Tripoli through the dey of Algiers. As early as January 1802, the Algerian ambassador offered to broker peace in exchange for a small financial consideration. O'Brien declined to pay, but Algiers continued to try to orchestrate peace settlements. In April, Secretary of State Madison made it clear to Cathcart that he must not allow Algiers to get involved in the negotiations—but it must seem like the bashaw was the instigator behind the Algerians' removal. Madison instructed Cathcart instead to consult with the Swedes, who were also trying to settle peace with Tripoli. However, the two countries could not be seen as colluding with each other, and any peace settlement had to be completely separate from a peace between Tripoli and Sweden.[67] It was important for the United States to maintain its ties with the Mediterranean community, but only on its own terms.

In June 1802, the *Franklin*, an American merchant vessel traveling without convoy, was captured off Cape Palos on the Spanish coast by a Tripolitan corsair.[68] Its captain, Andrew Morris, and its eight crew members were taken to Tripoli via Algiers and Tunis. When he learned of the capture as the prisoners passed through Tunis, William Eaton lamented that the captives "will be cried for sale at public auction, like so many cattle; or, perhaps, stationed on the batteries to slay & be slain by their Countrymen."[69]

When the *Franklin* was captured, the importance of the Mediterranean community became clear. Though the United States did not wish to be seen as equivalent to the Scandinavian countries, the Americans had to accept help from them. In particular, they received help from Nicholas Nissen, Denmark's consul to Tripoli, who had been an unofficial mediator between the United States and Tripoli even before the declaration of war. Seemingly motivated by nothing other than kindness and a close personal friendship with James Leander Cathcart, he immediately tried to convince the Tripolitans to give Morris, at least, his liberty within the town. The British chargé at Tripoli, Bryan McDonogh, claimed two of the *Franklin*'s officers and a seaman as British. As subjects of a non-belligerent nation, they could not be taken captive, so they were released. Two other seamen were also released because they were "foreigners." This left only Morris and three crew members captive in Tripoli.[70]

As American consuls learned of the capture, they tried to ransom the captives in different ways, without consulting any of their counterparts. For instance, William Eaton wanted to leverage the obligations Tripoli had to the Ottoman Porte, recalling that a retroactive prisoner exchange might be possible because the United States had released some Turkish prisoners to the bashaw of Tripoli the previous year. Eaton was counting on the fact that the grand signior owed a debt of honor to the United States, and the bashaw owed allegiance to the grand signior.[71] James Leander Cathcart likewise speculated about how to redeem the prisoners, though he noted that the brig itself and its cargo were surely unrecoverable, as they were good prize.[72]

But no one came to negotiate for ransom. The lack of naval leadership meant that the *Franklin* situation unfolded without intervention from the commodore. On July 21 Murray, patrolling off Tripoli with a Swedish frigate, noted the arrival at Tripoli of the two galleys carrying the *Franklin* prisoners, under the nose of the blockaders. But he did not try to capture those galleys or free the prisoners.[73] In the end, the mutual connection with Algiers proved the mechanism for getting the *Franklin*'s crew released. Through negotiations by a combination of Nicholas Nissen and representatives from the Algerian government, the bashaw of Tripoli agreed to release the prisoners into the custody of the dey of Algiers. Thanks to Nissen's involvement, the crew had been taken care of during their stay in Tripoli, and on September 22, 1802, Nissen reported their departure for Algiers.[74] When they arrived in Algiers on October 6, the dey ordered them released, as a "present" to the United States.[75]

Algiers was not a neutral party in this negotiation. By intervening on the United States' behalf now, Algiers could call in a favor later, and even go to war if that favor was not granted. The dey framed the whole negotiation in terms of friendship. He declared the United States his "best friends" because the *George Washington* had carried his cargo to Constantinople. But, he claimed, this redemption of the captives should not be construed as a quid pro quo for that action.[76] Though Eaton expressed gratitude for the assistance in redeeming the captives, he remained suspicious of the dey's motives. His suspicions turned out to be accurate. In January 1803 the dey requested $6,500 from the United States as a present for rescuing the *Franklin*. Eaton was incensed at that request. He believed that even if they paid the money, the dey would not consider the score to be even, instead hobbling the United States with "an Imaginary weight of obligation the value of which at some future period may be very considerable."[77] Eaton had discovered one of the perils of being part of an international community—the possibility that the United States might be under obligation to rulers it could not trust.

In July 1802 Nissen was approached secretly by Sidi Muhammad Dghies, the prime minister of Tripoli, about settling with the United States. Dghies suggested that the government had turned considerably less hawkish, so now was the time to negotiate a peace.[78] In order to get the Americans to the table, Nissen wrote to Alexander Murray, the only commander Nissen had seen much of during the year, rather than Richard Valentine Morris.[79]

The secretary of state had given Cathcart authorization to negotiate a treaty, but the secretary of the navy had also given Richard Valentine Morris authority to negotiate. The Americans could not come to a consensus about how it should be done, or who should be included—especially regarding the dey of Algiers. The *Franklin* incident was just one of the ways in which the dey tried to work his way back into the United States' peace negotiations with Tripoli after being turned away earlier in the year. Cathcart had warned previously that "the interference of the Dey of Algiers will never militate in favor of the United States." Instead, "their is a very great probability that he will interfere in favor of his brother pirate of Tripoli."[80] Eaton appealed to the bashaw of Tripoli himself to exclude Algiers, suggesting that the dey's interference would reduce the bashaw's honor and taint the negotiations against both parties and in favor of the dey.[81] He further urged Morris not to include Algiers, since Tripoli had declared war in 1801 after Algiers had reneged on its role as guarantor of peace between the United States and Tripoli. He argued that the United States should take a lesson and conclude negotiations with Tripoli only.[82]

Cathcart believed the *Franklin* matter had hurt relations with the other Barbary states and had put the United States into a compromised negotiating position. He wrote dejectedly to the secretary of state, "To have our vessels captured while the squadrons of the U, S of America & of Sweden are lending their aid to protect our commerce implies something very unfavorable to our energy & undoubtedly will be construed much to our disadvantage by the heads of the Barbary States."[83] The capture—and subsequent lack of vigor in trying to get the *Franklin*'s prisoners back—had certainly laid bare to the bashaw the fragility of the American blockade, deepening the rift with Tripoli.

These fracturing relationships raised tensions between consuls Cathcart, Eaton, and O'Brien, whose feud continued. Cathcart and Eaton believed that O'Brien was trying to collude behind their backs to bring about a treaty using Algiers without official authorization. Cathcart was very protective of the position as negotiator that he had been granted by the secretary of state.[84] He reminded O'Brien that he was the only person authorized to make treaties with Tripoli. Thus, any agreement O'Brien had entered into with Algiers was not only

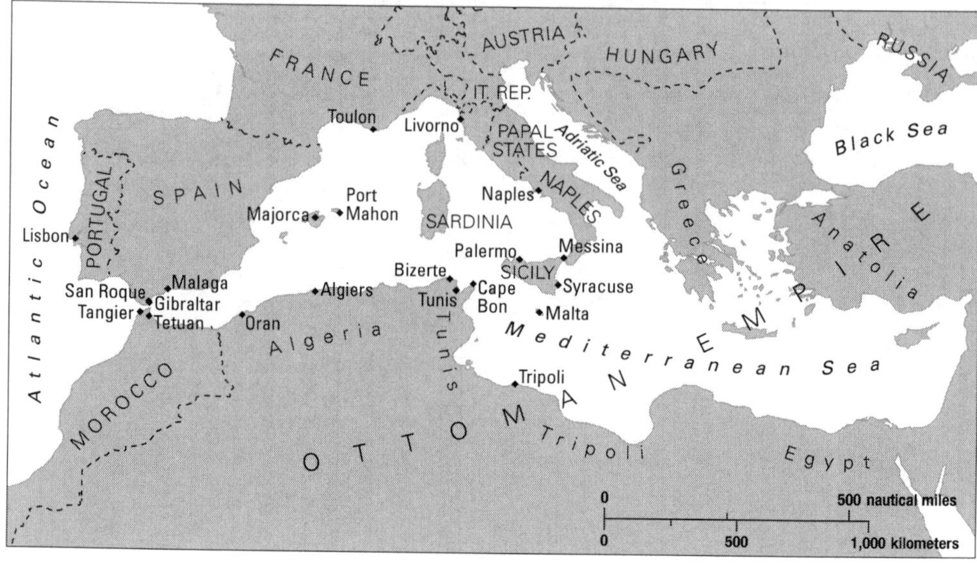

Figure 3.2 Sites important to the Americans in 1802. Map by Nat Case.

ill-advised but also illegal.[85] In fact, Richard Valentine Morris was also authorized to make treaties in concert with Cathcart, but Morris was in Morocco and so did not have a large part in any negotiations.

As the negotiators scrambled to regain the advantage after the *Franklin* capture, the commodore also had to reevaluate the navy's strategy. Seemingly unaware of how many different directions the navy was being pulled in, the secretary of the navy had suggested that Morris go to Tripoli and stand off that port with as much force as possible, "holding out the olive Branch in one hand & displaying in the other the means of offensive operations."[86] Secretary of State Madison made a similar suggestion to Cathcart—if the entire squadron could rendezvous at Tripoli in a show of force designed to intimidate, then Cathcart could tread lightly in his initial advances.[87] However, Eaton felt that friendly overtures had failed—"experiment has already demonstrated that nothing will render our nation respectable here and secure the faith of treaties but a decided dread of our resentment."[88] Of course, Alexander Murray had a contrary opinion. He did not think a show of force, even a skirmish with Tripolitan gunboats, would make the bashaw any friendlier to American interests.[89]

While he was in captivity, Andrew Morris, the *Franklin*'s captain, expressed to William Eaton his irritation about the navy's performance. He sidestepped the consuls' frustrations about ships not using the provided convoys by blaming the navy's ineffectiveness at maintaining the blockade: "It was the assurances

I had from all quarters of the impossibility of their Cruizer to evade the vigilance of the Blockade that led me to sea without convoy or *Arms*—fatal experience has convinced me to the contrary, for their small Vessels can go out any night in the week that they please and penetrate as far to the westward as Malaga, *which is manifest on a late occasion* except a different plan is adopted by our fleet." He suggested that two ships be posted to Tripoli to "keep up appearances," and the remainder sent to cruise between Cape Bon, Susa, and Sicily, where the real danger lay.[90]

Morris's ideas about how to correct the blockade might not have been possible, but he was not alone in his criticism of the strategy. Alexander Murray noted that the small Tripolitan galleys could easily get in and out under the cover of darkness despite the fact that his ship, at least, maintained the blockade "with all our diligence."[91] In July, when the blockade should have been at its most vigorous, sometimes Nicholas Nissen did not see any American ships for five days or even more. When the galleys that were fitting out left, they would surely get out and back in with their prizes without interference from the American squadron. The grain harvest in Tripoli had also bounced back from the previous year's famine, so the blockade of foodstuffs had much less effect this year.[92]

During those summer months, presumably because of their commodore's apathy toward the blockade, none of the American squadron stayed off Tripoli for more than a day or two except Alexander Murray and sometimes Captain McNeill in the *Boston*. Even the coalition with Sweden, which was supposed to ensure full coverage at all times, had broken down—the Swedes were off getting supplies and would not be back until August. Murray would also have to return to Malta to re-provision soon, leaving the port of Tripoli wide open.[93] By September, Murray had completely given up. He thought that maintaining the façade of the blockade was merely wasting a ship that could be doing something more useful (presumably convoy).[94]

Despite his skepticism about the effectiveness of the blockade, Murray was one of the few captains who spent any time off Tripoli (as he noted). As a result, he was involved in one of the only skirmishes with Tripoli during 1802. On July 22 the *Constellation* and the Swedish frigate *Thetis*, patrolling together, encountered nine gunboats near one of the forts of Tripoli. Firing between the antagonists commenced around 11:00 A.M. It concluded by 11:30, so it was by no means a pitched battle. Murray reported that as the skirmish progressed, Tripolitan landsmen began to congregate on the shore, eventually numbering around 6,000. The two frigates fired in their general direction and dispersed them.[95]

Sweden was not going to be the United States' partner forever, though. Swedish diplomats brokered a treaty with Tripoli in the summer of 1802, a development that William Eaton castigated as cowardly. Part of Eaton's scorn was for the French, through whom the Swedish had brokered the deal. He argued that though the French saved the Swedish $100,000, "the national honor and independence of Sweden are thrown into the scale to balance the obligation!"[96] Eaton saw greed as a pervasive problem among the European powers: "I know we have some politicians among us who talk of reliance on the *magnanimity* of the great powers of Europe to interfere in our behalf—When the *lion and the lamb shall lie down together* this event will take place; but while jarring interests agitate this world and while the greater powers of Europe are actuated by a counting-house policy, in stead of relying on their *magnanimity* we must think of defending ourselves against their intrigue here."[97]

With Sweden's support drying up, Commodore Morris had to make hard choices. His options for fighting the war demonstrated some of the core tensions of the conflict. He had to decide which Barbary state deserved priority—the state that was actively at war but with less power to interrupt American shipping, or the state with whom peace was essential to protect Americans in both the Mediterranean and the Atlantic. Morris also had to decide whether to expend his resources on the blockade, in which he had little confidence, or to allocate his men and vessels to a more active strategy protecting American shipping via convoy or an aggressive attack.

Trouble with the Other Barbary States

Whatever Morris decided to do, concern about the other Barbary states consumed the attention of both the consuls and the navy. In Tunis, the American inability to provide promised tribute exasperated the bey, Hamouda. Eaton scuffled with the bey over the question of presents in April 1802, and the bey ordered Eaton to leave Tunis immediately. Eaton instead announced that he had voluntarily chosen to leave the consulate; he had not been evicted. He then refused to grant passports to any Tunisian vessels. Hamouda requested that he be replaced by someone who was friendlier to Barbary interests. When Eaton informed him that James Leander Cathcart was the new appointee, the bey—who had requested a consul "with less *fantasia* & more friendly to the Barbary interests"—refused to allow Cathcart to enter Tunis at all, much less speak as the representative of American diplomacy.[98]

Hamouda's ranking of the United States in the hierarchy of nations upset the Americans. From afar, Cathcart reported that Hamouda considered the United States on par with Sweden or Denmark—in other words, a minor power. Cathcart wanted something better for the United States: acknowledgment as a major power such as Britain or France. He observed the disparity in treatment between those nations and his own. The major powers paid less in tribute and received appropriate salutes from the port when their warships came in, whereas

Cathcart regularly felt that American honor was affronted. If the United States was recognized as a major power, then it would be able to set its own agenda and appoint its own representatives to the Tunisian government. Perhaps Cathcart was feeling personally attacked by the bey's particular antagonism toward him. But he also argued that acquiescing to the bey's every whim reflected dishonor on the United States.[99]

While Eaton was in the midst of negotiations with Hamouda, Alexander Murray arrived in Tunis with some of the gifts promised. Though the bey accepted the gifts, he then demanded that the United States build him a ship of war as they had built the *Crescent* for Algiers. Eaton reminded him that the treaty did not allow for such a gift, privately noting to the secretary of state that if the United States did choose to build one for Tunis, it would almost certainly have to build one for Tripoli as well.[100] As these negotiations dragged into the fall, the bey wrote directly to President Jefferson with his demands for a warship. Couched in terms of conciliation, Hamouda's letter expressed hope that Jefferson would honor his demand in order to "strengthen ever more the ties of our friendship which, on my side, I will preserve as firm and inviolable."[101]

Tunis also became a battleground over the legality of captures made by the American navy. In May 1802 the *Boston* captured four Tunisian xebecs, small trading ships, that Captain Daniel McNeill believed were intending to run the Tripolitan blockade. The bey demanded that the xebecs and their cargo be returned, as the United States was not at war with Tunis. There followed a dispute between Eaton and Hamouda about international law and the differing authorities each nation claimed. The bey invoked a precedent of an encounter with Venice. Eaton countered with examples from Britain and France. The bey turned an American maxim against Eaton: free bottoms make free goods. Eaton countered that blockades were a clear example where that principle did not apply. The bey again tried to use the Americans' words against them, citing the president's letter to him as a promise that his ships would not be spoiled. Eaton reinterpreted that letter, stating that a "fair construction" of Jefferson's intent was to maintain peace so long as Tunis did not violate neutrality. At that point, the discussion devolved into threats of further violence from both parties.[102]

In his report about the dispute, Eaton argued the United States should hold firm about the legality of the capture. "Whatever restitution may be in future conceded," he wrote to the secretary of state, "this is not the moment to yield in the smallest matter that will go to deminish that opinion of our energy with which these pirates begin to be impressed—It will be Seasonable enough to be generous when they shall be taught to appreciate duly our generosity."[103] However, a few weeks later, Eaton wrote back to the secretary of state to tell him that all of this resolution had been irrelevant. The captures had not been made by

Captain McNeill, but by the Swedes, a turn of events that "relieves me from in-calculable perplexities" with the bey.[104]

McNeill again found himself in the middle of manufactured controversy when a Captain Norman returned to the United States from the Mediterranean with news that McNeill had intervened in a chase between a Neapolitan frigate and a Tunisian squadron. Norman reported that McNeill had sunk two of the seven Tunisian warships, dismasted two, and frightened off the other three. Norman lamented, "The imprudence of that Mad Man will I fear have brought a Severe Enemy upon us," since McNeill had no legal right to fire on the Tunisians unless they were running the blockade or firing at him unprovoked.[105] By the time the story had made the rounds in the newspapers, some were claiming that nearly all the *Boston*'s officers were killed in the battle. Others expressed doubt that the incident had ever happened.[106] No matter the specifics, the news alarmed the cabinet. Albert Gallatin, secretary of the treasury, suggested that the United States prepare some financial compensation for Tunis in case McNeill had fired first.[107] McNeill's well-deserved reputation for erratic behavior made the story entirely plausible, but fortunately for McNeill, the rumors were (once again) not true.[108] In fact, McNeill had not encountered a Tunisian squadron at all. But the story did not completely die out until early 1803, highlighting once again the perils of slow communication. For nearly six months, government officials in the United States believed that it was at least possible that one of their naval officers in the Mediterranean had acted in a way that would surely lead to war against Tunis, a circumstance the navy (and the treasury) could ill afford.

Actual actions by members of the squadron did jeopardize relations with Tunis. On May 12, 1802, Eaton wrote in a panic to the secretary of state about a report that an American schooner had looted a Tunisian xebec when it stopped the vessel on blockade duty. Investigation revealed that a marine and two sailors on Andrew Sterett's *Enterprize* had taken some money and a watch off one of the Turkish passengers on the xebec. Eaton smoothed things over with the bey of Tunis, but "it went very nearly to have produced a rupture with this Regency."[109] Charles Wadsworth wrote later that he hoped the three men would get the death penalty, and that they would be executed in the harbor of Tunis so that the bey could see that those men's behavior was not authorized by their superiors.[110]

Though relations were not as volatile in Algiers as in Tunis, the United States was by no means on sure footing. In May 1801 Commodore Dale had been given $30,000 to give to Algiers as a payment, but the dey wanted stores, not money.[111] In September 1801 Richard O'Brien was concerned that the dey was losing patience with the American inability or unwillingness to honor the terms of their agreement. "They are nearly of Opinion that I have been feeding Them with a

String of lies," he wrote to the secretary of state.[112] At the beginning of 1802, Algiers was still waiting for payment in both money and stores. O'Brien wanted to retire as consul, and the Americans were scrambling to find a suitable replacement for him.

The turmoil in the other Barbary states made convoy an even more important part of the navy's mission. Until July, the United States was able to partner with the Swedish because of Dale's agreement with Admiral Cederström.[113] But after the Swedish treaty, the American navy was on its own. As the year progressed, and relations deteriorated, Richard Valentine Morris personally recommended that ships wait for convoy at Cadiz before trying to pass through the Straits of Gibraltar because of the threat from Morocco.[114] The consuls also did their best to force the merchants to join convoys. Cathcart lamented that despite the entreaties of himself and Thomas Appleton, consul at Livorno, merchants continued to embark alone, "intent upon gain only." He solaced himself that at least he and the other consuls had tirelessly informed the merchants of the convoys available, and if they chose to go their own route, their fate would have to be on their own heads.[115] In 1802 close to 60 American vessels cleared from Livorno; it is not certain how many of them traveled in a convoy.[116]

Ironically, when Morris's suggestion that vessels wait for convoy in Cadiz garnered a few interested merchants, he wrote to Joseph Yznardi, consul at Cadiz, that no naval vessels were available to provide convoy, precisely because the situation with Morocco was so tense. If Simpson was able to bring Morocco to a peaceful settlement, Morris wrote, then no naval vessels would need to provide convoy. If not, he would eventually send the *Adams* to collect merchants at both Cadiz and Malaga.[117]

Although naval captains received instructions about how convoy ought to work, inevitably there were difficulties. In November 1801 Lieutenant John Shaw of the *George Washington* received instructions from Commodore Dale that he should plan to remain only a few days in each port, unless at least four or five masters asked him to wait. He was also to write to consuls informing them when he was coming to their respective ports and asking them to have the vessels wishing convoy already assembled.[118] However, when he arrived in Naples, he learned that one of these vessels had been detained by the government. Shaw asked General John Acton, prime minister of state, the reason for the detention of the brig *Traveller*, citing his desire for the convoy to leave at the first fair wind.[119] Shaw eventually decided that if the ship could not be released in time to sail, it would have to be abandoned, and the cost of its abandoned cargo would have to be claimed for its owner by the United States government.[120]

After about a week of inaction, on January 16, 1802, Acton suddenly decided to release the ship. The very next evening, Shaw and William Eaton, who was traveling with the *George Washington*, received an invitation to dine with General

Acton and his family, along with several other foreign dignitaries in Naples. As the party was winding down, General Acton's brother took Eaton aside. Though he said he could not speak freely with the British and French officials there, he wanted Eaton to know that Naples supported the United States' fight against Tripoli, and that Acton and his government would do anything they could to help. This was perhaps one of the first times the Americans had found themselves the supplicated rather than the supplicant in Mediterranean affairs. Eaton afterwards observed that Naples was trying to "profit of the interprize of our Nation to obtain some kind of succour against the piracy of Barbary." However, this desire might prove the catalyst for signing a commercial treaty with Naples, thus strengthening American ties to the Mediterranean community.[121]

When the *George Washington* moved on to Livorno after the delay, Shaw found that nearly all the commercial vessels had sailed without waiting for convoy. Shaw picked up 3 vessels in Livorno and 11 more when he arrived in Marseilles. Shaw found convoy frustrating, and when a storm separated the convoy, he did not seem to make too much of an effort to corral the ships again, commenting later, "The[y] pay but very little attention to Convoy I apprehend the[y] will repent—when its to late."[122]

In contrast to Shaw's at least half-hearted attempts to work with the convoy system despite its trials, Daniel McNeill clearly saw convoy duty as pointless or beneath him. When McNeill put in to Naples, he gave the merchants one day to assemble, despite being told that several merchants would be ready in just three or four days. The *Boston*'s purser wanted to write to ports that would be part of the *Boston*'s route going forward, but McNeill's determination to spend just one day in each port made that communication impossible.[123]

Richard Valentine Morris also spent much of 1802 on convoy duty. During 1802 Morris never came even close to Tripoli. The closest he got was a large convoy the *Chesapeake* and the *Enterprize* escorted from Gibraltar to Malta in August, stopping in at Malaga, Livorno, and Palermo.[124] Circumstances beyond his control conspired to keep him away from Tripoli. Morris noted that the passage from America alone took 55 days (an exceptionally long time), and then he had to stay in Gibraltar to superintend the Morocco affair. He intended to go to Tripoli, but November and December had such bad weather that he did not think it likely he or any of the squadron would be able to remain on station.[125] Facts seem to bear out his concern. Because of an outbreak of influenza on the *Chesapeake* in December 1802, Morris could not get out of Malta for almost three weeks, as he feared "risking the increase of their complaint, by exposing them to the inclemency of the weather." When the crew was well enough to sail, the *Chesapeake* still could not sail for several days because of adverse wind. Before Morris left for Tripoli, he stopped in at Syracuse in December for supplies, but discovered that they were much more expensive and scarce than in

Malta. Though the *Chesapeake* tried to sail from Malta in January 1803, it remained trapped due to the weather for many days, sailing for Tripoli after several detours on January 22, 1803.[126]

Since he spent almost no time on blockade, Morris was more dependent than ever on foreign friends for official needs. For the many months he remained at Gibraltar, he depended on the goodwill of the British officials there to keep his ship supplied. Morris also prioritized convoys over the blockade, which left his officers plenty of time to visit the ports they stopped at. As the *Chesapeake* prepared to leave Livorno in November 1802, Midshipman Henry Wadsworth observed that "20 or 30 days will generally satiate us with any place," which was a great deal more time than the recommended time to wait for a convoy. Instead of cruising off Tripoli, Wadsworth and the *Chesapeake* spent weeks in each port, giving him and his comrades plenty of time to visit the theater and tour the countryside. Though Wadsworth and his fellows made some local friends in places such as Syracuse, and perhaps accustomed local people to seeing American naval officers in the region, it is hard to make the case that sightseeing did much to further the goals of entrance into the Mediterranean community or the defeat of Tripoli.[127]

The continued pleas of both diplomats and naval officers for more ships finally bore fruit. The *John Adams* (not the same frigate as the *Adams* that had arrived in July) arrived in September, and the *New York* in November, though their purpose was to protect against possible Moroccan trouble, rather than deal with Tripoli. The *New York* came bearing orders for the *Constellation* and the *Chesapeake* to return home, but Morris was to transfer his command to the *New York* or the *John Adams* and stay in the Mediterranean to superintend negotiations.

The *Essex*, one of Dale's original squadron, had stayed well into Morris's tenure, but returned home in July, where it was laid up in ordinary.[128] Daniel McNeill and the *Boston* too were recalled. McNeill's shenanigans finally proved too much for the secretary of the navy, and when he returned home, he was dismissed from the service ostensibly under the Peace Establishment Act.[129] The Peace Establishment Act of 1801 had ordered that most of the navy's ships be laid up in ordinary after the Quasi-War, in an effort by the antinavalists to avoid keeping a peacetime navy.[130] Fewer ships on active duty meant fewer officers needed, though most of the officers whose positions were terminated under the Peace Establishment Act had not been sent on further duty after the Quasi-War. Clearly the secretary of the navy was just using the legislation as a convenient way to get rid of McNeill.

If 1802 seems like a year of disarray, it was. Historians have typically characterized Morris's cruise as one lacking in action, as Commodore Morris spent much of the cruise at Malta, Gibraltar, and other safe ports. This cruise may not have furthered the mission with Tripoli, but its events did complicate the United States' relationship with Europe and the other Barbary states. Morris's tenure shows how the differing priorities among the leadership manifested in confused and lethargic strategic decisions, complicated again by the struggle to maintain a squadron with no bases. Nevertheless, the year was not completely without consequential events, such as the *Franklin* affair. During 1802 the rift also widened between the navy and the consuls of the Mediterranean. Lack of leadership in both camps meant that neither camp was willing to work with the other. This infighting resulted in the loss of a unified front before both Tripoli and the other Barbary states. The capture of the *Franklin* demonstrated the ineffectiveness of the blockade strategy, as William Eaton's continued scheming about a coup against Yusuf Karamanli wandered toward an eventual end.

CHAPTER FOUR

Not an Idle Vessel

We are narrow sighted Mortals, we know not when we do right,
or wrong.

—Alexander Murray, January 11, 1803

The year 1803 began with stormy seas in the Mediterranean. For almost two weeks, the *Constellation* tried to cross from Gibraltar to Tangier, eventually sailing instead to Tetuan to avoid the fate of 14 other vessels, dashed on the rocks attempting the crossing.[1] On the *Chesapeake* in Malta, Midshipman Henry Wadsworth complained, "The Deck directly over my Cot leaks very much, of course my bed & bedding are much wet as the Element water is continually in boisterous weather washing over the Gun Deck."[2]

The winter storms were an apt metaphor for the situation of the United States in the Mediterranean. Richard Valentine Morris continued to struggle to lead his squadron, in part because his time and attention were still divided between Tripoli and the other Barbary states that threatened action. These fractures highlighted Morris's command inability as well as the impossible situation he faced. When the new commodore arrived in the fall of 1803, he inherited not only the lowest ebb of American naval power but also the nadir of Americans' relationships with each other and the rest of the Mediterranean world, thanks to Morris's mismanagement. It would take months to overcome all of Morris's poor choices.

Negotiation and Capitulation

In Algiers the diplomatic situation at the beginning of 1803 was so precarious that Richard O'Brien asked John Gavino, consul at Gibraltar, to address his letters to the Swedish consul at Algiers rather than sending them directly.[3] The dey still demanded naval stores instead of the $30,000 in cash O'Brien could pay. O'Brien entreated the government back home to take the demands seriously, as the dey tended to declare war first and then backtrack rather than waiting for diplomatic resolution. In Tunis, where the bey's mood toward the United States was still sour, William Eaton lied to one of the bey's courtiers that the new, more powerful American squadron would soon be arriving off Tunis. Knowing that the courtier would report this news to the bey, he hoped that the threat of force would bring the bey into a more conciliatory frame of mind.[4]

Eaton had reason to be concerned. On January 26 the bey summoned him to the court in order to make restitution for the *Paulina*, an Ottoman vessel that had been carrying Tunisian cargo when the *Enterprize* captured it trying to run the Tripoli blockade on January 17. After conceding that the *Paulina* had violated the blockade, Hamouda raised the same legal questions that he and Eaton had clashed on in 1802. Which law? Which precedent? Whose legal practice should prevail? As before, the argument devolved into threats. Eaton protested that the United States wished to be at peace with Tunis, but the actions of the Tunisian merchants indicated that Tunis wished a war with the United States. In the end, the question of international law was subordinated to local authority; Eaton had to bring the matter before Commodore Morris. Because a US naval vessel had made the capture, Morris held the legal authority to restore the prize (though Eaton maintained that if Morris did restore it, the act was one of goodwill, not one of legal justice).[5]

Morris had already made up his mind about the legality of the capture—he had given the *Enterprize* orders to lie in wait for the *Paulina*.[6] Nevertheless, he appeared as demanded at Hamouda's court to make his case, along with James Leander Cathcart, who came to provide diplomatic advice and to translate (from Italian) for Morris. After the niceties were observed, "the ceremony of shaking hands and drinking coffee," Hamouda demanded that the legal questions about the *Paulina* should be settled at Tunis. Morris suggested that the ship be sent to Gibraltar for adjudication in British admiralty court. This was a surprising suggestion, since the British had no jurisdiction over American prize cases. If the ship was not adjudicated in Tunis, Hamouda countered, the United States would find itself at war with Tunis as well as Tripoli. Morris quickly backed down, agreeing to leave the *Paulina* in Tunis, provided all the evidence was weighed fairly. Hamouda, perhaps sensing weakness, pressed his advantage. He promised that if Morris would not allow the Tunisians through the blockade of Tripoli, for every Tunisian ship the Americans captured, the bey's cruisers would take two American merchant vessels.[7] Morris refused to give free rein to Tunisian vessels, but he did agree to bring back the *Paulina*'s paperwork for inspection.

The *Paulina* dispute highlights the fact that proximity in both time and space were critical to keeping the peace. The two antagonists of this disagreement conceived of law and neutrality very differently. If the differences had to be ironed out via letters back to the United States, the dispute would have dragged on for months or even years, or the bey would have gotten tired of waiting and declared war. Instead, Hamouda seemed to enjoy arguing face-to-face with the Americans on questions of law.

These personal exchanges offered more than the opportunity for two combatants to lock horns, however. In diplomatic practice between Europe and the Barbary states, signed and ratified treaties held less weight than custom or precedent as the rule of law in disputes, and the victor in those disputes was the one who could spin in their favor the history shared between the two antagonists.[8] Since the United States had little history with Tunis or the other regencies, the Americans had to build experiences that would establish that history. Consequently, the social niceties such as coffee with the bey, salutes in the harbor, and other ritual forms of acknowledgment were much more important than the words of a far-off president or secretary.

Cathcart's presence as translator also allowed the negotiations to be done verbally, rather than through written means, thus establishing that needed precedent. Written treaties generally had to be written in Turkish, often alongside a copy written in the language of the other party. The Turkish was the canonical sealed version; any disputes were settled by the wording of that version. The use of Turkish was an acknowledgment of the sovereignty of the Porte, but the beys of Tunis sometimes could not even read the Turkish without difficulty.[9] Face-to-face meetings circumvented the need to write up official documents that had to be translated in multiple languages and verified by multiple people. Since Cathcart spoke several European languages, he was able to provide translation services typically performed by European captives in the court of the bey.[10] As a former captive of Algiers, Cathcart might have been both familiar and jarring to the bey. Instead of performing services as a slave, he now advocated for peace that would prevent the taking of more slaves like himself.

A few days after the initial meeting, on March 2, Morris and Cathcart returned to the bey's court, bringing the ship's manifest from the *Paulina*. The two Americans and Hamouda determined that a large portion of the cargo was not intended for Tripoli (though perhaps some of it was), and Morris agreed to restore it to the master of the ship. The agent representing the *Paulina*'s master agreed not to demand any of the cargo that might have been bound for Tripoli, nor to make any further claims. Morris's quick acquiescence to the Tunisian interpretation of the law probably kept the peace.

The *Paulina*'s agent, like the bey, pressed his advantage. Reneging on the agreement, he returned on the next two days with fresh claims for the rest of the cargo. After the second day, Cathcart "lost all patience at so barefaced a falsehood, [and] called him an impostor destitute of shame." But after being detained by the bey for a day, Morris agreed to settle all his claims, fearful that the bey would not let the Americans leave the city at all. After another two days of arguing about debts, particularly a debt owed by William Eaton, Morris finally left Tunis and returned to the *Chesapeake*. Cathcart returned to bring the bey the new consul in place of Eaton, Dr. George Davis. After yet more posturing and arguing over the details of various financial transactions, on March 13, Cathcart, Morris, and Eaton weighed anchor from the Bay of Tunis, "the abode of happiness."[11] (Tunis really was called this by its own denizens; Cathcart's use was obviously dripping with sarcasm.) After this point, Eaton was no longer welcome in Tunis. Instead, he headed back to the United States to drum up support for his plan with Hamet.

Despite the resolution of the *Paulina* dispute, Morris recognized the fragility of the settlement. A few weeks later, he wrote that the peace between the United States and Tunis would not last, because the "Northern Countries," Sweden and Denmark, had renegotiated their annual tribute treaties, but the United States had not agreed to further payments. Despite all of the Americans' protests, Morris realized that the United States was still a minor power in Tunis's estimation and would be treated as such.[12]

After the frustrating negotiation with Tunis, Morris's bad luck continued. On April 25 an explosion in the *New York*'s hold killed four men. The accident was almost much worse. But for a fortunately open passageway, the "explosion would momently have been followed by the magazine & then adieu." The *New York* limped back to Malta, arriving on May 1.[13] The other ships of the squadron spread out across the western Mediterranean. The *John Adams* patrolled off Tripoli for several weeks, skirmishing occasionally with gunboats that ventured out from the harbor.[14]

Though the crew of the Tripolitan flagship *Meshouda* had long since found other ways home, the ship itself still lay at anchor in Gibraltar. In September 1802 the emperor of Morocco had claimed the ship as his property, so consul James Simpson had granted the ship a passport to travel out of Gibraltar. But Hugh G. Campbell and the *Adams* had stayed in Gibraltar, leading the captain of the *Meshouda* to complain to the emperor that the Americans were lying in wait to capture him, passport or no passport.[15] When the *Meshouda* attempted to leave the harbor after signing on a new crew, Campbell had no choice but to honor the agreement made with the emperor and let it go. The *Meshouda* immediately set sail for Tripoli, in direct violation of the emperor's promise that he would honor the blockade. As the vessel approached Tripoli on May 13, it encountered the *John Adams* and was captured. When Captain John Rodgers brought the *Meshouda* to Malta, he discovered that it was carrying naval stores for Tripoli, which were contraband under the laws of the blockade. The stores had been taken on board in Algiers after leaving Tangier, in order to avoid trouble at

Gibraltar. Commodore Morris offered no advice for how Simpson should handle this "detestable Fraud."[16] If the emperor had ordered the *Meshouda* to Tripoli, it would be difficult to avoid a fresh declaration of war, which the United States did not want.

The wheels of communication among the Barbary regencies started turning almost immediately after the *Meshouda*'s capture, demonstrating that the United States was not truly up against only one opponent in this war. An agent of Tripoli in Malta wrote to the Moroccan emperor informing him of the capture and expressing concern that the *Meshouda* be given a fair trial.[17] The close relationship between the Barbary states had manifested itself before—from the beginning of the war with Tripoli, the other Barbary states had been providing both moral and physical support by giving supplies and obstructing the Americans. Historian Kola Folayan argues that because of commercial and religious ties, the Barbary states worked together to dismantle the American blockade of Tripoli.[18] The other Barbary states were not acting purely out of concern for the bashaw. Rather, they worked to maintain the communal ties that made them all stronger at the expense of nations that did not have the resources to fight them all at once.

James Simpson believed that the emperor was colluding with Tripoli, writing to Secretary Madison, "We have seen the Emperour since the commencement of the War with Tripoly, do what he could to favour them. All Nations experience the like conduct from every State in Barbary, when they have War with any of the others."[19] But the emperor vowed that he had not authorized Omar Reis, the captain of the *Meshouda*, to sail for Tripoli or to carry contraband. The governor of Tangier, Alcayde Hashash, likewise expressed astonishment, and "even after a long conversation he could not be made fully to believe that Omar could have committed such a mad Action, and so diametricaly opposite to the Instructions he had given him, by His Majestys Command." Hashash even went so far as to demand that Omar be delivered up in irons and forthwith be beheaded.[20]

Simpson suggested to Morris that it would be politic to take the emperor at his word and release the ship back to him, especially considering that peace had been so recently restored. Morris, however, was determined to send the ship to an international court for condemnation. Though Simpson acknowledged that the Americans had a strong case for condemnation, he judged it more important to make a gesture of goodwill toward the emperor.[21] While the two men worked out their plan for the *Meshouda*, it remained in Malta.

It was May 1803 before Commodore Morris turned to the primary task he had been given: negotiating peace with Tripoli. In April 1802 the secretary of the navy had ordered Morris to post the majority of his squadron off Tripoli while Cathcart went ashore to negotiate peace with the bashaw. Morris was to show the squadron in a grand naval gesture intended to bolster Cathcart's credibility, but he was not to get involved himself.[22] When these orders were issued, Morris was still in the United States. But by August 1802, when he was finally in the Mediterranean, he received orders that he should be a "superintending agency in the negociations." Cathcart should be consulted if possible. Eaton was not to be consulted, and Morris had the final authority to negotiate even if Cathcart was not available. Morris was also "empowered to negotiate an adjustment of our differences with Morocco or with any of the other Barbary powers that may have declared or waged War against us."[23] Morris had taken seriously this directive to negotiate with other nations. Since his arrival in June 1802, he had negotiated with Morocco and Tunis but had barely even seen Tripoli harbor.

When he decided to open negotiations with Tripoli, perhaps Morris was feeling the sting of humiliation in his negotiations about the *Paulina*—he informed Cathcart that his services would not be needed. This decision infuriated and confused Cathcart, who reminded Morris that he was still a newcomer to the Mediterranean world. He did not know the rituals that must accompany any audience with the bashaw, nor did he (seemingly) know the history of negotiations with Tripoli.[24] Morris had also chosen not to communicate his intentions to his superiors in the United States, a decision that the secretary of the navy found concerning.[25] Leaving Cathcart in Livorno, Morris sailed for Malta, and, on May 19, for Tripoli.[26]

When Morris's *New York*, along with the *John Adams* and *Enterprize*, arrived off Tripoli on May 22, 1803, the Americans found the Tripolitan resistance active. The first day the *New York* was on station, a Tripolitan felucca tried to escape the harbor. The *New York* and the *Enterprize* drove the vessel on shore, but Isaac Hull, acting as the *New York*'s flag captain, ordered the American ships to back off rather than pursue it under Tripoli's batteries. A disappointed Midshipman Wadsworth wrote, "Had she been but an oyster boat t'would have been amusement for us to skirmish a little."[27] Wadsworth got his chance to skirmish a few days later, when the squadron found nine gunboats and a xebec off the coast. These boats were not corsairs, but only harbor defense. Nonetheless, the Americans wanted to destroy them. In the afternoon, Morris signaled for the *John Adams* to lead the attack. Even then, Wadsworth did not get all the battle he was hoping for. As darkness fell, he wished for "anyone on board who like Joshua of Old could have commanded the sun to stand still," for then "Thy Gun Boats would have been ours Tripoly, & thy people our Slaves." The squadron disengaged around 9 P.M., unable to see their quarry anymore.[28] This was just one of several skirmishes the navy had with the Tripolitans.[29] Despite the success of the previous night, the next day Wadsworth watched two vessels run the blockade into Tripoli right in front of the squadron.[30]

Despite the skirmishes, Morris was at Tripoli to negotiate. On May 29 the *Enterprize*, using a signal set up by Commodore Dale in 1801, signaled the city of Tripoli, requesting that the Danish consul come out to the squadron.[31] A few days previous, Captain John Rodgers of the *John Adams* had requested that Nissen make overtures of peace to the bashaw, and now Commodore Morris wanted to reopen the discussion.[32] However, the bashaw wished to treat with the Americans directly, not through Nissen.[33] Once Morris had written to Yusuf himself, he received an invitation to come ashore and discuss peace with an official duly authorized by the bashaw. Morris went ashore to open negotiations on June 7.[34]

Though the white flag of truce was flying in Tripoli, Morris still felt uneasy about being on shore away from the squadron. He requested a guarantee of protection from three different consuls; only the French consul agreed to provide it.[35] It was a good thing Morris had insisted on this protection. The negotiations broke down after less than a day. To the bashaw's demand of $200,000 up front, plus $20,000 and some naval stores as annual presents, Morris replied, "Were the Combined World to make the demand it would be treated with contempt." Furious, the bashaw ordered the truce flag to be hauled down while Morris was still in the city. Only the intervention of the French consul kept Morris from being detained. Morris returned to the *New York* in the morning of June 9, whereupon hostilities officially resumed.[36]

By June 15 the *New York* was back in Malta. The ship was quarantined for 14 days as a result of its activities before Tripoli, so Morris could not go ashore to see his infant son, born on June 10 in Malta.[37] The other American vessels, including the *John Adams*, the *Adams*, and the *Enterprize*, remained off Tripoli. During their stay, the squadron's de facto commodore, John Rodgers, noticed some unusual activity by the gunboats in the harbor. He ordered the American vessels to spread out so that they could catch any vessel that tried to leave the harbor. Early in the morning on June 22, the *Enterprize* discovered a large armed Tripolitan vessel anchored near the shore. The squadron converged and began firing at the ship, as well as at the gunboats that rowed out to its assistance. After 45 minutes of constant firing from both sides, the crew of the Tripolitan ship "abandoned the Ship in the most Confused and precipitate manner." The *John Adams* had to wear back from the Tripolitan ship a little, as the harbor became shallow and rocky near their position, but the *Enterprize* was able to keep firing at the boat and at the military forces that had assembled on the shore. The gunfire from the shore meant that Rodgers could not capture the ship. Instead, some of the Tripolitan vessel's crew returned to the ship, though only to haul down its colors in surrender. While the colors were being lowered, the ship exploded. The blast "Burst the Hull to pieces and forced the Main and Mizen Masts perpendicularly into the air 150 or 160 feet." Rodgers declared it "one of the Grandest Spectacles I ever beheld."[38]

Figure 4.1 View of Malta, from the *Naval Chronicle*, vol. 8, 1802. Naval History and Heritage Command, NH 66001.

After this spectacular event, the squadron stayed on station for only four more days, departing for Malta on June 26 as ordered by Morris before he left.[39] The squadron remained in Malta, watering and resupplying, for the next two weeks. While the squadron lingered, orders were traveling across the Atlantic for Commodore Morris's recall. Though Morris had been stinting with his reports to the secretary of the navy, Robert Smith, others had not been. Allegations of Morris's lack of zeal for the blockade, and his ineptitude as negotiator, had reached Secretary Smith. Morris was summoned home to answer for his actions.

Frustration with Morris's poor leadership extended to nearly all the Americans in the Mediterranean. Cathcart summed up his irritation: "I long ere now expected to see Tripoli prostrate at our feet, one small effort would have establish'd our national character with that Regency for a century better than a million sterling, but for want of energy & a spirit of enterprize we bring our humiliations to their Bashaws foot stool."[40] Cathcart had traveled with the commodore for several months and had seen his inattention to the blockade of Tripoli. After he was dismissed from assisting in the negotiations with Tripoli, he wrote bitterly to Secretary Madison blaming Morris's wife for his diffidence; "I cant help thinking that neither the zeal for the service nor its activity would have been impeded or injured had Mrs. Morris been left to propagate her species at Balls town or Morrisina."[41]

The squadron's strategy was somewhat to blame for Morris's failures. Because the bashaw had come to terms with the Swedish delegation a few months previous, he had plenty of money to support both his people and the war effort. Nicholas Nissen observed that a good harvest had diminished the effectiveness of the commercial blockade, and the blockade was so porous that European supply ships came in and out of Tripoli at will.[42] William Eaton questioned the leniency with which vessels were allowed to legally run the blockade, writing, "What kind of a blockade is this, where the invested enemy is furnished with arms, amunition and provisions under the guarantee of the passports of our ministerial agents! Is it pretended that these submissions are the preservative of peace? The calculation is erroneous. They tend rather to precipitate a war; because they show that we dread it; and, it is on weakness and submission that these brigands make war."[43] Eaton referred to the practice of consuls granting passports to ships of neutral nations that allowed them to enter Tripoli. The passports were a calculated risk. Was it better to aid Tripoli, or to risk war with another power? In 1802 Morris had chosen the former, instructing Simpson to issue passports to Moroccan wheat ships. He reasoned that since Tripoli already had plenty of grain because of the good harvest, the wheat ships would not matter to the bashaw, but granting the passports might smooth relations with Morocco.[44] Simpson had also advocated for granting the Moroccan passports, concerned that unrest in Morocco might drive insurance rates so high that American commerce would suffer real consequences.[45] But Eaton thought this move, rather than improving relations elsewhere, would show the weakness of the American grasp on the Mediterranean and cause more war.

While some European ships were running the blockade with little difficulty, however, the American continuance of the blockade was actively injuring the cause of other members of the Mediterranean community. Aside from Britain and France, all the other nations who traded in the Mediterranean were on the same shaky ground as the United States. For example, the United States unwittingly caused the bashaw to increase pressure on the Dutch, who had no naval presence in the Mediterranean. The bashaw would not declare war with Holland while he was at war with the United States, because he could continue to extort money from the Dutch consul if Dutch ships were not getting through to Tripoli with their annuities.[46]

The blockade had to continue, no matter what the problems. After the failed peace conference in Tripoli, the squadron continued to cruise, stopping suspicious vessels to inspect their papers. Boredom set in, as vessel after vessel turned out to be benign, or at least not officially belligerent. The American officers struggled to tell the difference between Tripolitan sailors and ships and other North Africans, so they had to put special confidence in the passports issued to neutral ships by the American consuls in each port.[47] When his shipmates boarded a Tunisian galley only to find a passport from George Davis, Midshipman Wadsworth observed, "The Men were all hot for Battle, friends or Foes. The sight of a Turban soon enrages them."[48] The squadron also skirmished with Tripolitan gunboats and shore batteries throughout the summer, though nothing really came of any of the actions.

Since Morris could not leave the *Meshouda* unattended in a foreign port, the squadron brought the ship on the cruise off Tripoli. Meanwhile, in Morocco, Simpson waited in vain for Morris to decide what would happen to the *Meshouda*. Cathcart suggested that rather than sending it to Gibraltar for adjudication, Morris should instead give it to the bashaw of Tripoli as a gift. He argued that the ship, which had already divided the squadron between Tangier and Tripoli when it should have been unified off Tripoli, would never be condemned in a court that the bashaw or the emperor of Morocco would recognize. But it might be leveraged as a gift to the bashaw in lieu of a portion of the demanded money.[49]

Morris was never likely to have taken Cathcart's suggestion. But his failure to communicate any plans at all for the *Meshouda* caused James Simpson significant anxiety. Simpson had to wait and hope that the emperor would be reasonable when he arrived in Tangier from Mequinez in a few weeks. Under pressure to maintain peace, Simpson was also obliged to grant passports to two more Moroccan ships, the *Maimona* and the *Mirboka*, ostensibly cargo vessels. He felt certain that the two Moroccan cruisers had actually been authorized to capture American vessels, possibly because he would not return the *Meshouda*. However, he was not the only one under pressure—all the other consuls in Tangier had heard (and acquiesced to) the same demand for passports.[50]

Simpson also observed that there were a large number of both British and French privateers in the waters around Gibraltar.[51] American shipping was not immune to the depredations of European privateers. The Mediterranean community into which the Americans sought to enter was not a simple coalition of Europe against North Africa. On the contrary, relations between European nations were fractured—most significantly, the peace of Amiens between Britain and France had dissolved two months previous.[52] Alliances and antagonism shifted quickly and frequently, and the United States was caught in the middle.

The resumption of European hostilities also had indirect consequences for the Americans. The American squadron had been on fairly friendly terms with the kingdom of Sicily since the beginning of the war, but the rising tensions between Britain and France made Naples wary. When Morris requested the loan of some gunboats from Naples, the king's minister declined, expressing a desire to maintain neutrality with all nations until matters between England and France were settled. He was perfectly willing to allow the Americans to resupply in Naples and even keep prisoners there if necessary, but actually contributing arms to another nation's war effort was further than he was willing to go.[53] It was fairly clear that Britain and France were the controlling interests in the Mediterranean system.

Morris decided not to cruise off Tripoli after all. Instead the squadron sailed for Gibraltar with the *Meshouda* as well as a commercial convoy. As the squadron passed by a small Italian island in late August, the *Adams* came under fire from the fortification on the island. Though the *Adams* was not hit, Captain Hugh G. Campbell sent his boat to shore to discover the reason for this unprovoked aggression. The fortification was French, and the officer in charge demanded that the Americans pay him a guinea for each gun he had fired at the *Adams*. He held Lieutenant John H. Dent as a hostage until the money should be paid. William Smith, the former minister to Portugal who was a passenger on the *Adams*, went ashore and paid the money.[54] Commodore Morris was furious that Smith had paid the French off. He expostulated, "Well, by God if they had fired at me I would have returned it." Midshipman Wadsworth added privately that because of Campbell's "damn'd foolishness our country is insulted & we pay for it too. Blast him—if I were Com'r I'd arrest him & pack him off to the United States for Trial."[55] Most others in the Mediterranean wished that Morris *had* done more firing, and he was the one summoned back to the United States for trial. But the incident illustrated the point that the Americans might have to accept indignity from someone: fighting against Tripoli meant taking blows to their pride from many other sources.

As 1803 progressed into the fall, the Americans were pulled in many different directions. The squadron was slowly making its way toward Morocco, convoying vessels along the way, while diplomatic relations with Tunis and Tripoli remained uncertain. James Leander Cathcart had received orders from the secretary of state giving him full authority to treat with Tunis and Tripoli, but under terms that Cathcart despised. He railed at both Morris and the American government for their craven capitulation to the European system. His orders were to negotiate for payment to the bashaw, but he wanted the Americans to take their free trade by force. He felt that the Americans had lost any advantage that they had held earlier and were in danger of becoming like the Scandinavian countries, unless their advantage was "speedily retrieved by a brilliant act."[56] But Cathcart did not see Morris as capable of brilliance—his jealousy for personal glory rendered him unable to admit his weaknesses. "He acknowledges his being unacquainted with the usages of Barbary," Cathcart wrote. "How extraordinary then doth it appear that at the moment he contemplated a negotiation he should refuse to accept the assistance of a person legally authorized by government for that purpose & who was perfectly acquainted with their views usages and intrigues."[57]

As it turned out, this time Morris was all too happy to leave the negotiating to Cathcart. Morris wrote to Muhammad Dghies, the prime minister of Tripoli, to inform him of Cathcart's imminent arrival, which would, he hoped, "prevent the further effusion of blood."[58] Morris offered to send the *Enterprize* to bring Cathcart from Livorno to Tunis. However, Cathcart would have to find his own way to Tripoli—Morris claimed he needed the entire squadron off Morocco to deal with the *Meshouda* situation.[59]

Cathcart found himself again saddled with a naval partner reluctant to play by the rules of Barbary diplomacy. He was taken to Tunis by Hugh G. Campbell in the *Adams*, who took seriously Morris's instructions to remain at Tunis only four days. Campbell also declined at first to go on shore to pay his respects to the bey. Consul George Davis convinced him that Hamouda would insist on receiving a visit from the senior naval officer before any negotiations could start. The bey had seemingly retracted his former insistence that Cathcart would not be permitted into the country, instead telling Davis that Cathcart was welcome to come ashore with Campbell. After the traditional coffee was served to Cathcart and Campbell, it was clear that compromise was not in the offing. Though Cathcart still carried papers authorizing him to take over the consulship at Tunis, Hamouda's minister informed Cathcart that the appointment was impossible: "He cannot receive you as Consul resident, in this Regency, you having been the cause of the War with Tripoli." The bey also demanded the same things as he had demanded with Eaton—a warship, plus money and stores—and Cathcart refused. Finally, Hamouda insisted that Campbell make restitution for some prize goods sold at Malta illegitimately. Though Campbell protested that these questions were for the commodore of the squadron to decide, the bey decided to make Campbell accountable for them.

When Hamouda threatened to hold Campbell captive until the debts of the Tunisian prizes were paid, Campbell replied, "He may keep me to all Eternity; but the Ship Sails to-morrow; and I will write home for government never to pay the debt; I will remain here for ever, before I suffer such indignity to be offered with impunity." Campbell gave orders to the *Adams* to sail without him. However, Consul Davis was able to promise payment or restoration for all the disputed stores, and Campbell sailed with his ship.

As the *Adams* departed, Cathcart washed his hands of Tunis, writing, "To what a degrading situation are we reduced! the Commanders of the very Squadron which is sent out to preserve the Honor of our Nation and dignity of our Flag cannot land as the Officers of all other Nations do, and depart unmolested;

but have twice, in the small period of Six Months been subjected to arrest; and at this moment it would be the heighth of imprudence to land at Tunis, as certain arrest maybe imprisonment, would be the consequence." He waited until he and Campbell were safely back on board the *Adams* to write to the bey that Morris had revoked Davis's consular status, and therefore any agreement Davis had signed was invalid.[60] The *Adams* left Tunis on September 8 with no war, but no peace either.

At the end of July, the ships of the new relief squadron began to arrive in the Mediterranean. The *Philadelphia*, commanded by William Bainbridge, arrived in August. Upon his arrival, Bainbridge almost immediately encountered a Barbary ship whose nationality he could not discern. Bainbridge ordered the ship's papers brought on board the *Philadelphia*, where he discovered that it was the *Mirboka*, carrying passports from James Simpson and the other European consuls. Bainbridge had not heard from Simpson about the latter's suspicions of treachery regarding the Moroccan cruiser. Sailing with the *Mirboka* was an American brig, the *Celia*. Bainbridge sensed something amiss, and after the officer who brought the papers gave less than satisfactory answers about whether the brig was a prize, he had the *Mirboka* searched. Belowdecks, the search party found the officers of the *Celia*, who were clearly not on board voluntarily.

Since his men were already on board, it was easy for Bainbridge to take the *Mirboka*, which he did immediately, citing a violation of the passports. The capture was easy, but bad weather meant it took a full day and night to get the *Mirboka* and the *Celia* ready to sail. The *Philadelphia* had been headed for Malta, possibly to rendezvous with Commodore Morris, but after Bainbridge recovered both prizes, he turned back for Gibraltar to meet with Edward Preble, the commodore of the relief squadron that would be arriving soon.[61]

Bainbridge also set the chain of communications in motion. Upon his arrival in Gibraltar, he immediately informed consul John Gavino of his unsettling discovery: unsigned orders to Ibrahim Lubarez, captain of the *Mirboka*, to capture American shipping. Gavino then notified Joseph Yznardi, consul at Cadiz.[62] Bainbridge also sent a letter through William Kirkpatrick at Malaga to James Simpson.[63] These consuls presumably notified yet other consuls, spreading the news for American merchants to be on the lookout for Moroccan cruisers, who could no longer be considered harmless.

When Simpson heard that the *Mirboka* had captured an American brig, he immediately questioned the Moroccan government about its involvement. The answer to his appeal revealed that Morocco, just like the United States, suffered from poor communication and differing views about how to treat the Americans. Alcayde Hashash, the governor of Tangier, denied ordering Moroccan vessels to attack American ships, but the captains of the *Mirboka* and *Meshouda* identified him as the source of their orders.[64] When Simpson pressed the issue, he was detained in the governor's house in Tangier. Only the intervention of the European consuls convinced Hashash to release him. Simpson wrote directly to the emperor informing him of the circumstances. He resented the interference of Hashash, in whom "the Emperor has of late placed unbonded confidence, insomuch that we have seen acts of his of a most extraordinary nature sanctioned by his master."[65] The emperor summoned Simpson to Tangier along with Bainbridge and Ibrahim Lubarez and their respective papers to sort out the mess, assuring Simpson that Morocco was still friendly toward the United States.[66] Irate that Hashash had undermined his authority in front of the international community, the emperor wrote a circular to all the consuls at Tangier reaffirming that war could not happen without his express authority, and that if war occurred, he would respect the consul's safety while he was in Tangier.[67]

When the *Mirboka* arrived at Gibraltar, Captain Bainbridge faced a dilemma: where the ship should be held while its status was determined. To have the easiest access to Consul Simpson, Tangier was the logical place, but anchoring the vessel in that harbor was probably foolish. When John Gavino asked the government of Gibraltar to anchor the *Mirboka* there, he got a tepid response. Lieutenant Governor Thomas Trigge agreed to let the ship in, but only if the Americans did not intend to dismantle or sell it in Gibraltar. He also requested that its stay be as short as possible, as Britain did not want to get caught in the middle of the dispute between the United States and Morocco, "the Mischivious consequences of which you are well acquainted with."[68] Because Gibraltar was almost entirely dependent on Morocco for its provisions, any disruption to the relations between Britain and Morocco would certainly have unfortunate ramifications for Gibraltar.[69] Gavino could make no promises about either of the two stipulations, but he noted that neither the departing Commodore Morris nor the incoming Commodore Preble would likely involve the British in a dispute.[70]

The new commodore, Edward Preble, was a very different sort of man, with different experience from Richard Valentine Morris. He had served in both the navy and merchant service. In the Revolutionary navy, he had experienced both success and captivity. During the Quasi-War, he had commanded the *Essex* on the first voyage of an American naval vessel beyond the Cape of Good Hope. However, his health had been poor for much of his naval service, and it had prevented him from serving in the Mediterranean thus far.[71]

The transfer of power from Commodore Morris to Commodore Preble almost comically illustrates the difficulties of communication. The first ship from the new squadron to arrive was the *Nautilus*, commanded by Lieutenant Richard Somers, on July 31, 1803. Somers did not lack initiative. After taking on supplies from the American stores and purchasing the rest in Gibraltar, he stayed in Gibraltar for only two days before sailing to find the squadron.[72] Along his slow twenty-day journey, Somers "chased every thing that had appearance of Tripolitan." Despite good reason to think the squadron would be in Malta, as it had been there for the greater part of the year, Somers did not find any naval vessels when he arrived there. The next logical place to look for the squadron was off Tripoli, where Morris was supposed to be blockading. But again Somers did not find him. Returning to Malta, he learned that he had missed the *Enterprize* by one day, and that the squadron was at Livorno. He sailed for Livorno after anchoring at Malta for only half an hour.[73]

Near Sicily, Somers finally found one member of the squadron, Hugh G. Campbell's *Adams*, of which he inquired the location of Captain Rodgers. The fact that Somers asked after Rodgers and not Morris seems to indicate that he knew that the commodore had been recalled.[74] Campbell informed Somers that Rodgers had gone to Barcelona with a convoy. When Somers arrived in Barcelona after another storm-filled journey, he found that Rodgers and the convoy had sailed for Gibraltar two days previous. Making his slow way back toward Gibraltar, through storms that were so severe that the *Nautilus* was nearly driven onto land, Somers stopped in at Malaga. There, to his surprise, he found Commodore Morris. Somers was not pleased to see the commodore. He had dispatches for Rodgers, and having Morris there made his position rather awkward. Rodgers himself did not arrive till a day later, whereupon Somers was able to finally deliver his dispatches, a task that he confessed had been causing him considerable anxiety.[75]

Somers brought the squadron a lot of surprising news. He announced that the *Philadelphia* had taken the *Mirboka*, that there was war with Morocco (by that time, there was not), and that Commodore Preble was soon to arrive in the Mediterranean. Somers also delivered the dispatch that recalled Commodore Morris to the United States. Henry Wadsworth was astonished at the news: "We learn! Strange to tell!! We learn that the commodore is order'd home."[76]

Though Wadsworth was shocked to learn of Morris's recall, many others surely saw it coming. It was not surprising that a new squadron had been sent; after all, Morris had replaced Richard Dale after only a year. The difference was that Morris was not returning to the United States in glory or at least in the assurance that he had done his duty, but rather he was summoned to account for his misdeeds. The court of inquiry that tried Morris in November found him guilty of dereliction of duty—"two years sleep," as Thomas Jefferson later described it—and he was dismissed from the service.[77]

Morris's failures illustrate the larger struggles of the American squadron to support itself across the ocean from its leaders. The court—made up of three senior captains from the navy, Samuel Barron, Hugh G. Campbell, and John Cassin—alleged that Morris "did not conduct himself in his command of the

Mediterranean squadron, with the diligence or activity necessary to execute the important duties of his station," listing several long periods of time where neither Morris himself nor any member of his squadron had been maintaining the blockade off Tripoli. Surprisingly, they did not find enough evidence to censure his conduct between May 1802, when he had arrived, and January 1803. He had not been on blockade then either, but he had been trying to sort things out with Morocco. Apparently the court of inquiry found that activity a suitable substitute for his duty to Tripoli.[78]

The court repeatedly used the phrase "without necessity, or any adequate object" to describe Morris's decisions to remain away from Tripoli. Two of the three members of the court, Barron and Campbell, had served in the Mediterranean either before or under Morris, so in his defense, Morris appealed to their knowledge of the realities of the Mediterranean. Morris pointed first to the ambiguity of his orders. He argued that the government's priority was to protect American commerce, which President Jefferson had claimed as the mission of the squadron. His orders from the secretary of the navy indicated that a blockade was the proper means to that end, and that he should maintain the blockade insofar as it led to the protection of American commerce. Morris argued that when it became clear that the blockade was not preventing depredations, he had every right to interpret his orders to follow their spirit. He pointed out the vague terms in which the orders had been couched, written in that way because the secretary of the navy lacked familiarity with both the physical space of the Mediterranean and also the diplomatic climate, which could change frequently.[79] Morris's point was entirely valid, but even granting the ineffectiveness of the blockade, the court was right to judge that sitting in a port—particularly one where relations were stable—was not furthering a mission of any kind.

Once Morris dispensed with the philosophical and semantic defense, he turned to a more mundane argument: the difficulties of maintaining the squadron, and particularly his own ship. He observed that his Atlantic crossing had taken 55 days (by contrast, the *Adams* crossed in July 1802 in 44 days). He noted the time he had to spend repairing the *Chesapeake*'s bowsprit when he arrived in Gibraltar at the beginning of his cruise. Acting as a diplomatic agent in the Moroccan conflict caused yet more delays, until the weather made it impossible to get to Tripoli in the winter season.[80] The spring was supposed to bring better weather, but when Morris tried to take the squadron to Tripoli in March 1803, he turned back because of "the fury of a severe gale of wind." He appealed to Samuel Barron's own experience of wintering at Malta because of the strong storms in the Mediterranean.[81]

Provisioning the squadron was another barrier to Morris's success. Supply ships from America delivered their cargo to Gibraltar, so ships had to either return to Gibraltar periodically or rendezvous with one of the ships who had.

Morris detailed the difficulty of making these rendezvous points, particularly the frustration of having to return to Gibraltar so frequently. Morris adopted the viewpoint of the sailors of his ship in his defense: "The poor seaman, struggling with the tempest on a lee-shore, must have something to eat. While he cheerfully performs his hard duty, he looks up to his officer to provide for his necessities, and the officer could hardly appease the hunger of a starving crew, by describing the abundance heaped up in stores, at a distance of twelve hundred miles."[82] He further blamed Alexander Murray for not bringing the supplies out to the squadron as instructed.

Morris's defense of his actions rang true in many particulars. Communication among the squadron and with other parties was slow, unreliable, and likely to be outdated by the time messages were received. Provisions were hard to come by. The squadron's ships were worn down by hard use. The weather was unpredictable. Relations with other nations were neither simple nor always congenial. Morris also experienced the debilitation of sickness, though he did not bring it up during his defense. He likely suffered from malaria during a critical part of negotiations with the bashaw of Tripoli, when he initially refused to go on shore at Tripoli to treat with the bashaw's minister. Though he said he refused because he did not wish to be quarantined at Malta, it is also possible that he was not physically able to go.[83] Thus Morris's authority, already shaky, was compromised even further by illness. All of these factors were reasons the squadron struggled to make an impact.

Morris's tenure was not without merit. He had appeared in person before three of the four Barbary courts. Though his negotiations were largely unsuccessful, his personal attention to these matters was critical in maintaining tenuous relations where the American consuls had proved too abrasive. But Morris's deferential manner was not what the court of inquiry wanted. The court ruled that Morris had been negligent, and he was dismissed from the service.

A New Approach

On September 13, the day after Morris received his recall papers, Commodore Preble arrived in Gibraltar. Preble wanted to settle affairs with Morocco, but he lacked key information about the most recent developments. On September 7, as the *Constitution* neared Portugal, it had spotted a frigate, flying French colors, that turned out to be Moroccan. Preble boarded the frigate to inspect its papers. The ship carried all the proper papers, including a signed and sealed passport from James Simpson. Colonel Tobias Lear, incoming consul general to the Barbary states and passenger on the *Constitution*, certified the papers' validity. Since everything was in order, Preble let the ship go.[84] Preble did not know that this ship was the *Maimona*, carrying the same orders as the *Mirboka* to capture American vessels.

Upon his arrival in Gibraltar, Preble learned from Consul Simpson the news surrounding the three Moroccan vessels, the *Meshouda*, the *Mirboka*, and the *Maimona*. In each case, he was displeased with the American actions. He was vexed with Commodore Morris's determination to return the *Meshouda* to the emperor, stating, "Commodore Morris has the Controul of that business, and must act as he pleases, but if she came within my command, I should most certainly send her to the United States. The Captains and Officers of the Emperor, dare not act without his Orders." In the *Mirboka*'s case, he felt a similar passion: "You may acquaint the Emperor from me, that it is my intention in future to sink every such vessel as a Pirate, as he denies having given Orders to justify their conduct." Preble did not leave his own conduct unexamined, expressing regret that he had not acted on his doubts about the *Maimona*'s unusual behavior.[85] Though the American sailors must have been cheered by Preble's bold declarations, his brashness showed almost as much naiveté about the Americans' place in the Mediterranean system as had Morris's torpor.

By September 14, ships from both squadrons had converged on Gibraltar.[86] Morris was able to pass on to his successor information about all the various operations and negotiations the navy had undertaken in the past 12 months, a benefit Morris himself had not had when he arrived. Even so, the meetings were undoubtedly awkward. Morris was no longer commodore even of his own squadron, having given up the broad pennant to John Rodgers upon his recall. Rodgers was also technically senior to Preble, according to the secretary's list. Therefore, when Preble hoisted the broad pennant of the commodore, Rodgers felt his seniority had been ignored. Preble assured him that no offense was meant, quoting his orders from the secretary of the navy as proof that his squadron was separate from Rodgers's and therefore he could also be considered commodore. Rodgers did not agree. "It is not in the power (Even) of the Government," he wrote, "to place you or any other Officer in a situation which could afford an opportunity of treating me with Disrespect."[87] Eventually, Preble was able to bring Rodgers around by requesting that he join Preble in the negotiations with the emperor of Morocco.[88]

Preble also requested that Colonel Lear, who was ultimately bound for Algiers, stay in Gibraltar for a few days longer so that he might bring his diplomatic expertise to the negotiating table.[89] The juxtaposition of Preble's bold statements about Morocco and his desire to surround himself with good advisers set the tone for his tenure as commodore. Faced with many of the same problems as Commodore Morris, Preble prioritized communication and collaboration rather than isolation and defensiveness, at least in his earliest days.

As soon as he arrived in Gibraltar, Preble confronted the evergreen challenge of parceling out his ships in the most effective manner. Despite the problems with Morocco, Tripoli was the regency actually at war with the United States.

Preble chose to stay near Morocco, but he sent two of his ships to Tripoli, lest "the Tripolines would be induced to think we neglected them."[90] It took only a few days before the squadron was requested for convoy duty as well—Consul William Kirkpatrick wrote from Malaga that he had 14 vessels ready for convoy, if Somers and the *Nautilus* could be spared.[91] Preble sent the *Nautilus* once, but no vessels were indeed ready for him. Preble declined to send Somers back, instead dispatching the *Nautilus* and the *Vixen* to cruise looking for the *Maimona* and other Tripolitan or Moroccan vessels.[92]

Off Tangier, Preble and Rodgers waited for the arrival of the emperor, Mulay Sulayman. Consul Simpson worked tirelessly to find out the whole truth about the Moroccan ships in dispute. On the one hand, he had to quash the rumors spread by Hashash that the Moroccan crews had received poor treatment. On the other hand, new information from Captain Rodgers about the *Meshouda* led him to question whether he had taken the right approach. As the mediator among the three parties—the navy, the emperor, and the alcayde—it was paramount that Simpson have accurate information, which was difficult since he was essentially under house arrest. He grumbled to John Gavino, "There is no dependence on any thing in this country."[93]

While he waited, Preble took care of administrative tasks, such as sending out orders for the various ships in the squadron, as well as provisioning. He also met with James Leander Cathcart, who arrived on the *Adams* on September 23, and heard the news from Tunis of Cathcart's rejection as consul and the bey's demand for a frigate. Disgusted by news from both Tunis and Morocco, Preble wrote to the secretary of the navy, "I know not how long we shall be obliged to submit to this sort of treatment, the Moors are a deep designing artfull treacherous sett of Villains and nothing will keep them so quiet as a respectable naval force near them." Preble thought that the United States and all the other "Christian powers" must determine to pay no more in tribute to the Barbary states, but rather to "destroy every thing they can belonging to them."[94]

On September 24 Simpson received word from the Moroccan secretary of state, Mohamet ben Absalem Selawy, that the emperor would see them as soon as he reached Tangier. More importantly, Selawy directed, the American officers must be there with the *Meshouda* and the *Mirboka* if they wanted to treat with the emperor. "Beware of delays," he wrote. "Dont be slack or deficient in this matter of consequence for yourself."[95] In the meantime, the American officers seemed to be enjoying the company of the Moroccan crews. Preble shared his cabin with two of the *Mirboka*'s officers, the captain and what he called a priest.[96] Henry Wadsworth, transferred to the *Constitution* when Commodore Morris left for the United States, commented of the *Mirboka*'s captain, "A princely fellow invites me (after the War) to go home to Sallee with him & says he will give me four wives."[97] A less effusive Tobias Lear called

Captain Lubarez "a sensible, considerate and well informed man."[98] Neverthe-less, Preble wanted them off his ship, and after one too many conflicts, he eventually confined them.[99]

Storms impeded the emperor's overland journey.[100] While the squadron waited for his return, they engaged in short convoys and cruises off the coast, still looking for the *Maimona*. Letters of little import went back and forth between Consul Simpson and Minister Selawy frequently, as if both sides merely wanted to keep the lines of communication open but did not really have anything to say to each other. The Moroccan government demonstrated its good faith by releasing Simpson from house arrest. Colonel Lear announced Simpson's release in the circular where he also announced his own promotion to consul general in place of Richard O'Brien. He hoped to be taking up his post in Algiers soon, as relations with Morocco seemed to be improving.[101]

Finally, on October 4, word came that the emperor would be arriving the next day. Preble asked Simpson for guidance regarding proper (and safe) procedure for the meeting. Simpson suggested that it would be acceptable for Preble to wait to come ashore until Simpson had had a chance to meet with the emperor himself. He recommended as much pomp as possible from the ship, but to wait until after the garrison had fired its own salutes.[102] These details were just as important to Preble as they were to Mulay Sulayman, both of whom had a strong sense of honor and were easily affronted. In fact, the emperor was greatly pleased with the Americans' attention to him. Simpson reported that he watched another round of salutes the next day from a high place with a telescope. Simpson approved of the care Preble had taken: "Nothing could have been more apropos than your Salute just finished."[103]

However, when the emperor arrived, the Americans struggled to initiate conversations with him. After the ceremonies accompanying the emperor's arrival, Simpson began to make overtures toward the negotiating table. However, he was not permitted to come to the *Constitution* to discuss strategy with the commodore. His lines of communication to the emperor were also compromised. Written communications to the emperor had to be in Arabic, which Simpson did not know, so he employed the services of two interpreters from the Spanish consulate. They were willing to help Simpson, but they would not go aboard the *Constitution* to translate the affidavits of the officers of the *Mirboka*. Simpson had to find a different way to get the documents into a form the emperor could comprehend.[104]

Official communications struggles aside, the emperor continued to act friendly. When he brought an entourage onto the beach to view the squadron, Preble humored them with a salute in front of huge crowds, and the emperor's band played the Olester March, which signified friendship.[105] That day, the squadron received 10 bullocks, 20 sheep, and four dozen fowls as a present.[106] Given the struggles the squadron had experienced in the past with provisioning the ships, this present was eagerly received and quickly distributed. The emperor also ordered the release of an American ship, the *Hannah*, which had been taken into Mogadore a few months previous. As a sign of his good faith, Preble promised likewise to return the *Mirboka* once the treaty reestablishing peace was signed and ratified.[107] Though the Americans waited for several days to speak directly to the emperor after his arrival, their optimism increased as they waited. Preble wrote with confidence that the treaty of 1786 would be restored, with no further payments or presents to the emperor.[108]

On October 10 the American delegation—Preble, Lear, Simpson, Chaplain Noadiah Morris, and Midshipmen Izard and Wadsworth, plus "two mules and two Jews," carrying teapots, linens, sugar, tea, and other gifts—made their way to the emperor's court. After productive discussion, the next day Mulay Sulayman ratified the former treaty with the United States, restoring peace without additional payment. In exchange, James Simpson asked Commodore Preble to release the *Mirboka* back to Ibrahim Lubarez and let him raise the emperor's flag.[109] Preble was able to disperse his squadron, revoking the order to capture Moroccan vessels and turning his attention to Tripoli.[110] By October 14 the *Constitution* was the only American ship left at Tangier.[111]

On November 10 the secretary of state wrote to James Simpson giving instructions for how to negotiate with the Moroccans regarding the *Mirboka*.[112] When the letter was dispatched, it had been exactly a month since the Americans in Tangier had made peace.

While negotiations were proceeding with Morocco in October 1803, a conflict arose between Charles Stewart, captain of the *Syren*, and John Gore, captain of HMS *Medusa*, both stationed in Gibraltar. Stewart, who was charged with the keeping of the *Mirboka*, had discovered that three of his prize crew had deserted and found their way to the *Medusa*, where they were given safe haven. Stewart wrote to Gore, requesting that he return the men, as it was the only right decision as a representative of a country with whom the United States had amicable relations.[113] Gore refused to return the men, stating that one was not aboard and the other two had claimed the protection of the crown. He hoped the treaty of friendship between the two nations would motivate Stewart not only to revoke his claim to the deserters but also to hand over any other men of British origin who had shipped with the Americans while Britain was at peace but were now needed for the war against Napoleon. "As such Conduct [harboring deserters] is a violence against the laws of Nations," Gore wrote, "I must presume it Cannot be the intention of yourself and other Officers Commanding the Ships of the United States to persevere in it."[114]

More angry words passed between Stewart and Gore. Stewart finally told Gore that he had no authority to release anyone and referred the matter to the commodore. In his letter to Preble, Stewart acknowledged that Gore had the legal high ground: "We are liable to great inconvenience and contention with the Officers of the British Navy, as, many of our men may be claim'd on the same principle" as the one Stewart had claimed.[115] Preble too recognized that Gore was technically right, but he argued that he had no knowledge of his sailors' previous backgrounds, only that he had enrolled them as American citizens. This was not true—his crew was likely a majority non-American—but the American ships could not afford to lose the crew.[116] Ralph Izard, a midshipman on the *Constitution*, got to the heart of the matter: "It appears to me a matter of impossibility to draw a proper line of distinction, by which we may know an American from a British Seaman."[117]

Desertions quickly grew into a major dispute between the American and British navies. Midshipman Wadsworth alleged that the *Medusa* and HMS *Termagant* deliberately "anchored close to us in order to give our men an opportunity of swimming on board of them."[118] Just a few days after Preble told Gore he would go over his head to get his men back, Preble lost two of his own men to HMS *Amphion*.[119] Sensing a trend, Preble wrote to George Hart, the commander of the British squadron, requesting that he order his subordinates to return the deserters. Hart refused to do so. Preble invoked the character of Lord Horatio Nelson, who he argued would "not approve the late conduct towards us." Calling Preble's bluff, Hart said that he would write to Lord Nelson and ask him.[120]

This dispute affected more than just crew enlistments. It was the first major clash between the two navies, which was perhaps remarkable considering they had been sharing space in various ports for two years. Previously, the Americans had been concerned about British diplomats conspiring against them. For instance, in 1801 Cathcart thought that Murad Reis, the Tripolitan admiral, had been encouraged to violence by his friends Bryan McDonogh and Simon Lucas, British agents in Tripoli. But the US Navy's relations with the Royal Navy had been quite cordial—many American naval officers reported good reception by various British naval officers at Malta and Gibraltar.[121]

Desertions were a perpetual problem for relations between the United States and Great Britain. If the British were going to continue to encourage sailors on board American ships to desert, then Preble chose to make it hard for them rather than argue. Since both Gibraltar and Malta were in British hands, Preble chose to relocate the hub of his operations to Syracuse. The port was not as inviting as Malta, but Preble believed "we will find amusement enough in the necessary duties of our Ships," and as Henry Wadsworth observed, to Preble, "all places are alike. . . . He feels no pleasure in anything which does not forward his Favorite plans."[122] In the short term, the squadron moved from Gibraltar to the Spanish port of Algeciras, "because the English commanders have treated us with great indignity," though Gibraltar would continue to be the preferred port of entry into the Mediterranean.[123]

Disturbing news about the British came in from other quarters as well. Nicholas Nissen reported an alarming sight in Tripoli harbor: the arrival of an armed brig and a store ship with timber from Malta, flying the British flag. "Pray Sir," asked Nissen, "is Great Britain at War with the U States of America, that their flag is permited to protect the Cruisers & maratime & military stores belonging to the enemies of the United States of America?"[124] Not knowing of the conflicts and resulting shifts of operations, William Bainbridge, who had been sent on to Tripoli by Commodore Preble, stopped in at Malta on his way. There, he received permission from the British commander to store some spare spars and gunners' stores. Removing extraneous cargo from his ship was especially critical since he had left 13 men at Gibraltar and now had nearly 30 men sick, so he had considerably less than his full complement to run the ship. Given the likelihood of bad weather and high seas, Bainbridge did not want to waste manpower keeping the extra stores from rattling around.[125]

Supplies were hard to come by no matter where the squadron went. Disruptions in the Mediterranean had already hurt the American squadron, as the resumption of war between England and France had limited the supplies available for purchase at Gibraltar and drastically increased the prices on what was available.[126] But moving operations to Syracuse did not guarantee better supplies.[127] Preble wished to rely more heavily on the American supply ships, but they were also unreliable and costly.[128] Disease also caused the squadron difficulty in obtaining supplies. Though Preble left Gibraltar for Algeciras, he was unable to get water there because an epidemic of yellow fever at Malaga had closed all the Spanish ports between Malaga and Gibraltar. Instead, the *Constitution* and the *Enterprize* got water and repairs at Cadiz. The combination of desertions and disease had left the *Constitution* short of its complement of crew, though Preble did sign some crew on at Cadiz. The shorthanded *Constitution* nevertheless sailed back to Gibraltar as soon as it could to pick up Colonel Lear's family to deliver them to Algiers.[129]

On October 14 Bobba Mustapha, the dey of Algiers, wrote to Thomas Jefferson, "If you are my friends and wish to remain so," then the president must supply the dey with several long cannons and 60,000 bricks to build furnaces. He wrote to Jefferson directly because Richard O'Brien had refused to do so.[130] O'Brien did write to the secretary of state, James Madison, outlining all the ways that the United States would be in trouble whether it acceded to the dey's request or not. O'Brien wanted to break the Mediterranean system with force in a way that the Europeans had thus far failed to do: "We shall have to do it at last—if some great Event of Europe does not Curb the pride avarice & System of Barbary." However, European intervention seemed unlikely. The Danish, Dutch, Swedish, and Spanish consuls had already agreed to provide guns that the dey had also demanded of them.

O'Brien suggested that Madison write "at least 3 different letters—differing in words," which the consul (not himself, he hoped) could then use depending on how the situation unfolded. He recommended refusal, but only after several months so that the consul and other Americans in Algiers would have time to get to safety. He saw a conflict with Algiers as likely to lead to war with all the Barbary states, so he suggested more force should be built and sent over.[131] O'Brien took the liberty of drafting one of the proposed letters himself, in which he refused every demand, writing, "We have too great a regard to our Honor & dignity Then to condescend and acquise to all The Unjust and Extra demands of your Highness." He signed it "Jefferson" and addressed it to "The Meditteranian Don Quixotte."[132]

Disaster in Tripoli

On October 31 the focus of the war suddenly shifted to Tripoli. While cruising off Tripoli, the *Philadelphia* had sighted a Tripolitan vessel. Pursuing the vessel into the harbor, the frigate had run aground four or five miles east of the town. Despite cutting away anchors, guns, and even the foremast, the crew could not lift the *Philadelphia* off the bar. Four hours of fire from Tripolitan gunboats and shore batteries convinced Captain Bainbridge that he could not hope to defeat them. Around sunset, the *Philadelphia* struck its colors and the ship's crew were taken prisoner.

The United States' unofficial ally in Tripoli, Nicholas Nissen, took immediate action to get the prisoners into as comfortable accommodations as the bashaw would allow. The enlisted sailors were imprisoned in the bashaw's castle and made to perform hard labor. The officers were settled in the consular house formerly occupied by James Leander Cathcart, though the Tripolitans blocked their view of the sea, presumably to keep them from knowing whether American help had arrived.[133] Six days later, the blocked windows kept them from seeing the Tripolitans raise the ship off the bar, assisted by a strong westerly wind.[134]

Bainbridge acknowledged two faults regarding the capture. The first was in sailing alone, instead of with the *Vixen*, which he had been ordered to do. He had sent the *Vixen* away in order to cover more area for the protection of commerce.[135] The second was that he did not know the shoals existed because no charts of the area showed them. Unfamiliarity with the area had already set the Americans up for failure with the blockade, since their deep-draft vessels could not access the shoreline where the Tripolitan corsairs and commercial vessels slipped out. Now the deep draft of the *Philadelphia* had proved its undoing. Ironically, in 1802 the secretary of the navy had solicited the advice of Bainbridge, based on his cruise under Commodore Dale, about the size and trim of ships that would work best in the Mediterranean.[136] As a result, Commodore Preble's squadron had several smaller vessels—the *Vixen*, the *Argus*, the *Enterprize*, the *Syren*, and the *Nautilus*—that were better suited to navigating in shallow waters.

While the *Philadelphia*'s crew languished in prison, Preble, knowing nothing of the capture, went about the daily business of the blockade. He had prepared better for the dispersal of the squadron than his predecessor. Acknowledging that distance might prevent proper communications, he instructed Isaac Hull, new captain of the *Argus*, to charter a "small swift Sailing Vessel" to send him any urgent news rather than leaving his station.[137] That way, Preble could be informed of important occurrences without loss of blockade coverage. Dispatching his squadron to convoy duty and blockade duty, and steering his own ship to Syracuse to bargain for the use of the port as a base, he assured the secretary of the navy, "There shall not be an idle Vessel in my Squadron."[138] The blockade had essentially fallen apart over the past year, so Preble officially reinstated it, notifying the relevant consuls that all neutrals trying to enter the port of Tripoli would be detained.[139]

In November, the *Constitution* delivered Tobias Lear and his family to Algiers, where Lear took up the post of consul general. Though Lear was supposed to go to Tripoli to negotiate, he wanted to wait until the spring, when the weather was better, so that the squadron could accompany him and provide an appropriate show of force. Preble agreed.[140]

It was almost a month before Commodore Preble received the news of the *Philadelphia* from a passing British frigate. With the loss of the *Philadelphia*, Preble was now faced with the prospect of continued, and perhaps escalating, war in the Mediterranean: "The loss of that ship and capture of the Crew with all its consequences are of the most serious and alarming nature to the United States; and if it should not involve us in a war with Tunis and Algiers in consequence of the weakness of our squadron, yet still it will protract the war with Tripoly."[141] At the very least, it had seriously damaged the prestige of the United States, not only with the Barbary states but also among the Europeans.

The United States was already in a precarious position because of Richard Valentine Morris's struggles to negotiate. James Leander Cathcart outlined the stakes:

All Europe as well as Barbary has view'd our conduct in silent expectation, since the war with Tripoli commenced, the former with an intention to follow our example if worthy imitation, & the latter to know how to rank us among the nations of the earth, whether to class us with Great Britain and France the only nations

who make themselves respected, or with the northern nations whose miserable
pusilanimous aconomy has so far preponderated in their Councils as to induce
them in many instances to sacrifice their national dignity merely because it
cost's them something less to bribe those Regencys to confer the honor of per-
miting them to navigate the mediterranean sea, than it would to maintain a
Squadron in the Mediterranean.[142]

Cathcart echoed many others' concerns about the place the United States occupied in the Mediterranean community.[143] The Americans saw themselves as
far above the Barbary states, whom they considered savage, but they were less
certain where they fit into the European hierarchy. The loss of the *Philadelphia*
did not improve their standing, especially since some European observers, like
Antoine Zuchet, the Dutch chargé d'affaires in Tripoli, thought that the Americans had given up far too easily when the *Philadelphia* had run aground.[144]

But the *Philadelphia*'s crew needed the Mediterranean community. Bainbridge suggested that a mediator from a more powerful nation would be advisable, particularly Britain or France. He also advocated for an official treaty with
the Ottoman Porte, which he thought might have some influence on Tripoli.[145]
A commission to formally establish relations with the Turkish government had
fallen apart in 1799 and had not been revisited.[146] Thus, Bainbridge was the only
naval officer to have direct experience with the Ottomans, though his previous
encounter was under similarly degrading circumstances. His delivery of a menagerie of presents from Algiers to the Ottoman court had set a tone of subordina-
tion that the United States was still trying to overcome. But at this moment, the
navy might have to swallow its pride and take whatever help it could get.

Nicholas Nissen continued to act on behalf of the prisoners, including receiving and sending letters for them. Even before the *Philadelphia* loss, he often
wrote to Cathcart with news from Tripoli. When Cathcart passed on the information to Commodore Preble, he cautioned Preble to keep Nissen's role quiet
because "mentioning the source from whence you gain your intelligence . . .
might have serious consequences and might even tend to place Mr. Nissen's life
in Jeopardy."[147] Bainbridge wrote to Preble that he should send non-sensitive letters through the British consul at Tripoli, but sensitive materials should go to
the Danish consul at Malta, who could then send them on to Nissen while providing another layer of security.[148]

Bainbridge wanted help from another consul as well. One of the crew of the
Philadelphia, John Wilson, had been "telling the Bashaw numerous lies to exas-
perate him," expecting to be claimed by the Swedish consul as a subject of
Sweden. Bainbridge entreated Preble to write to the Swedish consul asking him
not to claim Wilson, as Bainbridge wanted him to "answer for his villainous
conduct."[149]

Commodore Preble could do little about the *Philadelphia* situation until he provided for the rest of the squadron, so he continued his path to Syracuse after leaving Consul Lear at Algiers. He arrived at Syracuse on November 28.[150] The governor of Syracuse agreed to let the American squadron use the port for its base of operations, giving Preble "the use of Magazines Gratis to deposite any provisions and stores." Other gentlemen of the town also paid their respects to Preble and offered whatever help the squadron needed. Their outreach was not entirely altruistic. Preble noted that they saw the presence of the squadron as "the means of protecting the coast from the depredations of the Barbary Cruizers."[151]

Preble needed help to supply the ships of his squadron because the supplies sent from the United States were not meeting their needs. He found an American store ship from the secretary of the navy in the harbor. When the stores were unloaded into the magazines, Preble discovered that the supplies were somewhat less than satisfactory. "Most of the Casks are the worst sort of fish Barrels, and very few of them full hooped; in consequence of which, the Pickle has leaked out, and the provisions spoiled. Several [barrels] have been condemned and thrown overboard, being too offensive to be retained in the ship," Preble wrote.[152] They had to re-pickle all the salted provisions in order to make them usable.[153] He also ordered his crew to make repairs to the *Constitution*. He allowed several officers to go ashore, where they found nothing but fruit for sale, though Preble assumed that they would eventually be able to buy "fresh Meat, Vegetables, Fruit, Candles, and Rice, cheaper than they can be purchased in America."[154] Alongside the ship, many bum boats, small harbor craft used by the townspeople as movable storefronts, offered their wares (likely alcoholic), but Preble would not permit them to sell to the crew, for the sake of "the duty of the ship." He had enough problems already with his crew being disorderly—he had punished five men in one day for drunkenness—and he did not need them causing problems in Syracuse when they had just arrived.[155]

Many of the *Constitution*'s crew members had been sick over the past few months, including the purser, who eventually died. To deal with these illnesses, Preble requested a hospital ship. The squadron had sent sick seamen to Malta and Gibraltar in the past, but now Preble was reluctant to do that. Grateful as he was for the warm welcome at Syracuse, Preble also did not want to put down roots too deep by building a hospital, "for it is uncertain how soon we may be disturbed by the French or English taking possession of this Country."[156]

Meanwhile, Tobias Lear settled in at Algiers in his role as consul general, replacing Richard O'Brien. Lear had served as President Washington's personal secretary until his death. He then became consul at Saint-Domingue (which would become Haiti) during the Quasi-War, so he had some experience in bringing together the navy and its foreign connections. When Lear arrived in Algiers, he found that the *Syren*, bringing the consular presents from Cathcart at Livorno, had not yet arrived. In consultation with O'Brien, Lear decided that he could not wait till the ship arrived, as the dey might view a delay in a consular visit as a snub. Accordingly, he went to the Jewish bankers of Algiers, the House of Bacri and Busnach, to request a loan. Bacri and Busnach was much more than just a lending house; it served as an intelligence service, advisory board, and maritime commercial house for the court of the dey. As diplomatic representative for the dey, Naphthali Busnach negotiated treaties and payments from the Europeans, and the consuls all went to him first.[157]

Lear's loan from Bacri and Busnach was not the first time the Americans had used their services. Richard O'Brien had used them several times, as early as 1800, to help pay the American debt to Algiers, but he was no friend of theirs. He had written in 1801 that he hoped the American government would provide consular funds for presents so as "not to be dependent on those leeches and extortioners the Jews."[158] Now the government had provided consular presents, but they had not arrived, so O'Brien and Lear were back in the same position. They contracted with the Bacris for the presents and also the remainder of the annuity the United States had not yet paid, a total of over $20,000. Lear thought that when the *Syren* did arrive, the presents originally intended for the dey could simply be sold in order to recover the loan.[159] It was perhaps for the best that Lear made the deal with the Bacris, as the store ship carrying naval stores for the dey had been lost off Cadiz on November 20, though Lear did not learn about it until December 10.[160] Only a few weeks later, the Bacris were refusing to pay the loans they had agreed to settle on with Tunis as well. Lear believed that David Bacri was "determined to throw obstacles in the way to obtain advantages which he ought not to have."[161]

Lear gave O'Brien credit for keeping the United States out of war with Algiers despite the tardiness of the promised gifts. "I should not apprehend much difficulty in keeping fair with this Regency," he wrote, "provided we are *punctual* in complying with the stipulations in our Treaty, and proper measures are taken by the Consul here to keep on good terms with the leading men; but unless such punctuality is observed, and the Consul has the power or means to meet any sudden or unforeseen storm, I presume we shall always be in danger of a Rupture, and the situation of a public Agent here very precarious and unpleasant."[162] Historically, the United States had struggled with punctuality, so Lear's job was not quite as easy as he blithely asserted.

Lear also reached out to the French chargé in Algiers, Dubois Thainville.[163] Thainville in turn reached out to Bonaventure Beaussier, the French chargé d'affaires at Tripoli, to secure his assistance in providing for the American prisoners in Tripoli.[164] In 1800 Thainville had been consul at Algiers when Bainbridge came in the *George Washington*. Bainbridge had provided Thainville and his family passage on the *George Washington* when the dey ordered the French consul's immediate dismissal. Thainville had later returned to Algiers and forced the dey to back down on his demands for tribute, so he could be a powerful advocate in the Algerian court, an ally worth having. "As he considers himself under great obligations for his [Bainbridge's] friendly aid," Lear wrote, Thainville was now doing whatever he could to assist the *Philadelphia's* crew. Lear noted that Bainbridge's reputation among the nobles of Algiers was also favorable because of the *George Washington's* voyage to Constantinople, so Lear felt confident that Algiers would intervene on the crew's behalf if needed.[165]

In a strange twist, Lear also reached out to Thomas Trigge, lieutenant governor at Gibraltar, on behalf of the dey. A few months previous, the dey had dismissed the British consul from his court, and just a few days previous, some Algerian cruisers had captured a ship carrying a British passport and sold it in Tunis. The dey wanted Lear to assure any British officials he knew that the dey wanted friendly relations with Britain, and these two incidents should not be taken as acts of aggression. It gave Lear great pride to be asked to intercede on the dey's behalf: "If any good should result from a communication of this disposition on the part of the Dey (let it proceed from what course it may) I shall feel peculiarly happy in having been the organ of it."[166]

Whereas his predecessors had felt no need to cruise off Tripoli during the winter, Commodore Preble thought he had no choice, given the capture of the *Philadelphia*. He knew the *Constitution* could not remain out all winter, but he intended to keep a presence off Tripoli as much as possible. He also changed the procedure for cruising—two ships had to be on station at any given time, and no ship was to cruise alone.[167]

Despite Preble's plans, the wind held the squadron in Syracuse for several days in December. The ships could not get out until December 19, whereupon they headed to Malta. There, Preble left a letter for Nicholas Nissen expressing his desire to speak to him about the *Philadelphia* affair.[168] He also encouraged Bainbridge to let him know the names of any other person who might be able to help the captives. In particular, he suggested Bryan McDonogh, who Richard O'Brien had said might be of assistance. This recommendation was peculiar, as Richard Dale had been convinced that McDonogh had encouraged the bashaw to declare war in the first place.[169] O'Brien, conversely, wrote to James Madison, "I believe the US has inadvertantly done an injury to McDonough. I believe he is a good man and has ever been a sincere friend to the UStates." O'Brien suggested that Cathcart's jealousy had poisoned the American relationship with McDonogh. As proof of McDonogh's good faith, O'Brien cited his assistance to the captured crew of the *Betsey* and the *Sophia*, a ship O'Brien had commanded after his release from Algiers that had been captured by Tripolitan corsairs.[170] Preble apparently believed Richard O'Brien's side of the story.

As the squadron sailed for Tripoli, finally a piece of good luck came its way. On December 23 the *Enterprize* and the *Constitution* captured a small Tripolitan ketch named *Mastico*. High seas caused the prize to get separated from the *Enterprize*. To prevent this from happening again, the *Enterprize* took the *Mastico* in tow and headed off to Syracuse. Following his own rule, Preble and the *Constitution* came with them, stopping in at Malta on the way. There, he requested that Joseph Pulis, the American consul, find someone to translate the papers he had found on board the *Mastico*, hopeful that they would contain useful information.[171]

The year 1803 was, for the United States, the pivotal year of the First Barbary War. Key changes in the strategy and logistics for the navy began to shift the Americans' focus. Though the contrast between the leadership styles of Richard Valentine Morris and Edward Preble could not be more stark, not all of Morris's problems can be laid on him. Preble benefited from the decision of the government to send more ships, a need that had been identified since the very beginning of the war. Because of his larger squadron, he was able to meet the primary opponent—Morocco—while still monitoring the other Barbary powers. Morris had not had that luxury.

Morris chose to prioritize Morocco over Tripoli. In the long run, this decision had larger ramifications than critics acknowledged. Though Preble sealed the deal with the emperor, Morris's less hawkish behavior set up the negotiations. By keeping both the *Meshouda* and *Mirboka* in the Mediterranean, instead of sending them to America for adjudication (Preble's suggestion), Morris had given Preble a bargaining chip that meant little to the Americans and a lot to the Moroccan emperor. With peace firmly established in Morocco, Preble could truly turn his attention to Tripoli, which he would have had to do whether the Morocco question was settled or not. The capture of the *Philadelphia* was a crippling wound to Preble's campaign against Tripoli. But it did energize the squadron, the government back home, and the international community of the Mediterranean to fight against Tripoli by whatever means necessary.

CHAPTER FIVE

A Secret Expedition

The Americans are true friends in time of Peace, but active
Enemies in War.

—William Bainbridge to the foreign minister of Tripoli,
February 20, 1804

The entire consular network in the Mediterranean jumped to help the *Philadelphia* prisoners—not just Americans, but Europeans as well. Consul general Tobias Lear and Commodore Preble were the only ones authorized by the American government to spend money on behalf of the *Philadelphia* captives, but others offered various other assistance. Charles Pinckney, American minister at Madrid, asked the French, British, and Danish ministers in Spain to solicit the help of their respective consuls in Tripoli. Pinckney promised to reimburse whatever expenses they incurred, up to about $3,000. Though he was not actually authorized to pay out any funds, Pinckney argued that the federal government could hardly fault him for having compassion for so many Americans in chains.[1] James Monroe, minister to London, reached out to the Swedish chargé in Constantinople for assistance as well.[2]

Robert Livingston, American minister to Paris, approached Charles Maurice de Talleyrand, Napoleon Bonaparte's minister of foreign affairs, about getting France's help. In response, Talleyrand offered the help of the French consulate in Tripoli, as well as a personal letter from Napoleon to the bashaw urging a quick peace. He assured Livingston that the French wanted to be friends with the United States. Napoleon's "greatest pleasure would be, to be able to effect or preserve the blessings of Peace in all civilized parts of the World. He holds a sincere attachment to the people & Government of America, depending on a just return on their part. In short, his natural feelings excite compassion for the misfortune of your Country Men."[3]

Even Russia offered aid to the *Philadelphia*'s crew. When Levett Harris, American consul to St. Petersburg, learned of the capture, he asked Count de Vorontsov, chancellor of the Russian Empire, for his assistance in the release of the crew.[4] Vorontsov immediately wrote to Constantinople encouraging the Porte to issue a firman releasing not only the crew but also the ship itself.[5] The emperor of Russia was very interested in helping the Americans. Perhaps the Americans represented a challenge to Bonaparte and the standard European practices in the Mediterranean.[6] Perhaps the Russians wanted to break British monopolies and establish better trade with the Americans.[7] In November 1803, Vorontsov's representative, Adam Czartoryski, had expressed a desire to build up the United States' West Indies trade with Russia, but the two nations did not have a commercial treaty.[8] The two countries were also trying to negotiate carrying rights through the Black Sea at the time, so perhaps the emperor wanted to do everything in his power to appear friendly to American interests.[9] Russia's intervention went through the Ottoman Porte, and not directly to Tripoli. Russia had relations with the Ottoman Empire on the Black Sea (and of course by land), but its ties to the Barbary states were minimal.

Not everyone was offering help. James Leander Cathcart heard rumors being spread about by the "Jews of Barbary . . . manifestly calculated to lessen our importance as a nation & sully our maratime reputation." Ever jealous for American honor, Cathcart requested specific details about the capture so that he could refute the stories "in the most pointed manner."[10] Likewise, British goodwill did not extend to claiming some of the crew as British. Marine First Lieutenant John Johnson reported a story he heard thirdhand at Cadiz that 140 of the *Philadelphia*'s crew had claimed British citizenship and requested Lord Nelson to acknowledge them. Nelson's response, reportedly, was, "if he done any thing in the Business, it would be to have the Rascals all hung."[11] Given the American squadron's tussles with the British over the question of nationality, it is not surprising that Nelson felt no obligation to either real or fraudulent British subjects.

In the early months of 1804, Commodore Edward Preble had to formulate his own plans for the liberation of the *Philadelphia* prisoners. At the same time, he had to address the vagaries of the other Barbary states. He also needed to reestablish better relations with many of his European counterparts, by goodwill or by bullying. Preble needed the help of the Europeans not only to resupply and repair his dilapidated squadron but also to increase his force in the Mediterranean in order to bombard the port of Tripoli. And, of course, the blockade had to be maintained, though by the middle of the year Preble's focus had shifted away from blockade enforcement and toward bombardment of the town. Preble kept the navy very busy. We will use six captures the navy made to illustrate the many tasks Preble faced in 1804.

Mastico

The first capture of importance occurred at the end of 1803. The *Mastico*, ostensibly an Ottoman ketch, had been sailing from Tripoli for Benghazi when the *Constitution* and *Enterprize* captured it on December 23, 1803, and brought it to Syracuse. It was carrying enslaved people and presents for the Ottoman emperor, as well as Tripolitan officers. The captain and crew were Turkish and therefore were neutral. Preble intended to release the captain and his part of the crew, giving them a passport to continue on to Constantinople. But the Tripolitans on board, civilian and military, as well as the enslaved Black people, Preble planned to keep as prisoners, unless Yusuf Karamanli thought it "proper according to the custom of other Nations, and as humanity dictates, to enter into a negotiation for an exchange of prisoners."[12]

Preble received news on January 28 that changed his assessment of the *Mastico*'s neutrality. The pilot Preble hired for the *Constitution* reported that the *Mastico* and its crew, under Tripolitan colors, had been involved in the capture of the *Philadelphia* after it grounded. This story was later confirmed by many others. Preble immediately decided to treat the entire crew of the *Mastico* as prisoners and declare the ketch a good prize, in retribution for its role in the capture of American sailors.[13] That same day, the *Mastico* finally received pratique in Syracuse after a quarantine of 29 days. Preble immediately took 26 prisoners off the ketch and began to prepare the vessel to sail.[14]

Though the Ottoman Porte had showed no signs of wanting trouble with the United States, Preble took precautions to keep the peace. He sent one of the Turkish officers—a chavush, or deputy, of the kapudan pasha—who had been captured on the *Mastico* back to Constantinople, bearing a letter of conciliation. Preble wanted to justify the strategy of the United States. The blockade in which the *Mastico* had been caught, he wrote, "is of the first importance in compelling them [Tripoli] to a peace that may be consistant with the honor and dignity of our Country." Because of his unfamiliarity with proper protocol about these sensitive matters, Preble sent the letter to the French ambassador, Guillaume-Marie-Anne Brune, and to the British ambassador for relay rather than directly to the sultan.[15] He wrote an additional letter to Ambassador Brune explaining the legal argument he hoped Brune would make to the sultan about the legitimacy of the capture. He argued that because the *Mastico*'s captain and crew had participated in the capture of the *Philadelphia* while flying Tripolitan colors, their subsequent attempt to run the blockade under Turkish colors amounted to piracy. Via Brune, Preble also sent several other statements that exonerated the Turkish government from blame for their ship's behavior, and laid the blame instead on the bashaw of Tripoli.[16]

He sent similar letters to the "Captain Pasha" (a bastardization of the term "kapudan pasha"), the grand admiral of the Ottoman navy, invoking the community's laws in hope of establishing commonality: "I hope and expect from the friendship & respect which the Government of the United States of America have for the Grand Seignior, and the Ottoman Nation that it will please him to grant us that Justice for which he is so renowned by ordering the Bashaw to surrender up to me, the Officers and Crew of the Frigate [*Philadelphia*], and by punishing in an exemplary manner those of his subjects who were concerned in this flagrant violation of the law of Nations."[17] Preble invoked the law he intended to follow—the Law of Nations—and the Ottomans' own law and justice. Given how much Ottoman piracy had shaped international law and customary practice in the Mediterranean, it was wise for Preble to try to situate his actions in the context of Ottoman norms.[18]

With the Ottoman concerns (hopefully) assuaged, Preble could turn to action. To develop his plans, Preble relied on intelligence from many sources, including the captive William Bainbridge, who wrote to him in cipher and then in an "invisible" ink of lime juice. Bainbridge's letters contained the information Preble needed to mount an effective assault on Tripoli. It was obvious to Bainbridge that the blockade was not working. He observed that a Russian vessel carrying Turkish soldiers had arrived around the same time Preble had, and since then a Tripolitan cruiser.[19] He noted a departure as well—a 12-gun polacre around January 8. Bainbridge suggested that Preble should destroy the *Philadelphia* during the winter when the ship was less well-guarded. The idea of destruction seems to have occurred to Preble, Bainbridge, and Lieutenant Stephen Decatur at roughly the same time, but only Bainbridge had intimate knowledge of the bashaw's security measures on the *Philadelphia*. Bainbridge reported the lack of guards at night, for instance, as though he could see them leaving. He also suggested an ideal time for the attack based on his observations of the weather.[20]

Bainbridge also provided valuable intelligence about other locations. He wrote to Preble about an attack planned on the squadron that lay at Syracuse, warning Preble not to take any vessel or crew's appearance for granted—"they intend to disguise their Crew in Christian dresses"—and not to assume that the American ships were safe while at anchor in the harbor.[21] Bainbridge knew that in order to keep the lines of communication open, caution and secrecy were paramount: "Keep it a secret that you receive any letters from me thro' Mr Nissen; and even better to not let it be known of your receiving any from me," he wrote.[22]

On January 31 Preble outlined for Lear everything he had done to regain control of the *Philadelphia* situation. He had written to Bainbridge several times, though Bainbridge had not received any of his letters. He had also sent money, clothes, and stores to the prisoners, care of Bryan McDonogh and Nicholas Nissen. He had written to the bashaw to request a prisoner exchange. He had listened to the bashaw's agent at Malta propose a 10-year truce or $120,000 as ransom for the captives along with an exchange of the *Mastico* and its crew. He had requested gunboats from Naples and Livorno.

Most importantly, Preble described his orders to Charles Stewart and Stephen Decatur. Stewart, in the *Syren*, and Decatur, in the *Mastico* (renamed the *Intrepid*), were to sail to Tripoli in disguise. Under cover of darkness, the *Intrepid* was to take a boarding party of 70 volunteers to the *Philadelphia*, which was anchored in the harbor, and burn the ship.[23] The *Syren* and the *Intrepid* were ideal for this task. The *Intrepid* was a Tripolitan vessel originally, and the *Syren* had never been on a cruise before Tripoli, so the two vessels should not arouse the suspicion of the Tripolitan harbor guards.[24] Preble noted matter-of-factly in his memorandum of February 3, "The *Syren* and *Intrepid* sailed for Tripoli to burn the *Philadelphia*."[25] The plans were closely guarded. The *Constitution*'s logbook recorded only that the two ships had gone on "some Sccrcte Expuditen."[26] The crews of the two vessels "were pleas'd to express their satisfaction by 3 hearty cheers" when they found out the exact nature of their mission.[27] However, poor weather slowed their progress toward Tripoli and their plans once they arrived. The two vessels lay for 10 days off Tripoli, waiting for the perfect weather conditions.

In the evening of February 16, the conditions were finally right for the assault. Decatur brought the *Intrepid* up as close to the *Philadelphia* as possible and boarded the ship. After subduing the guards, Decatur's men set charges throughout the *Philadelphia*. Decatur later described how he "immediately fired her in the Store Rooms, Gun Room Cockpit & Birth Deck and remained on board until the flames had issued from the Spar Deck hatch ways & Ports, and before I got from alongside the fire had communicated to the rigging and tops." As the ship burned, its loaded guns discharged into the city. The noise of the conflict raised an alarm on the shore, but the Americans were able to accomplish their mission before any relief arrived from the city.[28]

The boarding party quickly returned to the *Intrepid* and sailed away. Decatur reported that 20 Tripolitans had been killed, and many more had jumped into the sea or gotten off in a boat. Others reported smaller numbers.[29] The Americans had suffered only one slight injury. Decatur lauded his crew—both officers, enlisted seamen, and even the Sicilian pilot hired for the mission.[30] Charles Stewart, captain of the *Syren*, lamented that the *Syren*'s boats had not

Figure 5.1 Engraving by F. Kearney of the "Burning of the Frigate Philadelphia in the Harbour of Tripoli, 16th Feb. 1804, by 70 Gallant Tars of Columbia commanded by Lieut. Decatur." Naval History and Heritage Command, NH 56751.

been able to join in the fight and destroy some of the other Tripolitan cruisers in the harbor, but the expedition had nevertheless been a triumph.[31]

Even in this, the Americans' boldest act of aggression against Tripoli, they could not accomplish the mission all on their own. The Americans sought out some of the help they needed, but some they got by accident. Salvatore Catalano, the Sicilian pilot Preble had hired to navigate the *Constitution* in the waters around Tripoli, turned out to be a valuable asset.[32] February 16 was the third attempt the Americans made to get into the harbor. On the night Decatur wanted to try the first time, February 7, Catalano warned them not to do it, as the winds would drive the boat into the shore and they would not return. Furthermore, on February 16, Catalano was able to speak to the guards on the *Philadelphia* in Arabic, informing them that this ketch was in fact a vessel sent for bullocks for Malta.[33] There is no doubt that without him the mission would not have succeeded.[34]

The accidental help was no less important. When the *Intrepid* drew close to the Tripolitan shore, it was flying British colors. Seeing the *Intrepid*'s colors, the British consular house raised its own colors in response.[35] This recognition was not trivial. On the very day the *Intrepid* entered Tripoli harbor, the *Nautilus* was capturing the *Santissimo Crocifesso*, which the British expected to come collect bullocks for Malta. The British consul thought the *Intrepid* was the *Santissimo Crocifesso*. So during the critical period when the *Intrepid* was exposed to enemy fortifications, the ship was not invisible—it was vouched for by the British accidentally.

There were no mild reactions to the burning of the *Philadelphia*. In Tripoli, the bashaw put the American prisoners under intensified guard, increased their workload, and threatened fire and brimstone.[36] The Americans' strongest advocate, Nicholas Nissen, found more barriers in his way to helping the prisoners. For the past few months, he had been helping them in direct violation of the treaty the Danish government had signed with the bashaw, which specifically stipulated that he was not to interfere in any matters except his own nation's. After the bashaw tightened security on the prisoners, though, Nissen noted that they could not receive communications of any kind (though Yusuf lifted this restriction after a few weeks).[37] Nissen assumed that Preble would be arriving soon to negotiate for peace. Whether Nissen would be permitted to come out to Preble's ship when it arrived depended entirely on the bashaw's mood.[38]

This mission vaulted Stephen Decatur into the path of glory. The secretary of the navy was so pleased that he broke seniority (an action he had not been willing to do for anyone else thus far) to "send The Hero a Captain's Commission."[39] Congress gave Decatur a sword, and the crew of the *Intrepid* two months' pay, in gratitude.[40] The action garnered the respect of other nations as well. From Tunis, consul George Davis saw the mission as an atonement for the disastrous blunders of Richard Valentine Morris: "It has made much noise in Tunis, and is the only occasion, on which I have heard our Countrymen spoken of with due respect."[41]

Operating from a position of strength, Preble prepared for negotiation. He wrote a few days after the *Philadelphia*'s destruction, "My heart is fixed on obliging [the bashaw] to sue for Peace and I hope yet to make him consent to sign a treaty as favorable as ours with Morocco without a cent for Peace or Tribute. I had rather spend my life in the Mediterranean than we should ever consent to either."[42] The official negotiator for the United States, Tobias Lear, feared to leave Algiers in order to join Preble at Tripoli. The United States was in good stead with Algiers at the moment—in fact, Lear had just paid off the last of the annuities the United States had owed, after nearly four years in arrears. But relations between Algiers and Britain were tense, and Lear thought that war might break out soon. As Lear explained later to the secretary of state, if the

Algerians could not get what they wanted from Britain, they would need to get money from somewhere, presumably a weaker nation upon whom they could prey.[43] Lear feared that leaving his post would be an "act of relinquishment" that signaled that the United States was an ideal target. In his place, Lear suggested Richard O'Brien, who was still in Algiers assisting the new consul. O'Brien had many of the qualifications that were needed for a good negotiator with the Barbary states. "His knowledge of the language, Manners, and Politicks of these Regencies, must be highly useful to you," Lear wrote.[44]

Preble made overtures himself to the prime minister of Tripoli, Muhammad Dghies. Dghies had been fairly friendly in the past, but he had refused to answer Preble's most recent inquiries about prisoner exchange. When Preble wrote again to ask the reason for his silence, Dghies replied that he had heard that Preble had mistreated his Tripolitan prisoners, "against all laws." If Preble sent a prisoner to Tripoli and that man was in as good health as Preble claimed, then the negotiations could commence.[45] Preble took exception to the accusation that he mistreated prisoners, noting that the wounded prisoner they had taken during the raid on the *Philadelphia* had fully recovered under the care of the *Constitution*'s doctor. However, he could not send him on shore without an exchange.[46]

During this negotiation, Preble took on board the French chargé, Bonaventure Beaussier, whose help Napoleon had promised.[47] Beaussier made the first overtures to the bashaw and Minister Dghies on March 27. He heard again from Dghies that the prisoners must be released in order to "destroy the general Credited opinion among the inhabitants that [the Americans' prisoners] have been Massacred."[48] Beaussier added his voice to the Tripolitans, urging, "I assure you from my own knowledge how much this condescention on your part, would facilitate obstacles, and not pass without Compensation."[49]

Santissimo Crocifesso

The capture of the *Santissimo Crocifesso* on February 16, the same day the *Philadelphia* burned, symbolized the new aggression of the American forces while exemplifying the legal problems that had vexed them since the beginning of the war. It also symbolized the American desire to keep good relations with the British. At the beginning of 1804, Preble had authorized passports for a few British ships to pick up bullocks that had been purchased in Tripoli for the British garrison at Malta. These vessels were to go directly from Malta to Tripoli in ballast and return straight to Malta with only the cows.

On January 13, 1804, Lieutenant-General William Villettes had requested just such a passport for the *Santissimo Crocifesso*, and Preble had granted it.[50] However, when the *Nautilus* stopped the vessel on February 16, so close to Tripoli that the ships could see the burning *Philadelphia*, the master of the vessel declared that he was not going to Tripoli at all; he was going to Djerba and had simply been blown off course. Thus, the cargo he carried—hemp, linen, planks, nails, and other building supplies—was not contraband because it was not intended for the use of Tripoli.[51]

The captain of the *Nautilus*, Richard Somers, did not believe the master's story. When Somers searched the vessel, he found seven Tripolitans who swore they were bound for Tripoli, plus a Sicilian who was being banished from Malta. He also found no bills of lading or invoices to Djerba, which would be necessary if the cargo were legitimate, and most damning, he found letters bound for Tripoli hidden in the ceiling of the cabin.[52] And since he had given it himself, Preble knew that this ship had been one granted a passport to carry bullocks. Nevertheless, the evidence was circumstantial, so Preble told Somers to send the vessel to Malta "for the Purpose of investigating more clearly the property of the Vessel &c." Preble kept four prisoners from the vessel on the *Constitution*, however. When he wrote to William Higgins, the navy's agent in Malta, asking him to help adjudicate the capture, he observed, "Of course she is good prize."

Whether the *Santissimo Crocifesso* was good prize mattered less than who would take umbrage if it were condemned. While committed to sending the ship back to the United States for adjudication, Preble was sensible of his awkward position with the British, who had been counting on that vessel to bring bullocks for the Malta garrison. The need for foodstuffs on the island of Malta was dire; the food shortages caused by the siege of Malta were exacerbated by attacks on British supply ships from both France and the Barbary states. From 1800 to 1802, Barbary corsairs had captured 23 food ships bound for Malta. Governor Alexander Ball repeatedly asked Lord Nelson to provide convoy protection, but the masters of the supply ships themselves often proved duplicitous.[53] The corn for Malta came from the Black Sea region, but the cattle came from Barbary.

Convinced he was in the right, Preble had to make sure that the British saw the vessel's actions in the same light as he did. Therefore, he wrote to Sir Alexander Ball. He started by describing the destruction of the *Philadelphia*, an action that was sure to garner Ball's respect and approbation. Then he explained the situation of the *Santissimo Crocifesso*: "I suppose he thought to smuggle in our Enemies & their property with impunity. I am confidant this transaction is without your sanction, and without your knowledge." Though Preble was planning to send the ship and cargo to the United States for adjudication, he first sent it back to Malta for Ball's approval.[54] Surprisingly, Ball did approve, acknowledging that the vessel was good prize, perhaps all too familiar with the ways crews tried to manipulate the British need for food for their own profit.[55]

Once Ball assented to the legality of the capture, Preble appointed Lieutenant Edward Cox to sail the brig to the United States. However, the *Crocifesso* had sustained damage on its way to Malta, and Cox assessed the brig as unseaworthy to make a long Atlantic voyage. Herein, Preble confronted one of the frustrations of fighting far from home. Prizes had to be condemned before prize money could be paid out, but the cost (and likelihood) of getting a prize to a place it could be condemned was almost insuperable. Cox believed that the repairs necessary to enable the *Crocifesso* to sail across the Atlantic would be so expensive that all the profits—and the prize money—would be washed away. So, with Preble's blessing, Cox left the ship in Malta and simply carried its papers back to the United States. Though Preble had authorized William Higgins to sell the ship, he ultimately deemed that even that was too much effort for this "Vessel of little value," and he decided to give the ship back to its Maltese owners "in order to prevent litigation and expence," for a consideration of $300 and the resignation of its contraband cargo, which still lay in Syracuse. He told Ball the release was a compliment to the British flag.[56] He had many more serious complaints about the British, so this potential dispute seemed easiest to just let go.

Madonna di Catapoliani

On March 22, 1804, the *Syren*, commanded by Charles Stewart, captured the *Madonna di Catapoliani*, another cattle ship, as it sailed from Tripoli to Malta. The *Madonna* was flagged Russian, but the cargo belonged to Gaetano Schembri, a merchant of uncertain nationality who was sometimes called the Tripolitan consul at Malta.[57] This capture too became a point of contention between the United States and other nations—in this case, Russia. However, the dispute over the *Madonna's* capture was not about whether the ship had purposefully run the blockade, like the *Santissimo Crocifesso*, but rather whether the blockade existed at all. If it did not, then the non-Tripolitan ship was not a lawful prize.

In November 1803, Preble had reinstated the blockade that Richard Valentine Morris had let lapse in early 1803.[58] Questions about the blockade's legality remained, however. On January 30, Talleyrand contested the blockade's adherence to the "principles which have become, in this matter, the basis of international law and universally accepted usage." Talleyrand cited several violations. First, a blockade must be equal to the force of the blockaded port. Therefore, the one ship Preble had cruising off Tripoli was not sufficient to legitimate the blockade. Second, a blockade could apply only to a specific port, and not to a general region or coastline. Preble could not claim the entire coast of Tripoli was under the blockade. How the Americans treated their blockade could have ramifications for how their own merchants were treated when other nations enforced blockades. Talleyrand was not ignorant of the advantage of American wartime trade. He wrote that the United States was probably "more interested than any other power in not adopting a system contrary to the rights and commerce of neutrals." He entreated Robert Livingston, the American minister in

Paris, to ask Preble to stop taking liberties with his orders and restrict his blockade to a legal version.[59]

The French were not the only ones concerned about Preble's strong rhetoric. When Secretary of the Navy Robert Smith received Preble's circular announcing the blockade, he wrote back to Preble clarifying a few points. Most pressing, a neutral who was not carrying contraband articles could not be taken as prize unless it was clearly attempting to enter the blockaded port. It could not be taken merely in the general vicinity—it had to actually be heading for the port of Tripoli. A neutral ship that did not know about the blockade could, and should, be turned away from entering the port; if it persisted, then it could be taken. When a ship was warned off from a blockaded port, it would receive a mark on its identifying papers. Thus, if it returned at any later time, the blockading force could easily determine that it had already been warned.[60] Secretary Smith further noted that Preble could not assume that the circular had reached every place, and even if it had, that was no guarantee that any ship's master had seen it.[61]

Preble knew the rights of neutrals. In his orders to Lieutenant John Smith of the *Vixen*, he wrote, "You are not to suffer the vessels of any nation to enter or to have commerce with Tripoly, but have a right to treat as an Enemy whoever may endeavor to enter that place or carry any thing to it whilst blockaded by us. You are to respect the rights of Nations with whom we are at Peace and not to capture Vessels within the Jurisdictional limits or under the protection of such nations." But his orders would not have made the French happy—his own concession to his blockade rules was issuing passports for two ships to go to Tripoli to pick up bullocks for the British garrison at Malta.[62]

When the *Syren* captured the *Madonna*, the Russian government also objected to the legal flimsiness of the blockade. The Russian consul in Naples, Nicolo de Manzo, claimed to John Matthieu, American consul in Naples, that the capture of the polacre was illegal because the *Madonna*, captained by George Morfino, had arrived in Tripoli in December 1803 before notification of the blockade had reached Smyrna, its port of origin, or Tripoli. De Manzo argued Morfino had "accidentally" run the blockade, and the United States therefore acted unlawfully to detain him.[63] However, according to Preble, the polacre's crew had admitted that they knew the blockade was in place and that they intended to run it anyway (perhaps with the encouragement of Schembri).[64] Matthieu forwarded the Russian agent's letters to Commodore Preble, noting that the Neapolitan government might intercede on behalf of the Russians, as "the strictest friendship passes between this court and that of Russia."[65]

The Russian chargé d'affaires at Naples, P. D'Karpow, also objected to the legality of the capture. His objections drew on long-standing disputes among the European powers about what constituted a blockade. Though most nations at least notionally espoused the principles in Emmerich Vattel's Law of Nations, the principles regarding blockade were sufficiently vague to admit many interpretations.[66] Thus, blockade law was hashed out in individual nations' admiralty courts. The objections raised by both Secretary Smith and Talleyrand point toward the fact that blockade law had been very hard to pin down in the past, but by 1804 the needle was shifting toward a more specific definition of what a blockade was and how it ought to function. The questions raised by Talleyrand about necessary force and restricted range both factored into the *Madonna* problem.

D'Karpow argued to Preble that the American blockade of Tripoli mounted insufficient force to be legal—"Towns & Ports should be blockaded, not by Manifestoes only, but by a military force." Here, D'Karpow invoked the idea of a "paper blockade," a blockade that was announced but lacked the force necessary to actually keep ships from coming in or out. In support of his contention that the American blockade was merely a paper blockade, he observed that the *Madonna* had entered Tripoli without difficulty, and if it were a real blockade, the ship should have been stopped on its way in.[67] D'Karpow and de Manzo argued that the universally accepted laws of blockade stipulated that a ship could only be stopped coming into a blockaded port, but not coming out. In this, the Russians were incorrect. A British admiralty court had ruled as recently as 1798 that both ingress into and egress from a blockaded port made a ship liable to capture.[68] However, the Russians often did not agree with British interpretations of maritime laws, so the ruling likely would have meant little to them.

Legal questions about the blockade continued to plague the squadron. On May 18, George Davis wrote that the bey had demanded his immediate departure from Tunis after a vessel bearing Davis's passport had not been permitted to enter Tripoli, and the Americans had (supposedly) taken some small vessels off Djerba. The American squadron continued to claim the same rule that had infuriated the Russians: the vessel "might enter Tripoli; but if he attempted to come out, the Vessel would be captured." Davis was able to conciliate the bey by reissuing the passport and apologizing for the mistake the squadron had made. But relations with Tunis continued to move toward a breaking point. Davis again underscored the difficulty of juggling multiple sets of fluid legal customs: "It is very certain, that we shall never be freed from similar complaints, and outrages on the laws of Nations, as long as our difficulty continues with Tripoli—*these are evils without a remedy*; for where one party alone, has the right to accuse, adjudge, & condemn—there is but a partial field for reasoning or argument."[69]

In between the capture of the *Madonna* and its eventual release, the squadron had to keep it somewhere that was safe not just from Tripoli but also from the European nations seeking to take American sailors for their own purposes. It was not the first time the Americans had faced this problem—Captain Gore's behavior on the *Medusa* was still fresh. But it was not just the British. In Syracuse, a sailor from the *Enterprize* had deserted and taken refuge on a French privateer in the harbor. Trusting the power of French protection, he did not even bother to hide from the Americans who were looking for him. The deserter sailed with the privateer on a cruise and returned sometime later as part of the prize crew on board a Maltese vessel that the French had captured. When Stephen Decatur heard of his arrival, he went on board the Maltese vessel and forcibly removed the deserter. The prize master appealed to the governor, Marcello de Gregorio. In response, Gregorio shut the gates of Syracuse, effectively detaining the American officers who had come to the town to get the deserter. Gregorio sent word to Preble that he would not release the officers until they returned the man to the French privateer.

In turn, Preble detained the messengers, including Gregorio's aide-de-camp, until the next morning, when he wrote Gregorio a stern letter informing him that he would be taking the matter to the king of Naples unless his men were released immediately. Apparently, in the light of the new day, the situation looked different to Gregorio. He immediately released the officers, opened the gates, and begged Preble's forgiveness for his "hasty conduct."[70] He claimed that he had reevaluated his actions once he was certain that American and French laws allowed the American officers to take the deserter. This was an unusual intrusion of American law into the Mediterranean—usually the Americans had to force their legal interpretations on others, rather than hearing foreign interpretations of their own laws. To make up for his behavior, Gregorio asked Preble and Decatur to dine with him the next evening.[71] Preble declined.[72]

Gregorio called on Frances Leckie, a British lady, to intercede for him and restore his credibility before the irate commodore. She did intercede, though perhaps not in the way he had hoped. She said what Gregorio could not say in so many words—that his position in Syracuse depended on cowardly capitulation to the French government. She did not ask that Preble not go to Naples, only that he would impute Gregorio's actions to bad counselors.[73]

Gregorio's plan worked. Preble replied to Mrs. Leckie, "The Governour in having prevailed on you to become his advocate, has acted wisely for once in his life." Nevertheless, he still planned to make his case at Naples, arguing, "He certainly has a very singular way of discovering that attachment to the American Nation which he professes to have for it."[74] Though Mrs. Leckie was sympathetic to Gregorio's position, it seems unlikely that she had any desire to maintain the bonds between Syracuse and the French. Her husband, Gould Francis Leckie, who was an honorary British consul in Syracuse, saw the islands of the

Mediterranean as a beginning point of an "insular empire" that Great Britain needed in order to combat France's control of the European continent. Syracuse was one such island.[75]

Preble recorded in his memorandum book simply, "Some difficulty with the Govt. of Syracuse respecting the detention of officers by closing the gates, which was adjusted next day."[76] But Preble had learned something from this clash with Gregorio: the governor of Syracuse could be bullied. The Americans would not forget this lesson. Preble was not an unfair man, though. The very next day, a soldier from the garrison at Syracuse tried to desert by swimming out to the *Constitution*. Preble immediately wrote to the governor to send someone to take the deserter back.[77]

Three weeks later, the squadron found itself in the same position again, only in Malta and with the British. As in previous disputes at Gibraltar, two deserters from the prize crew on board the *Madonna di Catapoliani* found their way to a British privateer in Malta. The captain, under orders from Governor Alexander Ball, refused to give them up. A week later, the captain of HMS *Narcissus* acted even more aggressively than the commanders at Gibraltar—his men boarded the *Madonna* and took three men off, saying that they had applied to him for release as Englishmen. Midshipman Thomas O. Anderson, commander of the prize, immediately went to the commander of the *Narcissus*, Lieutenant Hyde Parker, to demand his men back. But Parker would not give them up, citing an order he had received to take any Englishmen wherever he could find them. Anderson protested, but left without the men.[78] Preble and the squadron were reminded that they had little recourse other than civility if any of the more powerful nations of the Mediterranean wished to treat them with disrespect.

Tired of dealing with the legal questions surfaced by these ships of little value, yet determined to hold his ground about the legality of the captures, Preble began to look for a way out. After heated exchanges with D'Karpow, Preble received word that Russia had intervened on behalf of the *Philadelphia*'s prisoners. Because of the kindness of the Russian emperor, Preble chose not to send the *Madonna di Catapoliani* to America for adjudication, but released the ship "as a compliment to [the Russian] flag."[79]

Transfer

In between the captures of the *Santissimo Crocifesso* and the *Madonna di Catapoliani*, the *Syren* captured a vessel of significantly more interest to the American squadron. The *Transfer* was an English brig carrying 16 six-pounder guns that had been sold out of the British naval service during the Peace of Amiens.[80] It was yet a third ship meant to bring cattle to Malta. In his search after the capture, Captain Charles Stewart also found muskets, blunderbusses, cutlasses, pistols, and other valuable stores on board.[81] Preble immediately saw the value of acquiring the brig for the American squadron, in particular since the brig *Syren* and the schooner *Nautilus*, his two ships of similar size to the *Transfer*, collided with each other just two days after the capture, forcing both ships to seek repairs.[82]

Three of the ships the Americans had captured thus far—the *Santissimo Crocifesso*, the *Transfer*, and the *Madonna di Catapoliani*—all had something in common: the interest of Gaetano Schembri. Schembri, a merchant who did frequent business with Malta and Tripoli, had inveigled his way into the court of Yusuf Karamanli, receiving what he called the consulship of Malta from the bashaw. Somehow he made the leap from commercial agent for the bashaw to (unauthorized) negotiator for the Americans. After hearing about conversations between Preble and the commissary for the British fleet at Malta, Patrick Wilkie, Schembri took it upon himself to step into the role of negotiator. Preble received overtures of resolution from the bashaw "indirectly," he wrote to the secretary of the navy on January 20, 1804. These overtures likely originated with Schembri, speaking without any knowledge of the bashaw's actual feelings, but were presented to Preble by Patrick Wilkie. Supposedly, the bashaw offered a one-to-one prisoner exchange of prisoners from the *Philadelphia* for prisoners from the *Mastico*. Preble believed the remainder of the crew could be ransomed for $400 each and a peace concluded that did not include annuities. This arrangement seemed implausibly good, but Preble intended to "take the necessary steps for lessening the Bashaw's expectations" even further while waiting for advice from Consul Lear. Preble also had plans that he could not write about in case the communications were intercepted; surely those plans included the destruction of the *Philadelphia*.[83]

Once Wilkie presented Schembri's offer to Preble, Schembri seems to have determined to go to Tripoli to argue for his plan with the bashaw. Wilkie may have told Schembri that Preble was sure to approve, so Schembri set out on the *Transfer*, which he had purchased from the British navy in 1802. When he arrived in Tripoli, he tried to steer Yusuf toward a settlement with no tribute, only a $150,000 ransom for the prisoners.[84] (Preble did not wish to ransom the prisoners, but he was absolutely adamant about the end of further tribute.)

When the *Transfer* sailed back to Malta, Schembri shipped, along with the licensed cattle, several casks of his own. "In so withdrawing his property your Memorialist was so little apprehensive of incurring your Excellencys displeasure that the *Transfer* sailed from Tripoli in open day when some of your Cruizers were actually in sight," he wrote to Commodore Preble. He expressed surprise that his cargo should be so mistreated, in this ship and the other two, as the irregularities that existed were due "partly to his Zeal in executing your Excellency's commission," so that he could not adequately secure the proper paperwork.[85] Unfortunately for Schembri, Preble disclaimed all knowledge of him or his business in Tripoli.[86] Schembri seems to have been hoping that his helpfulness to the Americans would give him free rein to continue his business with Tripoli.

Preble was not amused. He wrote in fury,

> You have prefaced your appeal with circumstances which only exist in Idea. You arrogate to yourself the possession of the "confidence and esteem of the Bashaw of Tripoly": and the "particular acquaintance of Mr Wilkie His Majesty's Commissary for the Fleet at Malta"—This you seem to suppose a sufficient reason why you should (unasked) interfere in the Affairs of the U.S. of America—Insolent Medlar!—Have you sagacity enough to calculate the pernicious consequence of your Duplicity? Do you know, that your ill timed officiousness served only to raise the sordid expectations of a Barbarian?—No—You do not exactly comprehend the extent of the mischief you have done—but this you well know, that the motives of this fraud against the U. S. were to secure the money you had then due in that regency and to make as much more as you could by the Violation of the faith reposed in you by his Excellency Govr Ball.[87]

In Captain Bainbridge's report from Tripoli about Schembri's negotiations, he concluded that Schembri had "done some injury and not the least service." He made many mistakes in protocol and discernment, surprising for one who supposedly had been so close to the bashaw. Beaussier concurred, writing that Schembri advanced "absurdities, contradictions, and falsehoods" in his bumbling attempts to play the Tripolitans and the Americans off each other.[88] Richard O'Brien said later that Schembri tried to play a "double and treble game" between Tripoli and the United States (and Great Britain), "but he has been punished in some respects for his deception."[89]

After Preble denounced Schembri's attempts at negotiation, Schembri renewed his allegiance to the bashaw. He advised Yusuf to make peace with the Americans now so that the navy would leave, and Yusuf could restart his attacks without the navy's presence to hamper him. Despite the disastrous negotiations, the bashaw seemed pleased with Schembri. He reportedly gave Schembri an expensive breast pin as a thanks for his work on Tripoli's behalf.[90]

Instead of working with Schembri, Preble decided to give Beaussier a chance to assist in negotiations. Beaussier was very much a man of the community. He knew how negotiations had gone with Tripoli in the past, where the Americans stood in comparison to those previous attempts, and where he stood as a representative of Napoleon. He told Preble that a host of factors had likely inflated the price the bashaw would want for peace. These factors included the negotiation of the Portuguese treaty at Algiers (for a lot of money), a Swedish prisoner exchange, the peace signed with the Batavian government while its squadron (like the Americans') lay off the port, the unacknowledged strength of the Tripolitan fortifications, and perhaps most importantly, the negotiations of Gaetano Schembri. Taking into consideration all of these factors, Beaussier feared that the Americans would not be able to make peace for less than $500,000. He expressed concern that the more Preble bombarded the town, the more the bashaw would dig in his heels. He also wanted to ascertain his place in the negotiations. He needed to know all of Preble's ideas and his bottom line in order to properly fulfill the role he had been given.[91]

Preble was not pleased with Beaussier's assessments. He grumbled that the English, French, and Swedish consuls were all siding with the bashaw, and only Nicholas Nissen could be trusted as an advocate for the Americans. Since Nissen had been barred from coming to the American ships, "we must therefore depend wholly on our own exertions for effecting a peace," Preble wrote. He redoubled his efforts to get gunboats and mortar boats to bombard the town, incredulous about Beaussier's analysis of the Tripolitan fortifications.[92] He also believed that Beaussier and his government hoped that war with Tripoli would turn into war with Tunis as well. If that happened, the American navy would blockade both nations and prevent the foodstuffs of the North African ports from reaching Syracuse and Malta, which they assumed the British would take permanently.[93] Preble refused to be caught in the middle of the war between the two great nations of the Mediterranean.

The brig *Transfer*, which was taken into the navy as the *Scourge* and given to John H. Dent, gave the navy more firepower, but it also taxed the already strained resources the navy received from supply ships. The most recent store ship, the *Woodrop Sims*, had delivered a quantity of naval stores such as cordage and sailcloth, but 22 of the 27 bolts of sailcloth were moldy from a leak in the ship's storage and had to be scrubbed clean of the black mold. Sixty-two pounds of the 144 pounds of twine were damaged and could not be salvaged.[94] Foodstuffs were also in short supply. Nathaniel Haraden recorded throwing 233 pounds of cheese and two barrels of beef overboard, "stinking & unfit for men to eat," in addition to 66 pounds of moldy bread.[95] Luckily, fresh provisions and vegetables were available for purchase in Syracuse.[96]

The *Scourge*'s addition also put a strain on the manpower of the squadron. Preble sent several seamen home because of their poor health, and three officers from the *Constitution* joined the *Scourge*'s crew. Manning the *Scourge* required taking men from all of the other ships in the Mediterranean, and the 20 men that joined the crew were described by Charles Morris as "the refuse of the squadron."[97] Complicating matters, some of the crews' enlistments were well past expired, particularly on board the *Enterprize*. As no orders had come to send the schooner home, the crew were getting restless. "Can we then call ourselves Men if we do not cast our thoughts on our families, most of whom exist in that Country that we have risked our lives to defend and protect?" they asked. "Or may we expect to be impressed in a service, whose liberty and independence our fathers fought and bled to establish and defend—against tyranny & oppression?"[98]

Paulina

In addition to the complications attending the captures under Preble's own command, he had to continue the adjudication of the cases of his predecessors. Despite the awe Decatur's success had inspired in Tunis, the bey was not finished arguing about Richard Valentine Morris's treatment of the *Paulina*, the Ottoman vessel captured in 1802. He had written to Thomas Jefferson in 1803 about his grievances with the United States on this matter, and he again requested that the United States build him a frigate. When Jefferson wrote back on January 27, 1804, he declined the bey's demand for a frigate, but still averred, "We set a just value on your friendship, as we do on that of all other Nations with which we have intercourse; and as we presume those Nations do on ours." Jefferson was apologetic for the manner of Cathcart, who had incurred the bey's wrath by his rude and demeaning attitudes. "The consideration that the bands of Peace between Nations ought not to be burst asunder by the hasty and unauthorised acts of a Public Agent was worthy of your wisdom and Justice," Jefferson wrote, telling the bey that he would take better care when selecting the next consul.[99] In fact, Jefferson rather liked Cathcart. He had described him in 1802 as "the honestest & ablest consul we have with the Barbary powers: a man of very sound judgment & fearless."[100] Few of Cathcart's colleagues shared Jefferson's assessment.

The last time Hamouda had seen Cathcart, the consul had stormed out of Hamouda's court after a heated discussion about the *Paulina*. In 1804 the old grievance cropped up again. Under threat of captivity in 1802, Richard Valentine Morris had agreed to restore the *Paulina* to its owner, as well as any cargo that was not bound for Tripoli. After Morris left Tunis, the brig had been returned to its master. But David Valenzin, the passenger on board whose cargo *was* bound for Tripoli, had been taken prisoner and sent to America when neither the governor of Malta nor the governor of Gibraltar would adjudicate the case. Valenzin's portion of the cargo, partially made up of perishable foodstuffs such as raisins, was sold instead of being sent to America with him.

In February 1804 a congressional investigation into Valenzin's case against the government found the sale of the *Paulina*'s cargo and treatment of Valenzin to be illegal and inappropriate.[101] The investigation demurred on the question of whether the capture had even been legal, but James Madison was not so coy. He argued that because there was no legally justified blockade in place at the time of the capture in January 1803, Valenzin's treatment was unacceptable.[102]

Consul George Davis knew none of these proceedings while he waited in Tunis for instructions. The bey and the merchants who owned cargo on the *Paulina* continued to badger him. In September 1803, Davis had thought the *Paulina* matter closed, after the Tunisian cargo was all either returned or indemnified. But Davis had warned then that Morris's capitulation "has produced the effect which was anticipated[:] new, and extravagant demands."[103] Preble also did not know the outcome of the congressional hearing, but after Beaussier's abortive efforts, he headed for Tunis along with the *Syren* to show some force there while waiting for his gunboats.[104] Since Preble and his crew were all sickly, they intended to stay only long enough to get supplies, not to engage in lengthy negotiations.[105]

On April 5, Preble sent a letter to Hamouda via Davis explaining that he was not familiar with the details of the *Paulina* dispute, as his predecessor had been in charge then, so he had forwarded the correspondence on the subject to the United States where it would be properly addressed by Captain Morris and Congress. He apologized if Cathcart had given offense at the time of the *Paulina* negotiations, and he begged the bey to consider George Davis the official representative of the United States in Tunis. He further apologized for not coming ashore himself, but he pled illness and urgent business elsewhere—Tripoli—and informed the bey that Tobias Lear would be coming to help sort any problems out. He closed by telling (or warning) the bey that he was sure the warships that were soon to arrive from America would bring satisfactory resolutions to the bey's questions.[106]

Davis's meeting with the bey did not go well. Hamouda refused to open Preble's letter, insisting that no more delay would be tolerated. When Davis gave Preble the report of the meeting, Preble told him that the *Constitution* was leaving the next day regardless, but would return with more naval force if necessary.[107] Preble did indeed depart the next day, April 8, sailing through stormy seas back to Tripoli, leaving the *Syren* off Tunis to support Davis and to get further supplies.[108] Davis was able to talk the bey into a six-week extension on payment for the *Paulina*'s cargo, despite the fact that neither Hamouda nor Davis gave any specifics about what the payment should be. If this dispute should lead to war, Preble thought the bey "must have already resolved on it, without this frivolous pretext."[109]

Because Tobias Lear had taken over the consul general role in Algiers, Bainbridge urged Preble to send for Richard O'Brien, whose "knowledge of the Language and people with whom we have to negotiate, would," Preble believed, "give us advantages which we cannot otherwise have."[110] (It's not clear that O'Brien could in fact speak any of the relevant languages except perhaps a *lingua franca*, but he did know about the customs of the Barbary court.)

O'Brien had come highly recommended by Captain Bainbridge and others, but James Leander Cathcart had reservations (to say the least) about his ability and his integrity, calling him "arm'd with all the mean intrigue & low artifice of that sink of perfidy and corruption the Sanhedrim of Algiers [the House of Bacri and Busnach] sent on to beg a peace through the influence of such perfidious mediators." Cathcart offered to travel with Preble and help with the negotiations, as long as he never had to interact with O'Brien or Davis. He thought that both men were more interested in their own advancement than in helping the United States make its mark in the Mediterranean: "The one is cultivateing the good graces of the Bey of Tunis & ministers in order to be appointed Consul; the other has been the mere echo of the Algerine Jews ever since he has been in Barbary."[111]

After sailing to Malta and then rendezvousing with Preble at Syracuse, O'Brien took passage on the *Enterprize* for Tunis, where he tried to iron out the difficulties. He observed that "Malta is the Arsenal for Tunis." The Tunisian letters of marque that needed repairs at Malta brought cattle with them to sell in order to pay for their repairs.[112] When O'Brien arrived in Tunis on April 25, he expected that the bey would be looking for an annuity from the United States, in addition to his other grievances. He found that Davis had not received any instructions from Lear about an annuity. O'Brien declared that the Americans would pay between $9,000 and $10,000 per year, due every other year, "to secure the Peace and friendship of this Regency towards the United States," with a delay of eight months to receive the sanction of the American government. He also instructed Davis to acquire $4,000–5,000 from Lear in order to settle the claims of the Tunisian cargos from the *Paulina*.[113] O'Brien encouraged Davis to continue to speak to the bey through his ministers, authorizing Davis to pay any ministers $5,000 as "greasing fees."[114]

When O'Brien and Davis attended the bey, they delivered President Jefferson's letter that rejected Hamouda's demand for a frigate. In their conversation with the bey's minister the next day, they signaled what they thought about the United States' place in the Mediterranean community. The minister told the Americans that he knew they had 40 or 50 ships in their navy (not true), so they could spare one. If the United States wanted to wait until peace had been signed with Tripoli, then the bey was willing to wait. O'Brien told him he should not expect a frigate at all. The minister protested that the Americans had given Algiers a frigate. O'Brien countered that they had asked for it when the original treaty was negotiated, and not in addition. He offered the sum of $8,000 per year as a token of friendship. Again, the minister protested that the Americans paid Algiers much more, and again O'Brien said that it was part of the treaty stipulations. The minister asked O'Brien how they could deviate from the standard practice of Spain, Denmark, and Sweden "and most all other Nations." O'Brien's reply was simply, "Our situation is superior to those mentioned Nations."

The minister, who is not named, argued that the United States had sought peace with Tunis initially, when Tunis "knew nothing about your Country," and therefore the United States should go above and beyond the treaty in order to keep Tunis as a friend. Tunis did not want or need peace with the United States, as war was probably more lucrative than peace. Furthermore, the United States had spent three years in a pointless and expensive war with Tripoli, and Tunis had more power than Tripoli. O'Brien replied that despite some setbacks, the United States was winning the war. He ended the discussion by saying, "We repeat, that, our system is Peace and will continue the War to obtain it."[115] The Tunisian minister's assertions were correct. The Americans had forced their way into peace with Tunis. They had engaged in three disappointing years of war with Tripoli. And they were tired of war. But they also considered themselves superior not only to the Barbary states but also to the states that capitulated to the demands of those so-called barbarians. The Americans put up a bold front to their neighbors' faces, but they could not wage war with Tunis and Tripoli simultaneously and could not afford to alienate even one of the European nations vying for commercial space along with them.

War with Tunis did seem possible—in March, Preble found three Tunisian frigates and a number of smaller Tunisian naval vessels fitting out at Malta. Hearing that the Tunisians were going to target Americans, Preble lamented that his squadron could not be at full effectiveness in four places at once: blockading Tripoli, monitoring Tunis, monitoring Morocco, and convoying merchants. On March 13 the Tunisian admiral at Malta came to the *Constitution* to demand that he be allowed to inspect the prisoners on board, in case any of them were Tunisian. Preble rebuffed the admiral, noting that he had already released the one Tunisian he had found. The admiral made threats toward the American navy, which Preble feared might turn out to be true.[116]

While the Tunisian navy fitted for sea at Malta, the American navy made an impression in Tunis. The intermittent appearances of Stephen Decatur's *Enterprize* penned in a Tripolitan cruiser that had been refitting in Tunis. George Davis heard a firsthand account of the burning of the *Philadelphia* from Decatur, and he sent the *Enterprize* away before retelling the tale to the bey of Tunis, lest Hamouda try to detain the *Enterprize* in retribution for the *Philadelphia*, which was supposed to have been given to him (Davis said). The story quickly became almost a minstrel tale in the streets of Tunis, as "each wandering Bedouin, details the daring action, and augurs something dreadful to our enemy from this event."[117] Eventually, after the *Enterprize* appeared yet again, the Tripolitans abandoned their ship and perhaps went overland to Tripoli.[118]

After O'Brien left with Commodore Preble on May 1, Davis's conversations with Hamouda's ministers inevitably circled back to the same problems: the United States had treated Tunis as lesser than Algiers, and the Americans saw themselves as better than the other nations with whom Tunis interacted. Despite their aggressive words, the Tunisian government was also embroiled in disputes with the Turkish grand signior and the Russian government, and so could not devote full attention to the American problem. The Tunisians were willing to wait until the Americans settled with Tripoli.

Meshouda and *Mirboka*

The Moroccan captures continued to be problematic for the Americans. Small claims about the *Meshouda* and *Mirboka* occupied James Simpson's time, but the real problem was how to deal with the great successes that the two captures represented.[119] Thus far, 1804 had been the most successful year of the war for the navy. However, since the United States had no bases in the Mediterranean, success could be its own problem. Prisoners often had to remain on naval vessels indefinitely instead of being held on shore, causing overcrowding and a drain on supplies. Preble had kept the prisoners of the *Mirboka* on the *Constitution* for as long as he could, but "their want of attention to cleanliness was injurious to the health of my Crew." He was given permission to detain the prisoners in some castles at Syracuse, but he kept eight of the officers, whom he deemed too important to be placed under someone else's care.[120]

Early in 1804, a year after they were originally commissioned, 100 gun carriages finally arrived from the United States for Morocco. Unfortunately, even after all the communications about them—they had been ordered, canceled, and reordered depending on the federal government's knowledge about peace with Morocco—the carriages sent were useless to the emperor. He had requested gun carriages for his fortifications, but the ones sent were for ships. His batteries were mounted with 18- and 24-pounder guns, but the carriages sent were for 12-pounders. Only one handspike per carriage was sent. Simpson was able to acquire 100 more handspikes from Gibraltar, but he could not remedy the size problem.[121] Luckily, the emperor seemed pleased with the gift, wrong size or not.[122]

Gunboat Diplomacy

Even with the loss of the *Philadelphia*, Commodore Preble still commanded the largest American squadron that had yet been seen in the Mediterranean. Hard sailing and bad weather had begun to take their toll on the ships, though. Preble had to balance his desire to lose not a moment with the reality that if his ships did not get repairs, they would fall apart. He compromised by ordering the minimum possible work and the greatest possible haste. Just one day after Stephen Decatur returned in triumph from Tripoli, Preble ordered him to take the *Enterprize* to Messina to "give her such repairs as are absolutely necessary to make her a safe Vessel." Once he arrived, Decatur reported that the schooner was "in a much worse state, than I had any idea of."[123] Preble requested of John Broadbent, US naval agent at Messina, that "the repairs which Capt. Decatur directs to be made, may be finished in the shortest possible time."[124]

In order to be effective, Preble wanted two more frigates and the brig *Argus*. (The *Argus* had arrived in the Mediterranean and was on its way toward Preble.) For Preble's squadron, the secretary of the navy had tried to follow the advice received from the previous commodores about the need for shallower-draft vessels, but Preble thought the pendulum had swung too far in the other direction. He had five schooners but only one frigate now that the *Philadelphia* was gone. He also wanted more guns and more powder, as "I expect to spend a large quantity of Powder in Fire Ships, and Infernals to blow up the Bashaw's Works." Preble argued that the commerce of the United States was worth the expense to protect it, and that the Barbary states must be brought to submission soon in order to prevent their continued naval buildup.[125] President Jefferson agreed, bringing to Congress a request to provide more ships and more money for the navy in light of the *Philadelphia* loss. But any money Congress provided would not reach the Mediterranean in time for Preble to use it.[126] In the United States, the *President* and the *Congress* began to take on water and supplies in preparations for a cruise.[127]

In early 1804, even though Preble had moved his headquarters to Syracuse, the navy seemed to spend nearly as much time at Malta. Partially because it was a clearinghouse for information, but also because the British garrison on the island was more familiar to the Americans than the Sicilian officials, Preble and his ships found themselves at Malta quite frequently. Cementing Preble's preference for Malta was the assurance of the British admiral there that the Americans would not face the threat of impressment as they had at Gibraltar, though the case of the *Madonna di Catapoliani* argued against that assurance.[128]

Communication difficulty hampered the operations of the squadron as it came in and out of Malta, which continued to be the mail stop for most communications with Tripoli. Both Preble and Bainbridge also tried to communicate with George Davis at Tunis, but delivery of that mail was appallingly slow. Preble did not trust his letters to Davis to any but an American naval vessel, which made "unrestrained communication" impossible. Mail was slow in the other direction as well—Preble noted on January 17 that he had just received a packet of letters from Davis addressed to Commodore Morris, who had been gone from the Mediterranean for nearly five months.[129] It turned out there was one unusual reason for the sluggish mail. Joseph Pulis, the American consul at Malta, was supposed to forward mail to all the appropriate recipients, but instead he had kept many of the letters. Pulis had held letters from America, from foreign officials, and from the captives at Tripoli; letters that arrived for the captives, he was sending back to America instead of delivering to Tripoli. This, then, explained how Bainbridge had not received any of Preble's letters to him. Preble demanded that Pulis be removed as consul, suggesting that naval agent William Higgins be appointed in his stead.[130] Though Pulis remained consul, Higgins took over the task of mailman, whereupon the mail service drastically improved.[131]

After the legal complications engendered by the blockade in early 1804, Preble went searching for a more effective means of bringing the bashaw to terms. He wanted to bombard the city, but the American navy had no vessels adequate to that task. Therefore, he requested gunboats from Naples and Livorno, and he asked James Leander Cathcart to facilitate their acquisition.[132] Cathcart also put out feelers to Marseilles and Toulon about getting gunboats built to his specifications. In case the French government should be concerned, he assured Stephen Cathalan, the agent at Marseilles, that these boats were intended for the American navy's use only.[133] Cathalan thought that the French would indeed be concerned—exporting guns and ammunition was illegal in France, and the French might not want to get in the middle of a war with Tripoli. Cathalan also questioned the wisdom of bombardment. He recalled that when the Swedes planned to bombard Tripoli, the bashaw threatened to execute all Swedish prisoners. With 400 American prisoners of war behind Tripoli's walls, Cathalan was not sure the navy should risk the same outcome.[134]

The gunboats marked an attempt at a new level of integration into the Mediterranean community—they would be built in a Mediterranean port, by European workmen, and would be manned by European bombardiers hired by Preble. When the Americans had requested armaments from the community in the past, they had gotten a cool reception. This case seemed to be no different; Marseilles was a dead end.[135] The government of Livorno was more accommodating, granting Cathcart permission to have gunboats built in the port. Cathcart also found there some mortars that would suit for his gunboats. But when their owner heard that Cathcart wanted to buy the mortars, he destroyed them rather than selling to the Americans. Cathcart surmised that this action was because the merchant, who was Jewish, did not want the bashaw of Tripoli to take vengeance on Jews living in Tripoli if he heard that the Jews of Livorno were providing the Americans with implements of war.[136]

Preble had reached out to the government of Naples about building gunboats and had looked into buying some at Palermo or Messina.[137] Where the French were reluctant to get involved, Abraham Gibbs, de facto American consul at Palermo, felt certain that General John Acton, the governor of Naples, would be happy to sell to the Americans "upon giving Security that they are to serve against the Common Enemy Tripoli."[138] Taking heart from Gibbs's positive reaction, Cathcart wrote to Acton requesting the loan of four gunboats and four mortar boats. He reminded the general that the Americans had enjoyed good relations with Naples in the past, and also that the American presence in Syracuse was "in reality promoting the Welfare of his subjects, by giving security to their persons and property, and lessening the risk of navigating under the Neapolitan flag."[139] John Broadbent helped to publicize the benefits of assistance to the United States by sending the story of the *Philadelphia*'s destruction to the gazette of Messina, as well as to General Acton, noting, "Atchievments of this nature cannot be too well known; it will have a good effect on the Court of Naples, and may give courage to this Government."[140] On March 27 Cathcart learned that the king of Naples would give the Americans the gunboats and mortar boats they had requested, but he was less willing to give them the guns that went in the boats. Acton suggested that if Preble came to Naples personally, the American navy would surely be able to get everything it wanted.[141]

Preble could not wait for the gunboats. He planned to go back out on a cruise and wished to take Cathcart with him. As though he were inviting Cathcart on a holiday weekend, he wrote, "What think you of a cruise for a few weeks? I am in want of a volunteer who possesses your knowledge of the Nation we are at war with. My Cabin & table is at your Service, if you incline to favour me with your company; & I will engage to show you sport before the summer is out."[142]

Hamet

While Preble considered how to deal with Yusuf, William Eaton worked on his plan to depose him. The year 1803 had been disappointing for Eaton's plans for Hamet Karamanli. In mid-1802 he had convinced Hamet to go to Malta to wait for Eaton to organize a resistance, but Hamet had proved unable to resist his brother's enticements to return to Tripoli. By November 1802 Hamet had taken the offered rule of Derna, though his family remained in Tripoli under his brother's captivity. Cathcart dismissed him as useless: "There was a period when he might have been of service to us. That period is past. . . . I do not think it advisable to have any thing to do with him."[143] Instead of abandoning Hamet, Eaton began to strategize how to help him foment revolution from Derna in order to garner support for a larger coup, returning to the United States to rally the government back home to his plans. Unfortunately, Hamet turned out to be just as weak and unstable as alleged, and the support never materialized.[144]

In November 1803 Hamet wrote to President Jefferson via Richard Farquhar, a Maltese merchant who acted as Hamet's intermediary, requesting a loan of 40,000 Spanish dollars, along with guns and powder. In return, Hamet promised to give the Americans one fort in the city of Tripoli until he could pay back the loan. He requested these supplies as he was leaving Derna, unable to hold back a force his brother Yusuf had sent against him. Despite the obvious failure,

Farquhar wrote to Jefferson, "If the United States assist the Said Bashaw of Derna [Hamet] to be Bashaw of Tripoli they are certain of being successfull and it will be the means of keeping America at peace with all the other Barbary States."[145] Joseph Pulis wrote a few weeks later that Hamet had fled to Alexandria in Egypt, "dreading the loss of his head."[146]

In January 1804 Hamet, through another agent at Malta, again requested funds and supplies from the squadron, "to purchase some more articles of War & to collect some of his Freinds." He intended to go back and retake Derna, and from there to conquer Benghazi and then Tripoli. Salvatore Busuttil, the agent, must have realized that Hamet's position did not invite help of any kind. In case Preble did not know of the navy's previous informal agreements, Busuttil included a letter that indicated Commodore Morris's willingness to help Hamet.[147] In Malta, Commodore Preble met with Busuttil in person to discuss Hamet's situation. Busuttil had little evidence of Hamet's ability to lead an insurrection, but Pulis, whom Hamet had befriended during his stay in Malta, urged Preble to give Hamet a chance.[148] Busuttil requested that the navy collect Hamet from Alexandria and bring him to Derna in order to begin the fight in the summer of 1804. Preble demurred on going this far, even though Busuttil wrote him a letter reiterating his suggestion.[149]

Richard Farquhar also continued to advocate for Hamet. He reported that Yusuf's standing with the other political elites in the city of Tripoli was tenuous, and "when your Vessels appear off Tripoli with his Brother on Board they will Murder the present Bashaw." Hamet apparently waited eagerly for the arrival of an American ship to take him to Derna from Alexandria in order to begin the fight.[150] Hamet was nothing if not persistent. On February 8 a letter from Hamet to Joseph Pulis arrived at Malta, once again begging for the Americans' assistance.[151]

In Tripoli, Beaussier informed the bashaw of the American plan to assist Hamet Karamanli in his coup. That information did not strike the fear into Yusuf that Beaussier had hoped. Instead, the bashaw scoffed that "he only sent him from his Governm[ent] at Derne, because he had began to Vex & discontent the people, but not from dread of any injury he might be able to do—he added his Brother was without means, inclined to drunkeness and incapable of acquiring partizans." Beaussier added privately, "All these assertions are truths." Even when Beaussier invoked a much more potent opponent—Napoleon—the bashaw brushed off his concern by stating that he was sure Napoleon would not take away from him the advantageous position he had acquired through three years of war. In the words of Antoine Zuchet, Dutch chargé at Tripoli, "It seems as if the Bashaw does not pay much respect to the First Consul's wishes."[152]

For the first time, a naval commander seriously considered the possibility of helping Hamet Karamanli. Apparently, the badgering of Farquhar and Busuttil had been effective. Preble could only support Hamet's coup if he received reinforcements, but he seemed inclined to do so if possible. He wrote, "I am in hopes the arrival of some additional force to our little Squadron will enable me to do this before the season is so far advanced as to dry up the Springs, and prevent the march of Troops from Egypt to Bengaza & Tripoly." Preble must have realized that if the reinforcements were not already on their way, the long delays in communications and travel would thwart his plans. He intended to start an assault on Derna and Benghazi by the middle of May, with or without Hamet's cooperation. These towns would have to be destroyed in order to keep Yusuf from using them, unless Hamet's forces were there to secure the citadels.[153] (Preble eventually scrapped this plan.)

Though Preble's primary goal was to defeat Tripoli and secure respect in the eyes of the watching Mediterranean community, he also kept tabs on other areas in which the United States had a reputation. For instance, he suggested that a minister to Constantinople would solidify the United States' standing with the Ottoman Empire, and that connection by extension would provide checks on Barbary aggression. He found the American vice consuls in Sicily (Syracuse, Palermo, and Messina) to "have no respectability attached to them." They had purchased their consulships in Naples, a highly irregular and unethical practice. Though most American consuls were not paid by the federal government, they all had to receive a commission from Congress in order to act in an official capacity.[154] These Sicilian consuls were not Americans, some of them did not speak English, and it seems unlikely that they had received such commissions. Perhaps they were only calling themselves consuls when they had no real claim to that title. The best-case scenario was that they were guilty of graft against the distant and weak American government. The worst case was that they were agents of the Neapolitan government. Either way, Preble found them "the laughing stocks of their own Country Men as well as Foreigners."[155] These consuls were not the kind of men needed to help the United States find its place in the Mediterranean community.

In the upper levels of command, the Americans seemed to be getting along quite well with their European counterparts. The squadron commodores had enjoyed a good relationship with most of the British officials and naval officers they encountered. (The exception was Captain Sutton of HMS *Amphion*, with whom the American navy had had problems before. He was still impressing sailors off American merchant vessels, according to John Gavino.[156]) One British captain even allowed an American sailor to ship to Gibraltar on board a British naval vessel with dispatches for Consul Gavino.[157] The more junior officers were more irascible. Though they had been charged to get along with their counterparts, sometimes the temptation to boast was too great. Henry Wadsworth, at the time a midshipman on the *Constitution*, wrote, "The envy &

jealousy of the British officers is excited by our fine Ships & handsome manoeuvring: we meet on shore but to fight & insult each other. The Politeness of the American officers will always induce them to give the preference to such as *do not* claim it but we wage eternal war with those who arrogate superiority."[158]

Working with the fractious nations of Europe was a matter of necessity for the squadron. Preble needed to exploit every channel he could in order to come to terms with the bashaw. He was able to reestablish relations with Bryan McDonogh, British consul at Tripoli.[159] But Preble preferred to work with the French. He obviously admired Napoleon, whom he called "that great Man."[160] Preble also hoped to leverage France's standing in the Mediterranean community to get what he wanted from weaker states. He asked Robert Livingston to solicit Napoleon's help in getting the Neapolitan government to provide the American navy with the gunboats he wanted.[161] The squadron's standing in Naples was somewhat shaky, according to Joseph Barnes, American consul in Palermo. Having offered in 1803 to assist the American squadron, General Acton had apparently not heard anything from the American navy until he received Preble's request for gunboats. Acton thought that the failure of communication was because of the United States' preoccupation with the acquisition of Louisiana, but it seems more likely that it was a combination of a lax commodore, Richard Valentine Morris, and letters "being Lost either thro' neglect, or design; or from jealousy taken up by parties & destroyed."[162] Barnes's apprehensions were unfounded. Preble was able to get gunboats from Naples with little trouble.[163] Acton promised to have both boats and artillery delivered to Messina for the use of the American squadron.[164]

As the summer arrived in 1804, all of these negotiations continued, but Preble's focus shifted back to Tripoli, where he hoped that his strategy of bombardment would force the bashaw into submission. Despite all the offers of assistance for the *Philadelphia* prisoners, it was not at all clear that the United States had made any more friends in the European community, and victory against Tripoli was still illusory. Antoine Zuchet wrote privately that the bashaw's position was weak and the bashaw was afraid of the Americans' plans for bombardment, but he would not budge in his negotiations, so from the American perspective, it looked as though nothing had changed.[165]

CHAPTER SIX

A Considerable Force

A National character is yet to be established, with these States—it
must be dreadful to Barbary—or, we shall ever, bow the neck,
and receive the tributary yoke, of half a dozen Pirates.

—George Davis to Edward Preble, May 12, 1804

On May 27 Consul George Davis wrote to Captain William Bainbridge,

> The incalculable movements of all Europe, predict a *new era, big with the fate of
> Kingdoms, States, Empires, & Worlds.* An epocha, more replete, with the destiny
> of Governments, than any period since the downfall of Rome. Recent arrivals
> from Marseilles inform us, that *Bonaparte,* is actually declared *Emperor* of the
> *Gauls, King* of *Navarre & Italy,* to be continued in his descendants. . . . *The fate
> of the Northern Powers, the commercial existence of Great Britain, the Ottoman Em-
> pire, are all involved in such an event.*[1]

In the great struggles that accompanied Napoleon's rise, the United States
and the Barbary states were only bit players. They would be affected by any of
these epochal changes, but they would not be the ones effecting the change.
This reality was at odds with the triumphal rhetoric that Preble and the US
Navy had been trumpeting for the past year. Davis's view from inside Tunis,
fighting for its own survival amid stronger nations, looked quite different from
the view of Commodore Preble, who projected confidence in his position at the
head of a naval force that had done more to deflate the Barbary states than any
other navy had done so far.

Preble's main concern was rallying the powerful nations of Europe to his
side in the fight against Tripoli. Thus, he was disappointed in the results of Bonaventure Beaussier's efforts to succour the prisoners of the *Philadelphia*. "It is

probable," he wrote to Beaussier, "the First Consul [Napoleon] expected his mediation would have had more weight with the Bashaw of Tripoly than it appears to have had." He also warned Beaussier not to give credence to anything said by Gaetano Schembri or his English friend (probably Patrick Wilkie), as Preble had not given them authorization to "interfere in the affairs of the United States at Tripoly." Instead, Beaussier could assist Richard O'Brien. Preble reminded Beaussier that the United States would treat ransom of the captives as a separate matter from a treaty of peace, and "we will not pay one dollar for Peace."[2]

Beaussier did not appreciate Preble's implication that he had been remiss. He thought that the arrogant and ill-considered actions of the commodore had wasted his efforts to prepare the bashaw for a peace offer from the Americans. Without waiting to confer with Beaussier, O'Brien had made an offer of only $40,000 to ransom around 300 prisoners of the *Philadelphia*. This offer was "truly ridiculous and offensive abruptly made after an absence of two Months and a half, which breaks off all Conference and negociation that could only be renewed with difficulty." Beaussier called the offer "worse than that made by Commodore Morris at an Epoch when none of your Countrymen were deprived of their liberty." In Beaussier's view, the Americans could no longer plead ignorance of Barbary custom; they were just being obstinate.[3]

Preble also dismissed the ideas of his own advisers. O'Brien had brought him a letter from Tobias Lear, who was supposed to be the lead negotiator in the Mediterranean, suggesting that Preble offer $600 per prisoner to ransom them, if the bashaw would agree to no annuities or excessive consular presents for peace. Preble wrote, "I am confident was I to make the Offer it would be accepted immediately, but it would be imprudent to offer a sum which would stimulate the avarice of the other Barbary Powers." Instead, Preble told the captive Bainbridge to try to secretly make the offer of $40,000 to the prime minister of the bashaw, with an additional $10,000 kickback for the minister. Preble did not really believe that this tactic would work, but he preferred to bombard Tripoli into submission anyway.[4]

Preble had thus far flouted almost all the conventions for the most advantageous ways to approach a Barbary ruler, so Bainbridge hoped that whoever came to negotiate would follow the standard pattern of starting with the minister and then approaching the bashaw after initial contact with the minister.[5] Bainbridge did reintroduce Preble's offer to the Tripolitan court, but it was rejected. He pointed out that as a prisoner, he had no standing with the government. A designated negotiator would be better suited to make both the offer and the bribe.[6] Beaussier also argued that the Americans were trying too hard to break the system—their proposal was "too extravagant to be listened to."[7]

Bainbridge sometimes took a philosophical view of his captivity, seeing himself and his fellow captives as mere pawns in a bigger game. He frequently complained of the severe restrictions placed on himself and his fellow officers (with no mention of the enlisted crew), arguing that this cruelty was counterproductive, as he would be a better advocate for generous terms if he had more liberty. (It isn't clear whether he voiced these complaints to the Tripolitans themselves.) Furthermore, he argued, the situation of the prisoners would not likely change Commodore Preble's ideas about negotiating with the Barbary states. "You are equally with myself acquainted with the disposition of Americans," he wrote to Davis, "and know *that they may lead, but cannot be drove.*" He saw the *Philadelphia* captives' suffering in terms of the grander American project: increased "political union" with the "first Powers in Europe." He was right that the *Philadelphia* capture had attracted the sympathy of the first powers more than perhaps any other event. Where Davis had seen the United States as a small fish in a big ocean, Bainbridge saw American disruption in the Mediterranean as a catalyst for sweeping political change in Europe, as well as a change in the United States' national standing. "America's rising Glory will make her friendship Courted by the Nations which at present form an erroneous opinion of her strength & respectability," he proclaimed.[8] Bainbridge seems not to have grasped just how much Europe was already changing, entirely without Americans taking the lead. At the moment, in fact, the evidence validated European estimates of American weakness.

Preble continued to be suspicious of the Mediterranean nations, perhaps feeling, like Bainbridge, that the United States' rise made the Europeans feel threatened. He had once again written off the British consul, Bryan McDonogh, and he remained skeptical of Beaussier's motives.[9] He also observed that Spain had sent carpenters to Tripoli to help the bashaw build gunboats. They had passed through the blockade because they bore a passport from Charles Pinckney, American minister at Madrid, so Preble thought "they must have decieved" Pinckney about their intentions.[10] The squadron had also captured a Spanish bomb vessel coming out of Tripoli under a passport from Consul Davis. Finding the crew with 14 more men than the vessel had come with, the Americans declared *La Vergine del Rosario* to be in violation of its passport from Davis and sent it to Malta for adjudication. Preble released the vessel when he heard of the capture, but Davis warned the Spanish that from that point on, no vessel, passport or not, would be permitted to enter Tripoli. Apparently Preble had had enough of the questions about passport violations.[11] Thereafter, Don Joseph Noguera, the Spanish consul general at Tunis, wrote to Commodore Preble requesting "special permission" for a Spanish courier to be allowed through the blockade to deliver dispatches.[12] Preble refused.[13] The emperor of Morocco also complained about the revocation of the passports. Preble did not find their grumbling a threat, but Simpson wished to bring some American naval vessels back to the Straits in order to keep the Moroccans in line.[14] This Preble also declined to do.

Despite his frustration with the Mediterranean powers, Preble still wanted their resources. On May 13, 1804, General Acton, the prime minister of Naples, informed Preble that the king would gladly loan the Americans six gunboats and two bomb ketches, with corresponding artillery, for the assault against their common enemy.[15] The gunboats, which were not really meant for open-water ocean sailing, mounted a 24-pounder gun on their bow and had a lateen sail, with a flat bottom that made them hard to sail or even row.[16] Preble desperately needed these boats, as well as the ships he hoped were coming from the United States, if his aggressive plans against Tripoli were to be enacted.[17]

The reinforcements were coming. On May 22 the secretary of the navy wrote to Preble that he was ready to deal Tripoli a compelling blow, and to that end, he was sending four heavy frigates to the Mediterranean.[18] Preble did not wait quietly for the reinforcements to arrive; instead, he decided that he needed to reconfigure his squadron to make his force ready for a more aggressive approach—bombardment. He picked up the six gunboats at Messina, which he ordered to Syracuse under the command of Richard Somers. These new boats required him to hire some additional crew from Naples.[19] His hired Neapolitans were not enough; Preble laid up two of the schooners and used their crews for his gunboats. In addition, he designated the *Intrepid* as a hospital ship because so many of the crew of the *Enterprize* had fallen ill.[20] He sailed for Tripoli with his squadron plus the gunboats, rather than waiting for the bomb vessels that had not yet been completed at Messina. With this force, Preble wrote, "I think it probable the Bashaw's Gun Boats and Cruisers may meet the fate they long since ought to have met with; and his old walls rattle about his ears."[21]

Aggressive Strategy off Tripoli

June was prime cruising time for the squadron. The weather was reasonable, and there was enough activity along the coast of Tripoli to keep the sailors interested in the cruise. Despite the resumption of fever season, Preble was as good as his word about keeping all of his ships active.[22] Henry Wadsworth, now a lieutenant on board the *Scourge*, wrote to his friend that the *Scourge* had been out on a cruise for two solid months, which was the longest cruise Wadsworth had experienced since his arrival in the Mediterranean. The squadron often sent its small boats "on shore at a distance from the Town for Sand to scrub our decks: & for amusement, to chase & be chased by the Natives, but they always retire before the people begin to collect." They had been running a gunboat up near where the *Philadelphia* had grounded, but the commodore stopped that exercise because it gave the Tripolitans target practice.[23]

Sometimes the games the Americans played turned deadly. Wadsworth recorded a chase that ended when the *Vixen* ran a ship on shore after making a "riddling sieve" of its hull. The fire from the American vessels supposedly killed

150 on the shore, but four Americans were also killed in the return fire.[24] The skirmishes between the Americans and the Tripolitans on shore continued to escalate in intensity as the summer progressed, though little actual damage was done. A skirmish on July 7 led to the wounding of three Americans and the death of one.[25]

Getting the squadron ready for bombardment meant a lot of coordination. After waiting for a few weeks in the vicinity of Syracuse, Preble picked up his two bombard vessels at Messina. As he headed from Messina to Tripoli on July 12 to begin the bombardment, he left a letter at Syracuse for the coming reinforcements, requesting that they make their way as swiftly as possible to the coast of Tripoli to join the rest of the squadron. He needed their guns and their manpower.[26] After a delay because of heavy weather, on July 14 Preble and the squadron were finally on their way to Tripoli.[27] They stopped at Malta on July 16, where they met the *Vixen*.[28] There, the ships all received the assistance of the British fleet in taking on water.[29] Preble received visits from Sir Alexander Ball and other military dignitaries at Malta while his officers went ashore to purchase desperately needed supplies.[30] Due to continued high winds, the squadron was not able to leave Malta until July 21.[31]

Reunited off Tripoli on July 26, Preble's whole squadron included the frigate *Constitution*, the brigs *Syren*, *Scourge*, and *Argus*, the schooner *Enterprize*, six gunboats, and two bomb vessels. The American forces numbered over 1,000 men, but they were still in the weaker position. Preble described the setting:

> A city well walled, protected by batteries judiciously constructed, mounting one hundred and fifteen pieces of heavy cannon, and defended by twenty-five thousand Arabs and Turks; the harbor protected by nineteen gunboats, two galleys, two schooners of eight guns each, and a brig mounting ten guns, ranged in order of battle, forming a strong line of defence, at secure moorings, inside a long range of rocks and shoals, extending more than two miles to the eastward of the town, which form the harbor, protects them from the northern gales, and renders it impossible for a vessel of the *Constitution*'s draught of water to approach near enough to destroy them, as they are sheltered by the rocks, and can retire under that shelter to the shore, unless they choose to expose themselves in the different channels and openings of the reefs, for the purpose of annoying their enemies.[32]

The winds prevented the squadron from commencing operations until August 3. The battle of that day proved that the Tripolitans were more formidable—and more treacherous—than the Americans had anticipated. The American gunboats moved in closer to the shore to engage with Tripolitan gunboats while the larger vessels tried to both provide covering fire and assault the town. Gunboat No. 2, commanded by Lieutenant James Decatur, was able to overcome one of the Tripolitan gunboats, but as Decatur moved to take command of the gunboat after it struck its colors, the captain shot Decatur in the head, killing him. Lieutenant Decatur's older brother, Captain Stephen Decatur, who had been commanding one of the other gunboats, sought out the Tripolitan captain to avenge his brother's death. Decatur and the Tripolitan captain grappled in hand-to-hand combat, and when the Tripolitan tried to strike a blow at Stephen Decatur as well, a young sailor named Daniel Frazier stepped in and took the blow. Only then were the Americans able to secure the gunboat.

The battle took about two hours, ending around 5:00 P.M. The squadron disengaged with no ship losses, only one death—James Decatur—and 13 wounded. Preble commended the crews of all the gunboats, including the Neapolitans he had hired. Three Tripolitan gunboats were sunk, three were captured and brought into the squadron, and Preble thought that the bombardment of the town had "done great execution." He awaited the response of the bashaw.

On August 5 Preble took advantage of a passing French privateer to send some prisoners back to Tripoli for treatment of their wounds. "The sending these unfortunate men on shore, to be taken care of by their friends, was an act of humanity, on our part, which I hope will make a proper impression on the minds of the Barbarians," Preble wrote, "but I doubt it." In reality, Preble sent the prisoners back because he could not spare the food to feed them.[33] The *Constitution* sent back 14 "badly wounded" prisoners to Tripoli, but Preble chose to keep

Figure 6.1 The bombardment of Tripoli, 3 August 1804. Oil by Michael Felice Corne. Image courtesy of United States Naval Academy Museum.

on board 35 additional men who were not wounded, a significant strain on resources.[34]

On August 7 the French privateer brought back news from Beaussier that the bashaw was interested in treating with the Americans. Beaussier also sent the unwelcome news that Muhammad Dghies, the Americans' best advocate in the court of Tripoli, had been too ill to join the discussions.[35] If the bashaw wanted to talk, he did not show it. He did not raise a white flag from the castle, a sign that a boat going ashore would not be fired upon, so Preble instead began to bombard the town. The gunboats were able to raze a battery, but not without cost. Gunboat No. 9—one of the three captured Tripolitan gunboats— blew up when hit by a shot from the battery, killing 10 men in total, including its commander, Lieutenant James R. Caldwell. All told, the squadron lost 12 men that day and 2 later from their wounds.[36]

After two battles with little accomplished, Preble was buoyed by the arrival of the *John Adams*. Armed *en flute*, or without most of its cannons, the frigate functioned as a supply ship and tender to the squadron. Master Commandant Isaac Chauncey brought news that the frigates Preble wanted were indeed coming, so Preble decided to wait for the reinforcements before launching another attack. Unfortunately, the arrival of the frigates also meant the end of Preble's tenure as commodore. The captain of the coming frigate *President*, Samuel Barron, outranked Preble on the seniority list. In fact, Preble also ranked lower than Captain John Rodgers, captain of the *Congress*. Knowing that the loss of command would be a heavy blow to Preble, the secretary of the navy tried to placate him: "Be assured, Sir, that no want of confidence in you has been mingled with the Considerations which have imposed upon us the necessity of this measure." Preble grumbled, "I cannot but regret that our naval establishment is so limited as to deprive me of the means and glory of completely subduing the haughty tyrant of Tripoli, while in the chief command; it will, however, afford me satisfaction to give my successor all the assistance in my power."[37]

On August 9 the French consul raised a white flag over the castle. Preble sent a boat to the town to hear what the bashaw had to say. That afternoon he received a letter from the bashaw offering to accept peace for $500 per prisoner, with no additional payments, for a total of $150,000. Though this number was approximately $350,000 less than the bashaw's last offer, Preble turned it down instantly. He had already told Beaussier that his final offer was $80,000.[38] The bashaw proved to be as intransigent as Preble. Beaussier reported that "since the Effusion of blood had already commenced, his country [Tripoli] was bent upon continuing the war—that the Bashaw, electrified more than ever by the decision of his council, and by the patriotic transport of his People, is determined to wait the event, unless the sum is considerably augmented."[39] Preble felt certain that the addition of four heavy frigates would be sufficient to force the bashaw to release the prisoners with no ransom. But the long cruise was beginning to take its toll on the squadron. "Officers and men are worn out for want of necessary rest," wrote Purser Noadiah Morris.[40]

Preble waited almost two weeks for the frigates to appear. Water and supplies began to run low. The *Constitution's* sailing master, Nathaniel Haraden, was so concerned about the dwindling supply that he began recording how much water was left for the squadron in his daily logbook entries.[41] Crews began to fall prey to scurvy.[42] Preble had to order the *Enterprize* to Syracuse for water and fresh vegetables. The *Enterprize* returned on August 20, followed the next day by a store ship. On August 31 the crew of the *Constitution* received some potatoes and onions from a small supply ship, but were forced to heave overboard 1,200 pounds of cheese that had rotted.[43]

With no sign of the reinforcements, Preble launched another bombardment before the autumn weather prevented the squadron from remaining off Tripoli. The squadron bombarded the city on August 24, and again on August 28, taking significant damage as sails and rigging were shot away and hulls damaged by the cannon from the town. On August 30, after another day of bombardment, Preble decided to take more drastic action. He turned the ketch *Intrepid* into an "infernal," or a fireship loaded with explosives, that would sail into Tripoli harbor and be blown up, hopefully along with enemy ships. Richard Somers and a small number of other officers and seamen volunteered to go with the *Intrepid* and light the fuses from a boat nearby. The crew of the *Constitution* loaded the ketch with 100 shells and 50 grenades, plus 100 barrels of powder donated from several different ships in the squadron.[44]

On September 4, after the *Intrepid* was fully loaded with the explosives, Somers and a small crew began to sail the ketch into the harbor. The crew was supposed to light a small fire to distract any Tripolitans who might try to stop them, but instead, as the *Intrepid* reached its destination, the entire ship blew up prematurely. "The whole squadron waited, with the utmost anxiety, to learn the fate of the adventurers, from a signal previously agreed on, in case of success; but waited in vain," wrote Preble. All 13 men aboard were killed, including Henry Wadsworth, who had written just a few months previous, "God preserve my life . . . until with exulting heart I tread the land of Liberty among my friends." He had served longer than almost any other naval officer in the Mediterranean when he was killed.[45]

The loss of the *Intrepid* was a blow to morale at the end of a long and fruitless campaign. By September 5 the squadron was scuffed up and low on supplies and ammunition. The weather had started to turn bad, so Preble prepared to leave Tripoli. He wrote to his friend in Malta, Captain Schomberg of HMS *Madras*, "Our Gun boats want much nursing, & create a vast deal of uneasiness for their Safety in rough Weather," and he could no longer keep them on station.[46] On September 7 he ordered the gunboats back to Syracuse, along with the *John Adams, Syren, Nautilus,* and *Enterprize.* Captain Decatur of the *Enterprize* was to transfer his crew members whose enlistments were up into the *John Adams,* which was headed for home, and to take on whatever crew he needed from the *John Adams.* The *Enterprize, Syren,* and *Nautilus* had to take the unseaworthy Neapolitan gunboats back to Messina, towing them as needed.[47] After the campaign was over, Preble's assault on Tripoli had left 32 Americans dead and 22 wounded. Preble did not immediately know the casualties the American squadron had inflicted on the town of Tripoli, but, recounting the sinking of several Tripolitan ships and the visible damage to the fortifications, he told General John Acton, "I think I may safely say that these Barbarians never have suffered more from any Christian power." He made a special point of commending the bravery of the Neapolitan bombardiers and gunboat crews.[48] From inside Tripoli, Beaussier had a different view: he told Preble that the August 24 attack had accomplished nothing at all, and the August 28 bombardment did more damage to the European consular houses (which were right next to the walls) than anything else. Beaussier noted that one camel was a casualty of the night's work.[49]

On September 10 the *President* and the *Constellation* finally arrived off Tripoli. By then the only ships left on station were the *Constitution, Argus,* and *Vixen.*[50] Preble noted only that "the command of the squadron was surrendered to Commodore Barron, with the usual ceremony." Preble asked Barron to return to the United States in the *John Adams,* leaving the *Constitution* for Stephen Decatur. Barron agreed, ordering Decatur to take the frigate to some Mediterranean port for refitting.[51] Though the ships of Preble's squadron were now dispersed throughout the Mediterranean, Barron's squadron began to bombard Tripoli again, but this time without the gunboats—the frigates had to do all the work.

Commodore Preble had been a very different sort of commander from his predecessors. Hampered by similar problems—lack of manpower, lack of ships, poor communications, poor supplies—he had improvised ways to work around the problems. Though Preble's brashness and unwillingness to operate within the culture of the Mediterranean sometimes created controversy, for the first time, some of the arrogance with which the Americans had entered the Mediterranean seemed to be justified, and the weaknesses of the Mediterranean system exposed. Noadiah Morris wrote of the weakness,

> The existence of these States depend in a very great degree on each other—that their manners and custons [*sic*] are the same, there is no question, and that their strength and arrogance has rather proceeded from the duplicity of the Maritime powers of Europe, than from any superiority in bravery or enterprize is equally

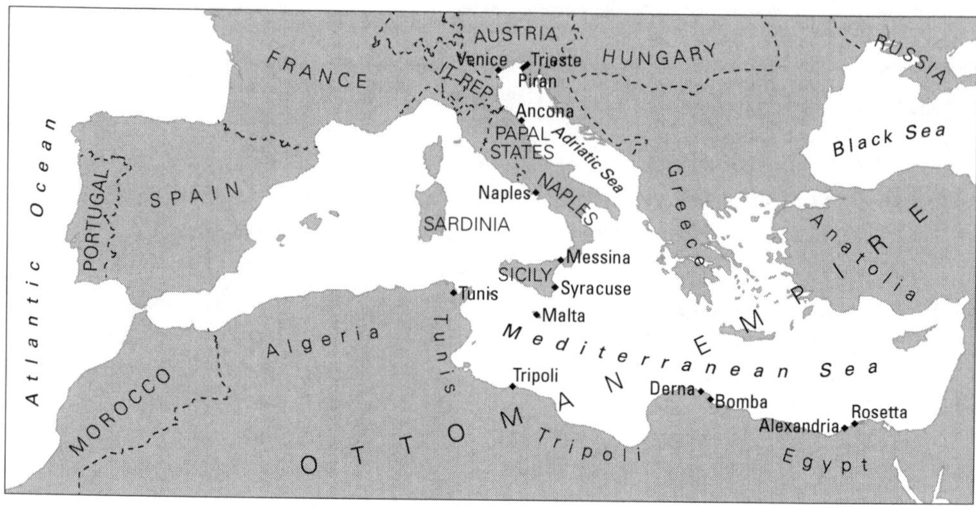

Figure 6.2 Sites important to the Americans in 1804. Map by Nat Case.

certain. The truth of this has been fully demonstrated by our small squadron.
The Americans have conquered them, hand to hand, one to five; and they have
reduced the insolent demand of the redoubtable Bashaw to the standard of
reason.

Morris thought that the commodore's actions regarding Morocco had set the
tone for his success. The resumption of the peace there had "been brought
about by his ready conception of the Turkish characters, which has been but
too long mistaken."[52] (Morris and most Americans called most North Africans
"Turks" whether or not they were ethnically or politically Turkish.) In other
words, where previous commodores had feared the bold threats of the Barbary
rulers, Preble had called their bluff. His men had followed his lead in their aggressive attitudes.

The arrogance and brutality of the more experienced officers sometimes
shocked the newly arrived officers. John Darby, the irascible purser on the *John
Adams*, wrote, "They seem to talk of butchering and cuting up a Turk with as
much indifference as one is acustomed to carve a Turkey or chicken."[53] These
men believed in their own superiority—and their prerogative to brutalize these
people they viewed as weak and cowardly. The irony was that even the experienced sailors in the American navy had had but few chances to conduct close
combat against anyone.

Noadiah Morris also noted how the Americans had acted as a foil to the
Europeans, including Preble's stern rebuke of the Neapolitan government when
it held American vessels under a more strict quarantine than other nations' ves-

sels.[54] His feelings were echoed by John Darby, who believed that the Europeans' familiarity with the Barbary states had engendered timidity: "This brave and dareing attack [the bombardment] will hardly be credited by the Europeans who know the greate Advantage of a fort and strong fortifyed Battery with their greate superiority of gun boats, nor do I beleive any other nation except the Americans woud have attempted it with the same force."[55]

With some successes under their belts, the Americans now asserted more directly how their difference made them better than the Europeans, who could not see past the familiar structures and contexts to imagine a different future relative to the Barbary states. Difference was a double-edged sword, but it was true that Preble had capitalized on American newness much more capably than his predecessors. The rhetoric surrounding Preble could not have been more different from the rhetoric that followed Richard Valentine Morris home. Consul George Davis wrote to Preble, "You have laid the foundation for a National Character; and on so solid a Basis, that Tripoli at least, will learn to respect, even its ruins; and in doing which, You have in a great degree removed the degrading opinion, they had entertained of Our Nation—Your example, will stimulate all the Secondary Nations; and I trust, finally destroy the false Policy of Europe."[56]

It was not just the Americans who appreciated Preble's zeal. When he heard the news that Preble was being superseded, Governor Alexander Ball of Malta, whose relationship with Preble had not been entirely smooth, wrote to him that when he gave the news to his government on Malta, "They join me in regretting that an officer whose Talents and professional abilities have been justly appretiated, and whose manners and conduct eminently fit him for so high a command should be removed from it."[57] Preble's conduct had thus achieved one of the aims of the war: the respect and community of at least one powerful nation in the Mediterranean.

Capitalizing on Preble's Success?

While Preble was cannonading Tripoli, the new commodore had stopped at Gibraltar to be briefed on the situation. He inherited relative calm in the Barbary states besides Tripoli, though he noted that the emperor of Morocco had again become fractious. As with the arrival of Preble in 1803, the appearance of Barron's two frigates had a calming effect on the emperor's complaints. The bey of Tunis likewise, though making a good deal of noise about his treatment, was unlikely to actually do anything while Barron's squadron was so close. Spain might represent a threat. Dissatisfaction with the United States' deals with France about Louisiana might spill over into harassment of Mediterranean commerce, according to Minister Charles Pinckney.[58] But by August 31 relations seemed more settled thanks to the work of the US consuls in Spain.[59]

Consul James Simpson remained concerned about the state of Moroccan affairs. He continued to refuse a passport to the Moroccan wheat ships bound for Tripoli, and it appeared that a rerun of the previous year's disputes might be at hand. Commodore Barron affirmed Simpson's decision to refuse the passports, and he also followed Simpson's lead about keeping American ships off Morocco as a preventive measure. He instructed the *Congress* and the *Essex* to remain at Gibraltar until Simpson's perceived crisis was past.[60] John Rodgers, captain of the *Congress*, instead chose to sail out to Salle to investigate the Moroccan navy and determine for himself whether they had hostile intentions. He ordered Captain James Barron and the *Essex* to stay at Gibraltar as Commodore Barron had instructed.[61] His inspection of Salle indicated that the Moroccan navy was not going anywhere, so after taking on water at Gibraltar, he headed for Tripoli.[62]

While at Gibraltar, Commodore Barron also met with William Eaton. Eaton outlined his still-unfinished plan for the coup under Hamet. He further requested that any treaty the Americans made with Tripoli ought to include provisions for both Denmark and Sweden. He wanted to repay the kindness of Nicholas Nissen and recompense the Swedish for the poor help the Americans had been in their alliance in 1801 and 1802.[63] Eaton decided to travel back to Tripoli with the squadron in order to superintend his plan for Hamet. Barron wrote orders for the *Argus* to refit and then provide convoy duty; however, he had other plans for the *Argus* that perhaps he did not wish to fall into the hands of the many Tripolitan agents in Malta. He verbally countermanded the convoy orders and instead dispatched the *Argus* with Eaton to Alexandria to find Hamet Karamanli and help him. William Eaton had finally found a commodore willing to go along with his plan.[64]

The *Constitution, John Adams,* and *Enterprize* were in such bad shape after their long cruises that they were almost unsailable. The *Constitution* headed to Malta to make the necessary repairs as quickly as possible, but the ship was hampered by a long quarantine imposed because of its lengthy stay off Tripoli.[65] When the *John Adams* arrived at Syracuse for refitting, Preble discovered that his officers had been bullying the government of Syracuse in his absence, "for which, I hope, they may suffer severely."[66] Lear observed that "the Americans are in fact commanders of the Town" in Syracuse, where they were able to manipulate and often ignore local laws, unlike in Malta where they were subject to strict quarantine and faced the constant threat of deserters claiming British protection.[67]

Barron arrived at Syracuse from Tripoli on September 27, along with Consul Lear and his wife.[68] Barron was in no shape to sail out on another cruise. His health was so poor that he could not be at sea during the winter months, and Eaton expressed doubt that he would be recovered in time for a spring cruise either.[69] In Malta, the *Constitution* was almost ready to return to Syracuse as well. The sick list had started to grow, due to "the quality of the water, which we daily receive from shore, & which from the late heavy Rains is white & empregnated with a limy substance."[70] In a mere two days, the sick list swelled from 20 to 60 because of "Graping with a flux," some kind of gastrointestinal distress.[71]

When the *President* sailed on a cruise in October, Barron stayed on shore at Syracuse.[72] He ordered the available vessels to continue the blockade of Tripoli as long as the weather permitted. The *Congress*, *Constellation*, and *Nautilus* kept up the blockade for another month, conducting nighttime tests about how close the American ships could get to the shore without being detected. John Rodgers bragged that one night he could "hear the People on Shore distinctly in common conversation." Armed with the knowledge that the Americans could get very close, Rodgers left the blockade in the hands of Captain Hugh G. Campbell of the *Constellation* and returned to Malta.[73]

Disease continued to affect the squadron's movements throughout the Mediterranean. No ships were able to touch at Gibraltar or Cadiz because a terrible yellow fever epidemic had virtually shut down the two cities. Consul John Gavino could not send or receive dispatches from the squadron because he could not speak to them (and he had been sick himself).[74] On October 29, one of the crew of the *Argus* fell sick with smallpox. Smallpox is transmitted through fairly close contact, so if one member of a ship's crew got the smallpox, it was extremely difficult to keep the other crew members from becoming infected. Since one episode of smallpox renders a person immune, certain ships in the navy built up a "herd immunity" to the disease. However, as new crew members came on board (navy enlistments were only for one year), collective immunity started to break down. To prevent an epidemic on board their ships, American naval surgeons practiced inoculation.[75] On board the *Argus*, a survey of the crew revealed 17 men who had not been exposed to smallpox before. The sailor who had fallen ill died of the pox; 16 others were sent to the hospital ship. It is not clear whether these men were inoculated, as the records do not indicate whether they were sent to the hospital ship to be inoculated or because they had contracted smallpox. In every other instance of smallpox in the squadron, men were inoculated, so it is reasonable to posit that the *Argus* sailors were as well.[76]

The smallpox on the *Argus* also indirectly affected the other ships of the squadron. No other cases appeared, but the Americans should have been subject to a long quarantine at Syracuse out of concerns about bringing the smallpox ashore.[77] However, because of the Americans' undue influence in the town, the port authorities gave the American ships pratique immediately, and were "much alarmed at having done so." To allay their fears, the *President*, which had 49 men on its sick list, went to sea for a few days to perform a pseudo-quarantine.[78]

One of Preble's last acts in the Mediterranean had been to establish a land hospital for American sailors in Syracuse, about two years after the idea had received authorization from the secretary of the navy, but it seems to have been a temporary structure.[79] In order to deal with the rise in illness among the squadron, Commodore Barron found a place for a permanent hospital to accommodate 75 men on shore in Syracuse and ordered the *President's* surgeon, Edward Cutbush, to set it up.[80]

On November 5 the *John Adams* left Syracuse with Captain Preble, bound eventually for New York. Preble had to deal with the Neapolitan government one last time when the frigate lost its anchors and had to borrow one from Naples. The frigate's journey back to the United States demonstrated once again the many ways that long cruises took their toll—the loss of anchors requiring help from both British naval vessels and the Neapolitan government; the crew made up of 60 able men and 80 invalids from all over the squadron; an outbreak of smallpox requiring the inoculation of 24 sailors; the poor condition of the water casks that caused the loss of over 2,000 gallons of water; and the loan of more than $10,000 from Preble himself for repairs just to keep the frigate afloat.[81]

Commodore Barron also asked Preble to negotiate the loan of more gunboats from the Neapolitan government for the spring campaign against Tripoli. Though General Acton was willing, the king of Naples declined. He reasoned that the Neapolitans had been especially harassed by all the Barbary regencies recently, so they needed all their armament. Preble thought that the king was under the thumb of both the British and the French, neither of whom wanted the United States to achieve peace with Tripoli while they were at war with each other. After this setback, Preble and the *John Adams* cancelled their remaining Mediterranean stops and headed straight for the United States in order to expedite the building of gunboats there.[82]

Barron's six-week assault on Tripoli did little to change the Americans' situation in the Mediterranean. From his confinement, Bainbridge hit on a key element that had been missing thus far from the way the Americans had interacted with the bashaw: "In making peace with these people we must not consider them as savages, but treat them as a nation with whom we wish peace."[83] Though most Americans would not have gone so far as to call the Barbary rulers savages, they certainly saw them as lesser, untrustworthy, and ultimately unworthy of honorable opposition. But Bainbridge had begun to understand that trust between sovereign nations had to go both ways.

Consul Lear planned to take a new approach with the negotiations. But he did not intend to begin until spring, when he thought the bashaw would be more inclined to talk. The dey of Algiers had permitted Lear to leave Algiers in order to negotiate with Tripoli, and even wrote the bashaw a letter ordering him to treat on American terms. Lear decided not to deliver the letter, because "we should not owe a peace, in any shape, to the interference of another power." The Americans' deference to Algiers had contributed to the break with Tripoli to begin with, so Lear was likely wise to decline their intervention.[84]

The squadron struggled to regroup from the fall's assault on Tripoli. In November, Commodore Barron ordered John Rodgers, now captain of the *Constitution*, to raise the broad pennant and take temporary command of the squadron. This was the second time Rodgers had taken over a squadron for an incapable commander—he had done the same in 1803 when Richard Valentine Morris had been recalled. Barron retired to the country near Syracuse, hoping that the pure air would improve his health. He invited Consul Lear to join him there in order to strategize about the next steps for the war effort.[85] The other ships of the squadron went back out to cruise off Tripoli for the month of November.

Affairs at Malta continued to be contentious, surprising given how friendly its governor had been. When the *Vixen* arrived at Malta on December 6, the ship received its fifth quarantine in two months. Steward Hezekiah Loomis wrote bitterly, "It appears by some of the arbitrary power which stimulates the English as much as virtue does the Americans, that they inflicted this imposition more for their own fancy than the Laws of their port or their Country."[86] An English store ship also took a boy out of the *Vixen*.[87]

The situation in Algiers and Morocco was somewhat better. Consul Lear, who was in Malta, had a brief scare when the dey of Algiers detained three American ships in retribution for the annuities he still had not received. Lear was able to pay the dey the money and set the ships free. He asked Robert Montgomery, consul at Alicante, to spread the news widely that Algiers was no longer a threat.[88] Likewise, Commodore Barron thought that the threat from Morocco was so minimal that he approved the release of the *Syren* back to Syracuse, leaving the port unprotected, provided Consul Simpson agreed with his assessment.[89] Simpson did not agree.[90]

On December 12 Spain declared war on England. Though the war created danger for American commerce, it would likely also leave the United States as the sole neutral in the Mediterranean, Charles Pinckney believed, as all the European nations would be forced to take sides. "I am convinced there is not one which does not wish us sunk in the Sea, & even England has but a splenetic cordiality for us," Pinckney wrote. "The increase of our Commercial Marine, now treading fast on her own—the probability of our being, if not the only, certainly always the most respected neutral flag in the world—the numbers & wealth this circumstance, connected with our freedom, will draw to us, & the consequent increase of our Commerce, & when we please, of our Naval force, will make England view us with jealousy."[91] Pinckney recognized that neutrality was a double-edged sword, but one that the United States should become accustomed to wielding.

The year 1804 was full of contradictions for the American navy. Edward Preble's efforts had been the strongest display of American force since the beginning of the war, but Samuel Barron could barely get out of bed, much less capitalize on Preble's success. The destruction of the *Philadelphia* had lionized the American navy's bravery and skill, but the captives of the *Philadelphia* remained imprisoned. The nations of the Mediterranean had rallied to aid the *Philadelphia* captives, demonstrating the integration of the United States into their community. They had also provided food, storage, clothing, men, and even munitions to the American squadron. At the same time, they had imposed regulations and harbored fugitives in a manner decidedly unfriendly.

For its part, the United States continued to insist that it would defeat the bashaw on its own, without interference from any other nation. Growing in familiarity with the Barbary system, Preble and others also grew in contempt for it. In December 1804 it appeared that the United States was little closer to peace with the bashaw than in January 1804. But the navy had slowly begun to garner respect in the ports it frequented, and the narrative of power and influence that the naval officers spun seemed to be working its way into the Mediterranean community. More dependent than ever on their Mediterranean neighbors, the leaders of the navy had talked themselves into superiority over the corrupt Mediterranean system. In 1805 they would have to try to convince everyone else.

European Complications

On December 30, 1804, Captain John Rodgers wrote to William Kirkpatrick, American consul at Malaga, "Every Effort is now using to give Tripoli her death blow next Summer, and no doubt it will be effected in a manner to prevent them ever again from feeling an inclination to make War on our Commerce."[92] In the United States, optimism about the prospect of peace was high. Expressing confidence in Samuel Barron's squadron, President Jefferson insisted that further tribute was out of the question. If the summer's expedition proved fruitless, Jefferson was prepared to keep a small force off Tripoli perpetually rather than pay tribute. He argued that it would cost the same amount of money to do so as to pay the tribute, but it would at least keep the United States from the disgrace of cowing to an inferior power.[93]

The squadron was in no shape to give anyone a death blow. In December 1804 the commodore's illness was so severe that many expressed concern that he would not survive, but the squadron's work had to continue.[94] Perhaps Commodore Barron had learned from his predecessors that English and French ports were minefields for diplomatic and social problems, so he ordered his squadron far and wide for refitting. But if he thought he could escape the long arm of the Napoleonic wars, he was mistaken.

Desperation for men and refitting led the navy into conflicts with its own consular service. At the end of 1804 the *Constitution* sailed for Lisbon to replace its depleted crew. By the time it arrived, the ship desperately needed repairs as well. Despite this urgent need, the *Constitution* sat in port for five days at the end of December without seeing the health officer or hearing word directly from the American consul, William Jarvis.[95] Jarvis attributed the delay to fears about the yellow fever in Spain and Gibraltar, which meant that the *Constitution* was in for a long quarantine. The only way to shorten the quarantine was to provide the health office with exact information about where the ship had been and whether its crew had been sick on the way.[96] Because Rodgers had already given this information to the vice consul who had come alongside when the ship arrived, he was astonished that Jarvis did not have it—and furious at Jarvis, who he felt had wasted at least four days of their time. He could stay in Lisbon for only 20 days, and quarantine would leave him almost no time for the needed repairs, which he had immediately begun to prepare for upon arrival. If Jarvis could not convince the health officers to take Rodgers's word about where the ship had stopped, then Rodgers would leave Lisbon and limp to Gibraltar, taking his chances with the yellow fever, "sooner than tamely subject the American Flag to such Disgrace"—a long quarantine.[97]

Jarvis was equally furious at Rodgers's accusation that he had neglected his duty, as health officers did not consult foreign consuls when assigning quarantine lengths, and Rodgers should have expected a long quarantine. Nevertheless, if Rodgers could not wait until spring or summer when sailors were easier to recruit, Jarvis would ready the sails and rigging for repairs for when the ship was released from quarantine.[98] Though Rodgers continued to rail at Jarvis for the perceived insults to his character, he accepted Jarvis's offer to provide the items for repairs.[99] Rodgers was also able to sign on nearly 80 men from Lisbon.[100]

Predictably, the signing of seamen provoked a conflict with the British. James Gambier, British consul at Lisbon, wrote to Jarvis to request that Rodgers hand over any British seamen he had signed on to the *Constitution*. British law stated that all British seamen must serve in the navy "whenever our fleets may stand in need of them," and with the war against Napoleon escalating again, Consul Gambier needed every man he could get. He invoked both the sailors' duty to their country and obligations imposed by American neutrality as reasons for the return of any British sailors.[101] Rodgers replied that he had not knowingly shipped any British sailors, but even if he had, he was not bound by British law, and there was no formal agreement between the United States and Britain that obligated him to give up sailors that he had found unemployed in a neutral port. However, he wrote, "The high respect I entertain for the British Government, will prevent my detaining one of its deserters a Single moment after I know him to be such."[102]

The Danish consul likewise requested that Rodgers deliver up four deserters believed to be on the *Constitution*. Rodgers disclaimed knowledge of them as well but promised to hand them over if they should appear.[103] Believing that Rodgers was lying, Jarvis hoped Rodgers would agree that "the Capt from whom they have absconded should regain them again."[104] The deserters were indeed on board the *Constitution*, but Rodgers put them on shore instead of giving them back to the Danish captain. He did not see himself as "bound either by National or Personal honor to deliver Men into the hands of an authority that would punish them for their wishing to serve our Country in preference to their own, particularly when at the same time, I had no Election in the motive that influenced their conduct." Rodgers did not have a high opinion of the conditions on board Danish vessels. He thought Jarvis wanted to punish the deserters for "prefering FREEDOM to SLAVERY."[105]

Political changes in Europe continued to affect the American navy on a larger scale as well. Great Britain threatened Portugal's colonies, making it likely that Portugal would not join the British against Napoleon. However, outside forces might affect Portugal's political future, as one of Napoleon's most aggressive generals, Jean Lannes, was soon to arrive in Lisbon.[106] Likewise, the British put the city of Cadiz, where the *Syren* was refitting, under blockade, limiting the Americans' ability to use that port.[107] At Messina, where the squadron had done business in the past, a change in government meant that the *Nautilus* was refused naval stores, which was especially unfortunate because the *Nautilus* needed timber not only for itself but also for the *President*.[108] The Americans believed that all of Europe was in turmoil, forming alliances and preparing for war. The smaller nations were arming, but Consul George Davis thought they could not withstand France's might, which would "annex them to the french dominions and as Nations wipe them from the face of the Earth."[109] Everywhere the ships of the squadron went, they encountered the changing alliances of the European states.[110]

While the *Constitution* was in Lisbon, the *Enterprize* was ordered to Trieste and Venice. The consul there, William Riggin, had negotiated with the government of Venice, which was governed by the friendly Austrian empire, to allow the *Enterprize* to refit and purchase stores at a fair price.[111] The schooner's captain, Thomas Robinson, gushed to Commodore Barron about the abundance of supplies and the helpfulness of the Venetian locals in repairing the *Enterprize*, which was in bad shape. The American vessel was able to take advantage of stores that had been abandoned when Italy had fallen under the control of

Austria. Robinson wrote, "There are piles of Timber in the Arsenal sufficient for twenty line of Battle ships." But the Italian republics too were subject to domination by French coalition forces or British-Russian coalition forces. In this unstable political environment, Robinson thought that when the war came to Italy, Venice would probably side against France.[112]

Like Rodgers, Robinson had only praise for the locals with which he interacted, and only scorn for the consuls. For one thing, the consuls handed out American passports unheedingly, to whoever desired one, not just to Americans. Robinson found their conduct degrading to the honor of the United States, and potentially harmful: "A designing man might under the character [of an American] do infinite injury to a Belligerent [power] with whom we are at peace and perhaps on terms of warm friendship."[113]

Access to friendly ports was more important than ever for the American squadron. The larger squadrons required more supplies, but their supplies from America were of poor quality and variable frequency. After several shipments of cheese were nearly all lost to rot, the *President*'s purser, Charles Wadsworth, wrote to the accountant of the navy suggesting that staples such as cheese, vinegar, and candles could be purchased more easily in the Mediterranean, with less cost to the navy department.[114] But the squadron had limited access to some of its favored ports. In Gibraltar, the yellow fever had ravaged the city.[115] When the *John Adams*, carrying Edward Preble home, stopped there to get water and supplies for the voyage to the United States, few supplies were available because of the tight quarantine and the lack of workers to load them. The health officer had died, as well as almost all the men responsible for loading ships. In addition, the weather was so bad that nothing could be loaded onto any boats for the entire first week of January.[116] The *John Adams* had to get fresh vegetables, eggs, and fowls by sending a boat to Tangier instead.[117]

Political struggles with the British also stifled American activities in the Mediterranean. The United States was getting a taste of its own medicine about blockades. An American brig had been captured and brought to Malta for a violation of the British blockade of Genoa. However, the judge ruled that the Americans represented a special type of neutral, different from neutral Europeans, and released the ship with only a fine to compensate for the captors' effort. The judge's ruling accentuated the ways in which the United States could not be part of the European community. The United States was not likely to entangle itself in the Napoleonic conflict directly, so it was different from other neutrals who needed pressure to keep them on the correct side (the British side, in this case).[118] When the United States found itself restricted by the blockade of Cadiz, it was the Americans' turn to ask for special treatment. Joseph Yznardi, consul at Cadiz, entreated Admiral John Orde to renew the agreement the Americans had enjoyed with Lord St. Vincent that allowed them to send produce in and out of Cadiz.[119] Just as the American consuls had declined to allow British vessels into Tripoli, so Admiral Orde declined to allow American vessels into Cadiz.[120]

Captain Hugh G. Campbell thought the turmoil in Europe would cause problems for any American action in North Africa. Acknowledging that the *Constellation* would need significant repairs, he set about getting them done quickly, as there was no guarantee how long the Americans would be permitted in European ports. "Intrigue has conquered Italy," he wrote. "Naples is intirely directed by French influence, in so much as to leave the King with little more than a name; and obliged many of its Inhabitants, like the Birds in Autumn, to rove in search of milder climes. Nor shall I be surprized if the European Wars continue much longer, to find ourselves debarr'd the Privilege of refitting our Squadron in their Ports." This prediction, which had already been proved true when the *Nautilus* was denied stores at Messina, left Campbell skeptical of the Americans' chances in their summer campaign against Tripoli.[121]

Just as Campbell thought, the European unrest kept resources out of American hands. On his way home in autumn 1804, Preble had requested 15 gunboats and 8 mortars of the government of Naples, but he had been rebuffed.[122] At the beginning of 1805, when Commodore Barron had recovered enough to transact some business in Syracuse, he entreated General Acton of Naples to intervene on behalf of the navy's request.[123] Preble had thought that the king's refusal to grant the gunboats had more to do with the French than the Barbary states, and he was probably right. But the Neapolitan forces had also stepped up their own attacks on Barbary vessels. George Davis informed Commodore Barron that the Tunisian warships that had been fitting out at Malta were now abandoned. The bey of Tunis wanted them returned to him, but he feared the Neapolitan forces. He therefore requested that the American navy convoy the vessels home to Tunis.[124]

Barron also had to mediate yet more complaints about the American blockade, including another one from Russia about the polacre *St. Michael*, taken in September 1804 by the *Constellation*.[125] Consul Levett Harris was able to convince Minister Adam Czartoryski that the capture was legitimate, and the crisis was averted. Czartoryski did have some bad news, though. The Russian attempts to force the Ottoman government to intervene on behalf of the *Philadelphia*'s prisoners had not succeeded—the Ottoman Porte had less influence on Tripoli than he had believed.[126]

The Ottomans had their own complaints about the blockade. The Ottoman court requested that Sir Alexander Ball at Malta intervene in several irregularities involving Ottoman vessels. The first was the *Mastico*, which had been captured over a year previous, and had been destroyed in Tripoli harbor as an infernal. Little remained of the *Mastico*'s cargo or crew, but Barron offered to return the slaves that the Americans still held, if Ball would tell him where to send them. The other two Ottoman prizes had been taken more recently, and Barron could speak more authoritatively about them. He thought there could be no dispute that they were trying to run the blockade, so they would be good prize. Because their cargoes were perishable, he had sold them, but (unlike Morris with the *Paulina*) he had kept the money in escrow until the prize court ruled. He expected to send them to prize court as soon as he received direction from the American government.[127]

The Barbary states were also in tumult, though some were more problematic for the United States than others. Tripoli felt the pressure not only of the American forces but also of "civil comotions" and famine. Tunis was "on growling order," which was not much different from its usual attitude toward the United States.[128] Algiers had been relatively quiet for the entire duration of the Tripolitan war. A few complaints and demands had been dispatched with relative ease by Richard O'Brien and Tobias Lear. On January 20, 1805, the dey sent word to Timothy Mountford, who had taken over for Tobias Lear while Lear went to negotiate with Tripoli, that he wanted a 74-gun ship of the line as a present. Mountford argued that a ship of the line would cost more than a million dollars, well outside the stipulations of Algiers' treaty with the United States. When the dey countered that a French ship of the line could be built for $100,000, Mountford emphasized the differences between France and the United States. In this case, materials for shipbuilding had to be shipped to the United States from Europe. In the face of this argument, the dey backed down on his demand.[129] To keep the peace, Consul Lear sent Algiers a ship full of wheat, which doubled as both an annuity and goodwill gift to the famine-stricken country. Mountford's eloquence and the gift probably counted for much less than another factor in the dey's retreat: he was dealing with the much larger threat of British influence in Algiers, interference that the Americans encouraged. When Lord Nelson asked Consul Lear to house a few British officials who came to Algiers to speak with the dey, Lear and Mountford were only too happy to oblige.[130] Additionally, Lear officially transferred diplomatic authority in Algiers to Mountford so that Lear could remain with the squadron and begin negotiations with Tripoli when the time was right.[131]

In Morocco, the emperor continued to complain that his wheat ships should be allowed to go to Tripoli. Simpson again refused to grant the passports. Fearing repercussions, he requested that Commodore Barron send two frigates and two smaller vessels to patrol off Morocco during the spring and summer, or whatever force Barron could spare immediately. In the meantime, Simpson wrote, he would continue to spread the story that an American force would soon arrive, hopeful that the mere threat of force would be enough to keep the emperor in line.[132] Ultimately, the secretary of the navy officially ordered the *Syren* to leave Morocco and join the squadron off Tripoli, no matter what Simpson said about the hostile intentions of the emperor.[133]

Despite the turmoil, the Americans had to continue their fight against Tripoli. The squadron began to prepare for another attempt to bring the bashaw to terms. The Syracuse countryside had not greatly improved Commodore Barron's health, and so at the beginning of February he decided to move back to Malta in hopes that the change would do him good. George Dyson, the naval agent at Syracuse, wrote privately to Edward Preble, "I am of opinion He can never recover."[134] The *President* stayed in Syracuse under the command of Master Commandant George Cox.[135] The *Congress* and the *Vixen* likewise converged on Syracuse while the *Constitution* made its way back from Lisbon.[136] The *Syren* remained near Gibraltar, where the port had been reopened on January 30.[137] Though Captain Rodgers could recall the *Syren* to Tripoli, he took Consul Simpson's concerns seriously and ordered the schooner to stay.[138]

Though Barron would not ship out himself, he ordered the *President*, the *Constitution*, and the *Constellation* off Tripoli for a cruise. The *Nautilus* was to cruise off Tunis after a quick convoy trip.[139] The *Essex* was ordered to Venice, where Captain James Barron was to try to acquire gunboats from the government there. Commodore Barron was not sanguine about Captain Barron's chances, but since Naples had not worked out, he felt he had no choice.[140] Captain Barron hoped to meet up with Captain Robinson and the *Vixen*, but he ended up in Trieste because the draft of the *Essex* was too deep for Venice's harbor. He found that either Trieste or Venice might be willing to let the Americans have gunboats, but getting them might require some diplomacy.[141] Robinson reported back that boats were easy enough to get, but mortars had to be approved by the Austrian government at Vienna.[142] While Robinson and Barron negotiated with Austria, Robinson also took matters into his own hands. He built out machinery on the deck of the *Enterprize* capable of holding a 24-pounder gun, which would give the schooner considerably more firepower than it had had during the previous summer. Though he had not completely secured it to the deck, in case Commodore Barron disapproved, Robinson was obviously quite pleased with himself: "I am certain she can carry it in almost any Sea, & if so what a nice tickler she will be for nightwork on Tripoly, & altho her seranades may not be so agreable as from the Guitar to a Turk, they no doubt will generally have as respectable an audience."[143]

James Barron continued to search for gunboats elsewhere as well. Though he found that he could have some built at Trieste, he anticipated some kind of trouble there, and recommended that any gunboats Robinson could acquire in Venice be routed through Piran, a port in Slovenia, rather than going to Trieste. The government of Trieste had just enacted a law that made it illegal for any citizen to sell a vessel without permission from the government. Captain Barron had found this out the hard way when the owner of a gunboat he wished to purchase was detained in the castle before completing the sale.[144] In the end, Robinson was able to purchase two gunboats in Venice, and Barron was able to acquire an American brig and two other gunboats in Trieste. With this addition to their force, Robinson predicted that "Tripoly certainly gets a severe dressing next summer."[145]

Commodore Barron's orders to Rodgers sounded similar to the orders the secretary of the navy gave to commanding officers, emphasizing the latitude given to the officers on station because of the rapidly changing circumstances and the poor communication. Barron advised caution around the Tripolitan batteries, as the squadron was not equipped to make many repairs while on station.[146] In essence, Barron was handing over the reins of the squadron to Rodgers.

The squadron's cruise off Tripoli was met with few challenges from the Tripolitans. However, the *Constellation* was struck by smallpox, and 30 crew members had to be inoculated. Campbell requested permission to leave the station, pleading that "should we Experience bad weather their situation will be truly unpleasant."[147] Rodgers consented, advising Campbell to go to Malta to fill up on water and supplies, so that he could return and relieve one of the other ships that would be staying longer in the *Constellation*'s place.[148] Campbell made a sudden reversal, however, informing Rodgers that he had enough supplies to last for two months, so Rodgers should return to Malta (presumably to get orders from Commodore Barron). Rodgers ordered Campbell to stay until the *President* arrived. Then either the *Vixen* or the *Constellation* could return to Malta. But two ships should always be on station at any given time.[149]

The Tripolitan navy, though numbering between 16 and 20 vessels, was by no means ready for sea. One of the vessels did not even have masts, and none had sails.[150] Rodgers suggested to Commodore Barron that a six-ship rotation, where two ships were always off Tripoli, would be an easy and efficient means of maintaining a strict blockade. The other vessels could cruise in locations where they would likely intercept the Tripolitan cruisers that were not in the port, or they could be available to do whatever other business the commodore might require of them.[151]

On January 27 Captain Bainbridge had written to Consul Lear that the bashaw seemed interested in peace. He hoped, however, that the Americans would improve their tactics from the last assault in August and September 1804. He advised Commodore Barron to bring a strong force, as "the Bashaw apprehens a very severe attack, and the apprehension perhaps would have as great an effect as the attack itself." More importantly, Bainbridge hoped that a negotiation would be done face-to-face, instead of through letters as Preble had chosen to do. Bainbridge assured Lear that a personal meeting would not be beneath the Americans' dignity, unlike in Algiers, where Lear had been required to kiss the dey's hand.[152]

Bainbridge also asked Commodore Barron to send a negotiator. Prime Minister Dghies, seemingly aware that Bainbridge was communicating via a secret method with the outside world, requested that he discreetly recommend that Barron begin negotiations. Bainbridge argued that if an American negotiator would come and offer the same terms as Preble had, he would likely be accepted. If not, the Tripolitan people would see that the bashaw's obstinacy caused the continuation of war, not the bloodthirstiness of the United States. But Bainbridge also thought that the United States would never be able to secure the release of the *Philadelphia* captives without payment, even if no money was given for peace specifically, unless it landed troops in Tripoli.[153] Nicholas Nissen also advocated for Dghies's plan. Nissen informed Barron that Dghies wanted to begin negotiations very soon because his poor health would soon drive him back to the countryside. Losing Dghies as an advocate would be detrimental to the American cause. Nissen admitted that Dghies had asked him to write to Barron, but he would not have done so unless he believed that Dghies really intended to help.[154]

Keeping up the force off Tripoli was paramount to the American strategy. Consul Lear wrote to Bainbridge, "We have a very Considerable Force now in this Sea, which, if exercised, must be productive of all the fatal effects of War; for our Country will never admit of any terms of peace which shall not be honorable and as permanent as we can expect." Whatever reservations the federal government had entertained about sending the navy, they were committed now. Lear argued that the expense was a secondary consideration to the acknowledgment of the "rising Character of our Nation" and the establishment of peace with honor. Furthermore, honor dictated that the United States no longer come to Tripoli as a supplicant for peace. "If the Bashaw wishes for peace it now remains for him to come forward," wrote Lear.[155] The only way to force the bashaw's hand was to increase the pressure on his city and commerce. After almost four years of attrition, the navy would have to finish what it started. Despite Lear's bold words, he also wrote to the European consuls in Tripoli to reestablish contact with nations that could potentially help his negotiations.[156]

Barron adopted Rodgers's suggestion of a rotation for the squadron. Since he had returned to Malta, the Americans had essentially moved their headquarters back to that port. Barron suggested that the *Constellation* should go to Syracuse when it came off station, however. The health officers at Malta would likely impose a stricter quarantine on the smallpox-ridden ship than those at Syracuse.[157] While the *Constellation* was in port, Rodgers urged Campbell to make preparations for an aggressive summer offensive against Tripoli. "Good Powder

& plenty of Shot will in all Probability, be as necessary to ensure success as good supply of Beef and Bread to give us strength to use it," Rodgers wrote.[158]

Rodgers felt that the time was quickly approaching to strike the death blow to the Tripolitans. Tripoli's fleet of gunboats had not increased since the winter, and Rodgers wanted to strike before the circumstances changed. In a letter of April 17, he wrote that if the navy could attack within six weeks, he felt confident in a mighty victory.[159] The American naval force had increased over the winter and was set to increase even more. In addition to the gunboats that Robinson and Barron had acquired, the secretary of the navy was sending the *John Adams* back to the Mediterranean as a troop transfer ship carrying 500 men, plus eight additional gunboats.[160]

The force that was already off Tripoli continued to cruise. The *Constitution* captured a Tunisian xebec and its two Neapolitan prizes on April 24, sending them to Malta with the *President* for adjudication.[161] Other than infrequent chases, the squadron saw little activity in its cruise before Tripoli. The real action was happening nearly 600 miles away, where William Eaton and a ragtag band of warriors prepared for an assault on Derna.

CHAPTER SEVEN

Rather a Rabble than an Army

There is reason to believe the example we have set, begins, already to work on the dispositions of the powers of Europe to emancipate themselves from that degrading yoke. Should we produce such a revolution there, we shall be amply rewarded for what we have done.

—Thomas Jefferson to Judge John Tyler, March 29, 1805

Having returned to the Mediterranean from a tour of the United States, in 1804 William Eaton continued to pursue his plans for the overthrow of Yusuf Karamanli. Eaton's operation is by far the most well-known aspect of the First Barbary War—the "shores of Tripoli" of the "Marines' Hymn" are the shores traversed by Eaton. But even though his efforts have been coopted in one of the most recognizable American anthems, the coup was not solely an American effort. As the First Barbary War wound to a close, American relations—good and bad—with Mediterranean stakeholders had the potential to either impel the American efforts forward or destroy them before they ever got off the ground. Relations with Tripoli were only one part of the story. The Americans continued to get help from nations such as Great Britain, and they continued to fend off encroachment from nations who wanted to take advantage of them. They also once again found themselves in the middle of conflicts that were much bigger and much longer than their own squabbles with Tripoli and learned how much their own affairs were influenced by those bigger conflicts.

It is also worth noting that for much of the year 1805, we have primarily Eaton's word for how his operation progressed; the only other accounts we have are from people peripheral to the events. Given the ease with which he lied to authorities when it suited his purposes, it is not unreasonable to imagine that his reports back home, or his requests for assistance, were sometimes less than the truth. However, he is the only narrator we have for much of his journey, so we will have to take his word for what happened.

Eaton intended to take passage with the *Argus* to Alexandria to rendezvous with Hamet Karamanli in late 1804. But the mission was not going to be easy. Other than allowing Eaton to have the *Argus*, Commodore Barron's interest in the plan did not extend to providing arms, money, or men to the cause. Eaton further discovered that his alternate source of money, a debt owed to him by a Sardinian noble, had been forgiven by the American government, so he could not collect it. Discouraged, Eaton wrote, "I cannot forbear . . . expressing, on this occasion, the extreme mortification I suffer on account of my actual situation; destitute of commission, rank, or command; and, I may say, consideration or credit." He had not received any official orders, or even guidance, about how to stage this irregular operation. With so little to work with, Eaton thought it would be a miracle if the plan succeeded.[1]

Eaton's mood fell further when the *Argus* spent nearly a month refitting at Messina instead of sailing to Alexandria. Upon its return to Syracuse, the brig was sent on a search mission for three American naval vessels that had been blown off course during a severe gale, and thus "the expedition to Alexandria [was] suspended."[2] In the meantime, Eaton roomed with George Dyson, Preble's navy agent at Syracuse, "a plain, frank, up and down, hospitable Yorkshireman."[3] Richard Farquhar and Salvatore Busuttil began to badger the new commodore, just as they had badgered Edward Preble, about when the American navy could be expected to sail to Hamet's aid.[4]

If Eaton doubted his prospects for success, Tobias Lear was downright certain that the plan would fail. He thought Hamet did not have the character to sustain a successful government in Tripoli and certainly would be no help to the American cause.[5] Captain Bainbridge felt the same, writing to Lear that he could "sincerely hope that such an Impolic & extraordinary measure has not intruded itself on the wisdom, of our Govt."[6] Bainbridge argued that it was Yusuf's rule that was sanctioned by the Ottomans and the Europeans, not the rule of his "poor effeminate fugitive brother."[7] Bainbridge believed that a fools' errand to help the hapless Hamet was not worth risking the ire of the rest of the Mediterranean community who recognized the legitimacy of Yusuf. Perhaps now, in the throes of Barbary captivity, Bainbridge was beginning to realize the limits of American ambition to be different.

Barron disagreed, authorizing Isaac Hull, captain of the *Argus*, to assist Eaton in whatever way he could.[8] Barron wrote to Lear, "I conceive that if no other use can be made of him [Hamet] there will be no difficulty in placing him in possession of Derne & Bengaze. It may have a good effect, On his Brother it cannot I think, have an ill one."[9] Perhaps Barron saw Eaton's expedition as a way

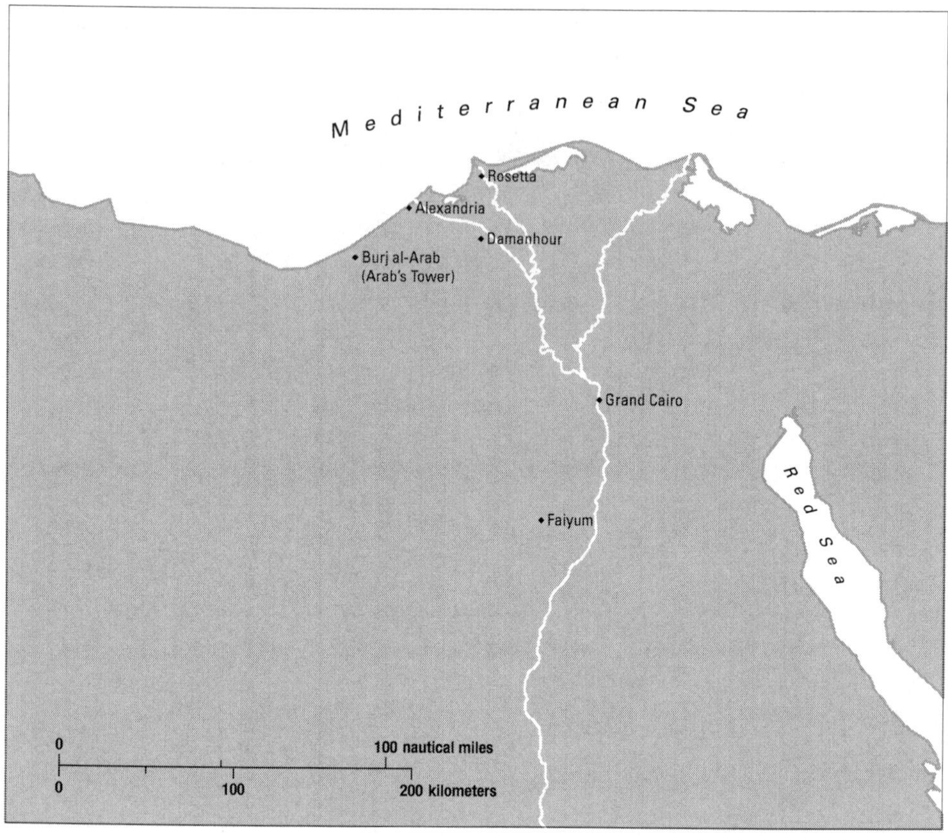

Figure 7.1 Egypt in 1805. Map by Nat Case.

to keep the pressure on Yusuf, as it was becoming obvious that Barron himself would be unable to do much to help the squadron.

The *Argus* finally sailed for Alexandria on November 14, 1804, with Eaton and Richard Farquhar on board. Eaton prepared to make a land journey from Alexandria to Derna with Hamet's forces, supported with supplies and munitions from the *Argus*.[10] Knowing he would need help from the British, Eaton wrote to Governor Alexander Ball to request an introduction to the British consul at Alexandria.[11] Ball agreed, giving him letters of introduction to both Samuel Briggs, the civilian consul, and Major Ernest Missett, the British resident at Cairo.[12]

The *Argus* arrived at Alexandria on November 25. After meeting with the British consul and Alexandrian officials, Eaton, Farquhar, Marine Lieutenant Presley O'Bannon, and a few others began the journey to Rosetta on November 28 in a smaller craft. From there they embarked toward Hamet's residence in Grand Cairo, a journey that Eaton predicted would be difficult because of the unrest in the country.[13] The evidence of the European conflicts in Egypt was everywhere on their journey. Eaton recorded that near Aboukir Bay he saw "the battle grounds of 8th and 21st of March 1801, yet covered with human skeletons."[14]

When Eaton arrived at Rosetta on December 2, the party met Major Missett, who had fled from Cairo because of the internal unrest in Egypt between the Turks and the Mamluks.[15] These two factions had been fighting for control of Egypt's government for some time. However, the French invasion in 1798 had disrupted everything. After an Anglo-Ottoman alliance forced the removal of Napoleon's army in 1801, a new power struggle had erupted between various forces in Egypt, which was only just being resolved as Eaton and his company arrived in late 1804. Both the Mamluks and the Ottomans thought that the British would help them regain power, and the British played both sides. By the end of 1805, a leader named Muhammad Ali would take power and hold it for 40 years. But when Eaton arrived, the country was in civil war.[16]

Eaton could not help sounding imperial as he evaluated the Egyptians' situation. He wrote to Alexander Ball, "Why this misery, and spirit of revolution? from a despotic or rather a total want of Government! Egypt has no master: though the most frightful despotism." He continued, "Egypt must have a new master—and the first comer will be welcome. One of the belligrent parties will be apt to join the foreign standard—The peasantry will embrace protection." He hinted that Ball should encourage the British powers to be the first comer, even providing him with tactical information (as if there were no British people in Cairo to provide it).[17] He thought that the glory days of Egypt were long past, however, even if Britain intervened. He found the geography, flora, and fauna of the area wanting in comparison to American alligators and the mighty Ohio River, but more importantly, he found that the channels of international commerce had taken their paths elsewhere and had left Egypt desolate. Reflecting on the rising glory of the United States in contrast to the fallen splendor of Egypt, Eaton concluded, "I almost lose the sensibility of pity in the glad reflection that I am a citizen of the United States."[18]

The American company was welcomed at both Alexandria and at Rosetta as saviors, come from England as the advance of a large British army. Eaton supposed that the *Argus* had given the impression of being British, as it had flown the British flag to ease entrance into the harbor at Alexandria, and the ship had been met by the British consul Briggs. Eaton and his company did nothing to dissuade the people from their mistake. "It would have been cruel to have undeceived them," Eaton wrote. "Consequently without positively assuming it, we passed in the character of Englishmen among the middle and lower orders of society, and as their allies among those of better information."[19] In other situations, Eaton had been furious at Americans who wished to fit in with their European counterparts, but here it suited his purposes very well.

From Rosetta, Eaton wrote to Hamet that he had come to honor the agreement he had made in Malta. He affirmed his belief in Hamet's claim to the throne of Tripoli. He averred that while Yusuf was ruling, America would never have peace with Tripoli, but "when God shall have restablished the rightful sovereign upon the throne of Tripoli we will seek peace with that kingdom." But Eaton did not want to cause more trouble than necessary in this volatile political climate. He requested that Hamet instruct him on the best way to communicate that would not cause suspicion among the Egyptians.[20] On the same day, December 4, Eaton's company, now numbering 18, started for Cairo.[21] Along the way, Eaton recorded several more instances of the Egyptians' excitement at the prospect of a British re-conquest.[22]

On December 8 the company reached Grand Cairo, where they settled into Missett's house for a few days. In Cairo, the people were interested in them because they were American, not because they looked British.[23] Eaton visited and was visited by many dignitaries. He took special time to see the Ottoman viceroy of Cairo, Ahmad, who wanted to know about the state of European affairs as well as about the commerce and power of the United States. Given the unrest in Egypt, Ahmad undoubtedly wanted as much information on potential threats as possible—including the United States itself. Though he had welcomed Eaton, he expressed suspicion that the Americans' visit was for more than "mere gratification of curiosity."[24]

In response, Eaton told him of their mission to overthrow Yusuf. The viceroy pledged his help, unless Hamet had joined the Mamluks, the Ottomans' perpetual enemy. He had. Knowing this, Eaton used his charm—and semantics—to argue that even if Hamet had joined the Mamluks, "it was more like God to pardon than to punish a repenting enemy." It was not the only time Eaton would try to essentialize Islam and Christianity to find common ground. When the viceroy agreed to search for Hamet, Eaton sent out his own couriers to find him as well. Even though the viceroy granted Hamet a pardon for colluding with the Mamluks, Eaton thought convincing Hamet to leave might be a challenge.[25]

The British took good care of the company while they waited for word of Hamet. Eaton asked Hamet to rendezvous at Rosetta when he was able to, but to send his troops directly to Alexandria, perhaps to keep the Rosetta authorities from discomfort with so many troops around who had just been serving under the Mamluks.[26] Eaton's perpetual enthusiasm for his project waned a little as he waited. Hamet was clearly a poor leader and a poor manager of both people and goods; he had chosen to join the "rebel Beys," increasing the difficulty of getting him out of the country and back to Tripoli; and Eaton was unable to directly communicate with him.[27] Because the viceroy had granted Hamet safe passage, Eaton instructed Captain Hull of the *Argus* to prepare for an influx of 300 to 400 men, though Hull needed to secure provision for only around 100 men in Hamet's entourage.[28] Hull told him there was no way the *Argus* could ship and provision even 100 men. He suggested that they should simply collect Hamet and repair to Syracuse to regroup before an attack.[29] Eaton appointed Francisco Mendrici, the viceroy's personal physician, to be agent for the United States in Cairo. Eaton and Mendrici had known each other in Tunis, when Mendrici had been the bey's physician, and they had both been thrown out of the country by the bey.[30] It was possible Mendrici could help in finding adequate provisions for the men, given his ties to many places in Egypt.

By Christmas, Hamet still had not appeared. Captain Hull and his officers spent the day with the British consul and his family, who had entertained the *Argus*'s officers many times during their wait in Alexandria. Hull continued to raise objections to Eaton's plans. Eaton had requested more money be sent to him in Cairo, but Hull had no money available. He reiterated his inability to carry the number of people Eaton wanted. But he also wanted to stop treading on the hospitality of the British, so he did not want to house the troops in the city of Alexandria either.[31]

As Eaton waited, he concocted more extreme plans to get Hamet moving toward Derna. Repeated missives to Hamet went unanswered. Eaton began to consider trying to pass through the Turkish and Mamluk armies to see Hamet personally. This was a last resort, however, as the task would be extremely dangerous: "We shall have three perils to encounter, danger of Robery and assassination by the wild Arabs; danger of falling into the hands of the Arnaut Turks and being murdered as Enemys, and danger of being executed as Spies by the Mameluke Beys; If we surmount these perils, we shall have carried a point, and gained an object."[32] The boredom of waiting got to Eaton's entourage as well— Richard Farquhar and Purser Robert Goldsborough's unsavory exploits at the billiard table resulted in a fistfight between them and black eyes for both. Eaton sent both Goldsborough and Farquhar back to Alexandria with dispatches the next day.[33]

By the new year, still without word from Hamet, Eaton began to suspect that Hamet was a captive of Eli Bey, the captain of the Mamluks. Since the Mamluks were fast closing in on Cairo, Eaton figured they would have an answer soon one way or the other.[34] Hull, in contrast, thought that the nefarious hand of the French was behind Hamet's silence. He again suggested that Eaton's plans were too grand; so much reliance on English hospitality made Hull uneasy.[35]

On January 3 Hamet finally responded. He rebuked Eaton for taking so long to come to him from Tunis, but he was no less eager to carry out the coup. He suggested a meeting in order to arrange the expedition.[36] When Eaton received Hamet's letter on January 8, he was elated, writing to Hull, "I cannot but congratulate you and felicitate myself after so much apprehension doubt and solicitude, that we now calculate with certainty on the success of our expedition, we are sure of the Bashaw." Eaton's grand words about certain success rang a little hollow, though. His next thoughts were of Derna and Benghazi, which he learned had been fortified more strongly in the past few months (this report turned out to be false). Eaton suspected Joseph Pulis of leaking the American plans to Yusuf Karamanli, but the expedition would carry on.[37]

Meanwhile, Hull and the *Argus* waited in Alexandria. Farquhar and his men were housed there at the navy's expense. Hull wanted to discharge them until Eaton's plans for returning to Alexandria were more secure. The *Argus* planned to leave for Malta on January 20 in order to report to the commodore the progress of the mission. Hull suggested that Farquhar should come along on that journey, since he had been with Eaton in Cairo and knew the details better than Hull did.[38] Eaton departed Cairo for Rosetta on January 12.[39]

Eaton thought that Hamet would come to Rosetta, as he had suggested in his messages, but when Eaton arrived there on January 14 Hamet was not there. Instead, Hamet had relocated to a village called Houissa, where he wrote to Eaton requesting clothes, animals, money, and tents for his men. "Friend, you must have courage," he wrote. "Do not think about money because the occasion demands heavy expenditure."[40] Eaton went on to Alexandria, and on January 20 he received a message from Hamet announcing his plan to decamp to some 190 miles inland in Fiayum. Though Eaton was still uneasy about inland travel, he saw little choice but to follow. He headed for Fiayum on January 22 with two officers from the *Argus* and 23 additional men.[41]

On January 23 one of Eaton's fears came true. Attempting to pass through Turkish battle lines, Eaton and his company were arrested in Damanhour by the kerchief, or kourchet, the military leader in the area. Eaton admitted privately to Edward Preble that though the arrest was inconvenient, he was impressed by the military acumen of the Turkish general, who was suspicious of a band of foreign military wandering through his camps. Exacerbating the problem was the French consul, who told the Turks that Eaton had come to Egypt with anti-Turkish intentions. Eaton was able to convince the general otherwise. After that, the general brought Eaton to a chief of a Bedouin tribe who knew of Hamet's troubles. The Bedouin chief was delighted with Eaton's plans and volunteered to find Hamet and bring him back, in addition to pledging 20,000 men for the cause.

To put the Turkish general at ease, Eaton decided to send back to Alexandria most of his company, leaving only himself and a few others to wait for Hamet. The general set up accommodations for the remaining Americans in

Damanhour. Despite their friendly words, the kourchet did not trust Eaton—armed guards around Eaton's quarters, supposedly to protect him, also kept him within close range. Though relations thawed between Eaton and the general, the Americans were still eager to leave as soon as possible.[42]

In Alexandria, the presence of the Americans was becoming a source of concern. After Hull spent some time recruiting men for the *Argus* in the city, the governor sent Briggs to tell Hull to stop recruiting, even though the governor had given Hull permission to do so previously. The governor claimed that the new orders came from the viceroy of Cairo, who had countermanded the governor's permission. Though this excuse seemed implausible, Hull did not want trouble, so he instructed Farquhar to dismiss all the men that they had signed on. Hull and Farquhar then returned to the ship, withdrawing from the town as much as possible.[43] Tales of Eaton's recruitment of men at Damanhour also caused concern in Alexandria. In an audience with the governor, Hull tried "to do away his fears, but find that he is as much alarmed as ever." The governor was concerned that the effort the Americans were making indicated an objective larger than simply unseating Yusuf.[44] Eaton denied recruiting any men at Damanhour, and he even suggested that Farquhar had overstepped his orders in recruiting openly in Alexandria.[45]

The French continued to make trouble for the entourage. When Eaton arrived at Alexandria on February 7, he was informed that Hamet would be denied entrance into the city. Despite the viceroy's decree of amnesty for Hamet, the French had convinced the governor of Alexandria to deny him admittance. Hull thought that the governor had then invented a letter from the viceroy instructing him not to let Hamet in.[46] Eaton prevailed on the viceroy of Cairo to issue Hamet a firman of amnesty (a document with much more weight). The viceroy did so, as well as fining the governor of Alexandria 25,000 piastres for violating his initial order of amnesty. He also granted Eaton's request to recruit Christians in Alexandria. Concerned that the governor might choose to exact retribution for his harsh punishment, Eaton advised Hamet to remain outside Alexandria. They made plans to begin their march on February 20.[47]

While the company was outside Alexandria, an envoy from Yusuf Karamanli, working on information from his old friend Gaetano Schembri, arrived to prevent Hamet from leaving. The envoy could not convince the town authorities that he had a case, however, and without force, he could do little. In fact, Eaton thought that Tripolitan expatriates who had fled the reign of Yusuf would join Hamet's forces and increase their ranks by 20,000 or 30,000. Armed with these hopes, and $10,000 that Hull had managed to acquire from the Briggs Brothers banking house, Eaton felt quite secure against any intrigue Yusuf orchestrated.[48] The company would also include fighters from Egypt. The firman of safe passage that the viceroy had granted Hamet contained a request: that

Hamet bring into his army the Arabs called Aulad Ali and allow them to march with him to Derna.[49]

Once Hamet and Eaton were together, it was time to begin serious preparations, but not everyone appreciated Eaton's style of leadership. Richard Farquhar, who Hamet had said was essential to his success, seemed inclined to abandon the whole mission because of conflict with Eaton. Farquhar insisted that he would quit unless Eaton "shall be *more reserve* in his manner of speaking, and that my Account shall be paid up till today, and that at least one hundred and fifty men shall go from this [Alexandria] to join the Bashaw, with three or four small Guns, and an agreement stating the pay and time of service."[50] Farquhar had become tired of Eaton's practice of making casual promises that he had no authority to follow through on and thought Eaton was going to dismiss all the men he had worked so hard to recruit. Hull thought that Eaton would never let Farquhar make any command decisions, so Farquhar should abandon any idea of going on the overland march and come with Hull on the *Argus*.[51] Farquhar did more than that; he apparently embezzled or mishandled the funds given to him by Consul Briggs for the expedition, delaying their departure for several days while the finances were sorted out. Eaton dismissed him entirely, though it seems he rejoined the expedition yet again at some point.[52]

The navy had a role to play in this coup as well. Eaton sent Hamet's prime minister—who is not named but may have been Farquhar—to Malta in the *Argus* to acquaint Commodore Barron of the events thus far. He also requested that Barron send him 100 firearms, two fieldpieces, and 100 marines to join his march across the desert. Neither Hamet nor Eaton had any illusions about the trustworthiness of the men they had signed on. As the two men had developed their plans, they had gone back and forth about if Hamet needed to accompany the men overland or if he could take the shorter and less strenuous sea route to Derna on the *Argus*. But after the whole company was assembled, it was clear that the troops he had assembled would not make the journey without him, so Eaton and Hamet would march with them.[53] Eaton wanted support from the sea, though. He intended to rendezvous at Bomba with the navy, who he hoped would bring supplies and reinforcements.[54] Marine Lieutenant Presley O'Bannon, seven other marines, and Midshipman Pascal Paoli Peck remained with the expedition. Eaton also signed on Christian mercenaries along with a French captain of light artillery, the latter to deal with the fieldpieces he hoped to get from the navy at Bomba.[55]

Eaton formalized the agreement with Hamet on February 23. The treaty contained all of the stipulations the two had already agreed on. To pay back the Americans for the expense they had gone to, Hamet agreed to give them all the tribute money paid to Tripoli by Denmark, Sweden, and Batavia. He also formalized his relationship with Eaton, officially making him the general of his troops. It was not uncommon for foreigners to have high military ranks in the Barbary states. Yusuf's own admiral, Murad Reis, was actually a Scotsman named Peter Lisle, though Eaton had no intention of converting to Islam like Lisle had. Though the agreement indicated a certain level of trust between the two parties, it also stipulated conduct between the two nations in case war broke out between them after Hamet was bashaw.[56]

Hamet had little to offer the expedition except some men and solemn promises. However, he too recognized the importance of establishing community with other Mediterranean powers, so he reached out through Barron to the kingdom of Sicily as well. He offered a similar treaty to the Sicilian king as he planned for the United States: a treaty with no tribute and most-favored-nation status. He also promised Eaton to hand over Yusuf and his court for the United States to hold hostage, and to give the United States any ships that had attacked their commerce.[57]

After such difficulty in getting into Alexandria, Eaton found his way again barred when it was time to leave the city. He and the other Americans were free to go, but Hamet's servants, who had come to help with supplies, were forbidden to leave. Patrols of Turkish soldiers were also sent out close to Hamet's camp, which was now about 12 miles from Alexandria. Consul Briggs intervened to let the company leave, and Lieutenant O'Bannon was able to keep Hamet from fleeing from his camp. A crisis was, for the moment, averted.[58] As he was leaving, Eaton wrote a scathing letter to Monsieur Drovetti, the French chargé d'affaires in Alexandria, who he believed was responsible for the Egyptians' unfriendly behavior. Drovetti had spread rumors that the Americans were British spies, and he had refused to allow French subjects in Alexandria any contact with the Americans. These actions were, in Eaton's mind, a "singular and calculated insult." He asked for "your explanations to our respective governments and to the world, for the open indignity you have shown the flag of the United States in this port."[59]

Drovetti was not finished interfering with the Americans. To Consul Briggs, he made a now-familiar claim: French subjects, sought by the government, had possibly taken refuge by signing onto the American expedition. He requested that Briggs deliver them up. Briggs demurred, however. He was only assisting the Americans; he had no jurisdiction to return any member of the expedition, whether he wanted to or not.[60] Briggs also informed Eaton that Drovetti had been monitoring their forces and reporting back to Yusuf about their numbers and armament. Eaton welcomed this espionage, writing, "The information he sends forward of our movements, will be essentially serviceable to us; as it goes from a quarter which will attach full credit, and of course leave no doubt with the enemy of a coalition which he most dreads, and which he has used all possible means to counteract: it will through [throw] his Capital into convulsions."[61]

Despite his bold words about the coalition, Eaton had problems within the company as well, including a persistent lack of funds. Sheik il Taib, one of the Arab chieftains, insisted that he would not march unless paid more money. As Eaton had no money to pay soldiers, he had to placate the sheik by promising him money later. Eaton did spend money to purchase 190 camels, for $11 apiece.[62] Dr. Mendrici and the Briggs brothers collaborated to charter a boat to sail to Bomba, where the expedition could rendezvous to pick up supplies and intelligence. They cautioned, though, that supplies would be difficult to acquire, so Eaton should not expect much from the boat.[63]

On March 6 the company, numbering about 400, marched to Arab's Tower to begin its journey to Derna.[64] In his journal, Eaton recorded details about nearly every day of the march from this point forward. His journal and correspondence are basically the only sources we have for the expedition. The group Eaton had assembled was an unusual example of collaboration among the people of the Mediterranean. It included nine Americans in addition to Eaton (eight of whom were marines); 25 cannoneers, commanded by a Frenchman; 38 Greeks; 90 men that Hamet had accumulated in Fiayum and Alexandria; and a group of Arab cavalry. It also included the camels and a few donkeys.[65] In bringing these factions together, many of whom were expatriates from the city of Tripoli, Eaton capitalized on generations of conflict between the city of Tripoli and the country around it. The money brought in from tribute payments to the bashaw and the sale of prizes rarely made it out into the countryside. The difference between the city's mode of survival and the country's stronger reliance on agriculture often caused political disputes that Eaton hoped to channel into anger at Yusuf.[66]

Despite their common enemy, the factions did not have much love for each other. Keeping all of these groups happy with him and with each other was Eaton's most difficult task during the march. Near-mutinies were at minimum a weekly occurrence. Conflicts between the Christian and Muslim factions were also frequent, neither side trusting the other not to betray them. Each faction had its own commander and its own supplies, but they all looked to Eaton to supplement those supplies.

For the first part of the journey, water was plentiful—in fact, sometimes too plentiful. The camp flooded at least once, and the mud made it difficult for the troops to march. Money was scarce, and Eaton had to make many promises of future payment in order to keep members of the company from turning back. While negotiating one of these conflicts about payment, Eaton wrote in despair, "We have marched a distance of two hundred miles, through an inhospitable waste of world," and now the expedition was in danger of falling apart. He determined to press on, as "pilgrims, bound across this gloomy desert on pursuits vastly different from those which lead to Mecca; the liberation of three hundred Americans from the Chains of Barbarism, & a manly peace" (which to Eaton no doubt also meant the end of any kind of payment).[67] He wrote later, "Cash, we find, is the only deity of Arabs, as well as Turks."[68]

While Eaton and his company struggled through the desert, Isaac Hull reported to Commodore Barron at Malta. Upon receiving Hull's report, Barron sent Eaton $7,000, which he suggested Eaton should retain possession of instead of handing it to Hamet—though even Eaton himself would not receive the money for quite some time. While Barron encouraged Eaton's efforts and lauded his perseverance, he also began to lay the groundwork for the United States to get out of its agreement with Hamet in case he turned out to be the ineffective leader so many had warned that he was.

> You must be sensible, Sir, that in giving their sanction to a cooperation with the exiled Bashaw, Government did not contemplate the measure as leading necessarily and absolutely to a reinstatement of that Prince in his rights on the regency of Tripoli—they appear to have viewed the cooperation in question as a means, which provided there existed energy and enterprize in the exile, & attachment to his person on the part of his former subjects, might be employed to the common furtherance and advance of his claims and of our cause, but without meaning to fetter themselves by any specific or definite attainment *as an end*, as the tenor of my instructions . . . and the limited sum appropriated for that special purpose clearly demonstrate.

Barron reiterated twice more to Eaton that he could not definitely sanction Hamet's ascension to the throne of Tripoli. Nevertheless, he hoped that Eaton would press on in his expedition, and he would provide whatever support he could. He sent the *Argus* and the sloop *Hornet* to Bomba with supplies, though he was unable to acquire the requested fieldpieces.[69]

The supplies could not arrive soon enough. Eaton recorded on March 22 that the company had no cash to purchase produce from the Arab tribes they passed by, so they traded rice for dates. The grain for the horses had also been used up.[70] As more troops joined the expedition, the lack of food and money became more alarming. Eaton had no way to pay the 80 horsemen that joined the company on March 23.[71] On March 25, 150 more soldiers arrived, along with their families.[72] News that Yusuf had amassed 500 soldiers to confront the expedition frightened some of the company, however. The camel drivers fled, and the Bedouins threatened to leave as well. Eaton (not for the first time) stopped their rations until they would sit down and discuss the problems.[73] Sheik al Taib took his soldiers off in rage when Eaton called him a coward, but the next day they returned after Eaton ignored all attempts to conciliate. Apparently they respected his unwillingness to beg them to come back.[74] This incident illustrated the fragility of the coalition as well as Eaton's drive to complete the mission one way or another.

The expedition continued in fits and starts, with perpetual delays because one group or another (including Hamet) wanted to withdraw, and sometimes did, only to return a few days later. Eaton tried to galvanize his soldiers by proclaiming to the people of Tripoli their intentions, at least in part to shame his soldiers if they chose not to follow through. In his proclamation, he drew parallels between the tribes of Tripoli and the United States, emphasizing how the United States had been able to transform a fragmented group of colonies into a powerful nation-state. Unlike many Americans, who viewed Islam as the exact opposite of the Christianity of grace and peace, he also averred that the common God of Islam and Christianity was worshiped freely in the United States: "People of every nation, every tongue and every faith could come to us and dwell in safety, because our religion teaches us to fear and to worship God and to be kind to all his creatures." He accused Yusuf Karamanli of breaking faith with his God when he "sent out his armed pirate ships against our commerce and even brought some of our ships into the port of Tripoli, and without provocation had their crews put in chains and reduced to slavery; thereby outraging every obligation of honor and decency, and transgressing against the law of God which forbids us to be the first in aggression." Eaton explicated a litany of ways in which Yusuf had betrayed the faith of his fathers in his treatment of Americans. Eaton invoked Yusuf's counselors, the Jews, as one of the signs that he had fallen away. Antisemitism was a trait shared by Christians and Muslims, and Eaton put that connection to work.[75]

This call to arms was one of the first times in the war that religion had been invoked in a significant way. Eaton wrote, "Oh, Moors, oh, Arabs, can you calmly behold the shedding of your children's blood, without avenging yourself! Will you meekly allow them to be put in chains and reduced to slavery in order to satisfy the cruel and savage cupidity of a usurper, a traitor, a barbarian, who fears not the Lord and who has no regard for human rights!" Eaton argued that this war had nothing to do with a particular religion, but rather only with morality: the downfall of a morally bankrupt ruler who would be condemned under any religious system. In the end, though, the war—for both sides—really was about national prosperity and understanding one's place in the world: "Be faithful unto God. Be loyal to the Grand Signor. Be loyal to the rightful prince, Hamet Bashaw of Tripoli, and let us not doubt that the Almighty will grant us his succor and his assistance to accomplish his wishes. A lasting peace; free and extensive trade, wealth and fidelity will be the result."[76]

The actual recipient of this proclamation is uncertain. Eaton could have no real idea of who would hear or read it, especially considering that it was written in English, and most Tripolitans could not read in any language. Historian Seton Dearden argues that it shows how great was the disparity between Eaton's idealism and the realities of his situation. Though Eaton did view his entire project optimistically, this proclamation seems more like Eaton's internal monologue he set to paper, his self-justification for his actions under both American and Muslim ethical codes.[77]

Eaton had to cling to those self-justifications as the expedition continued and the obstacles loomed larger. On April 6 he recorded that the horses had not drunk any water for almost two days, and the men had only gotten some foul water from a well near a ruined castle.[78] By April 8 a mutiny had broken out in earnest. Only the intervention of Lieutenant O'Bannon kept the Arab soldiers from turning on the Greeks in order to take their provisions. Eaton berated Hamet for his inability to keep his soldiers in line and praised O'Bannon for his quick and decisive action to protect the coalition. But the situation was still extremely tense. Provisions were once again nearly expended.[79]

Captain Hull had arrived at Bomba on April 2. Not finding Eaton's company, he cruised for a few days in the area, stopping in at Cape Razatin for news, where he found a messenger with information about the company's whereabouts. He also encountered some Arabs who said they were from Hamet, but Hull did not believe them and so refused to give them information. Because the weather was poor, Hull could not stay anchored at Bomba. Instead, he continued to cruise in the vicinity, stopping in every few days to see whether the expedition had yet arrived. He sent Eaton word of his plan by the messenger he had taken on board.[80]

On April 10 a courier that Hamet had sent to find news of the *Argus* returned to the company. He brought tidings that the *Argus* had indeed arrived at Bomba, and none too soon—the company was in danger of yet another mutiny. "In an instant the face of everything changed from pensive gloom to inthusiastic gladness," Eaton wrote, and Hamet promised to redouble his efforts to reach the meeting place. Even this promise had to be broken, though. Hamet fell desperately sick that evening, possibly from drinking water from a well that had been contaminated by two dead bodies. After a day of slow marching because of Hamet's illness, the company resumed a brisk pace on April 12 despite near-famine.[81] By April 14 the company was completely out of food.[82]

News of Hamet's march had by this time spread to Tripoli. William Bainbridge learned of it from Muhammad Dghies, who informed him that Yusuf was now taking the fight personally. Before, the conflict had been a simple commercial dispute, but now that the Americans were trying to dethrone him, he would hurt the Americans (presumably, the prisoners) in the manner in which his feelings of honor had been injured. Bainbridge, who had expressed his disapprobation of the coup in the past, informed Barron of this threat, declining to elaborate on his feelings about it, assuming Barron felt the same.[83]

On April 15 the expedition arrived at Bomba after a march of more than 500 miles. The *Argus* was not there. The various parts of the expeditionary force spent the rest of the day deciding what to do, each accusing the other groups of treachery. They all separated for the night. In the morning, one of the men spotted the *Argus* off the coast. "Language is too poor to paint the joy and exultation which this messenger of life excited in every breast," Eaton wrote. That morning, Eaton went on board the brig, and provisions were distributed that afternoon. On April 17 the *Hornet* arrived with more provisions, and over the next few days the company found a good harbor for the ships and an "inexhaustible cistern" for the troops. With food and supplies finally plentiful, the company began to make plans for the assault on Derna.[84]

Since the field artillery had not yet arrived, Eaton asked Hull if he could spare a few carronades from the *Argus*, as well as ammunition for small arms. He hoped that Hull would follow the company to Derna and provide bombardment from the sea, if possible. He also asked Hull to allow the marines from the *Argus* to remain with the expedition until Derna was secure.[85] Lieutenant O'Bannon seconded Eaton's request to stay with the land forces, and Midshipman George Mann made the same request.[86]

Hull made use of his time off Bomba. On April 22 the *Argus* captured an Ottoman vessel carrying Tripolitan passengers and cargo. Hull sent the vessel to port for adjudication, though he admitted that the capture might not be good prize. He was uncertain whether the blockade could be considered enforceable some 700 miles from Tripoli, and he could not be sure whether the vessel was carrying contraband.[87]

Eaton and the expedition resumed the march toward Derna, which was still 40 miles away, on April 23 in driving rain. As they began to approach more cultivated areas, Eaton made sure that the whole group knew not to spoil fields or harvests along the way.[88] The company had to take care not to alienate anyone because Hamet needed as much popular support as he could get. Surprisingly, Eaton never mentioned that Hamet had a history with the city of Derna, where he had once ruled—and where Yusuf had offered him a chance to rule again. But perhaps the order not to spoil the fields came from Hamet's desire to rebuild relationships he had once had and bring the citizens of Derna back to his side.

As they had marched, more and more soldiers had joined the expedition, giving credence to Eaton's belief that many on the fringes of Yusuf's control had little loyalty to him. However, Yusuf still had loyal followers. When the expedition camped about five hours' march from Derna, Eaton's men learned that Yusuf had indeed known they were coming and had sent troops to fortify the town. It was likely that those troops would arrive before Hamet's assault could begin, especially since the rainstorm had blown the *Argus* and the *Hornet* out to sea. The leaders of the various groups met to discuss strategy—without Eaton.[89]

By April 25 the *Nautilus* was close to Bomba, bringing the fieldpieces Eaton had requested.[90] But the expedition had not yet seen the ship, and from the closer vantage point they took up, the situation looked even more grim than before. The town had been fortified, and even though some of the local rulers had come out to express support for Hamet, they also brought news that the governor of Derna had an 800-man army in addition to the forces from Yusuf that would be arriving soon.[91] The next morning, in desperation, Eaton wrote to the governor of Derna, asking him to join Hamet's forces or at least let them pass the city unmolested. The governor's answer came back the same day: "My head or yours."[92]

After a discouraging few days, April 26 brought hope for the expedition. The *Nautilus* arrived off the coast where the company was encamped. It brought the fieldpieces and a quantity of ammunition, as well as some other stores for the expedition.[93] When the men began to move the fieldpieces the next morning, they realized that the hill up which they were attempting to get the fieldpiece was extremely steep. They managed to get one to the top, but Eaton decided not to waste time getting the other. With the artillery in hand, he intended to attack that day, April 27.

The expeditionary force began the attack at 2:00 in the afternoon. At the same time, the *Nautilus*, *Hornet*, and *Argus* began bombarding the town from the sea. Astonishingly, the town's defenses crumbled quickly. By 3:30, O'Bannon had raised the American flag over the fort. By 4:00, Hamet's forces, which by that time numbered around 2,000, had come in from the rear. The expeditionary force had complete control of the town. Eaton himself took a musket ball to the left wrist, and 13 men were wounded altogether, but only one man was killed.[94] Against all odds, despite mutinies, famine, storms, and grumblings, Eaton and his men had accomplished the first part of their mission: they had taken Derna.

After the remarkable initial victory, momentum disintegrated. Eaton realized now that Hamet could not be trusted to continue the campaign on his own, writing to Commodore Barron,

> I cannot conceal my apprehensions, grounded on experience, that when arrived there [in Tripoli] he would effect little, without more military talent & firmness, than exists either in himself or the *hordes* of Arabs who attach themselves to him; They are . . . rather a rabble than an Army, & in our affair here, they held safe positions to catch fugitives, untill the doors of the Enemy were open'd for plunder, when they became at once brave, & impetuous. If therefore the co-operation is to be pursued with him and its direction is to be confided to me, it must be on condition that detachments of regulars may be occasionally debark'd from the Squadron, or procured elsewhere, to aid and give effect to such operations as require energy.

Eaton felt he had to stay on to guide Hamet's affairs, but he did not know how long the navy would continue to back his plan. If the American government intended to cast Hamet aside once his usefulness was expended, Eaton felt honor-bound not to pursue the coup any further. Now that the first part of the plan was complete, Eaton did not really know what to do. He had reflected on the consequences of failure, but not, it seems, on the consequences of success.

If the navy came to an agreement with Yusuf now, Eaton hoped that the government would insist that Hamet be treated fairly, perhaps allowed to stay in Derna with his family returned from their captivity under Yusuf.[95] While Eaton waited to hear from Barron, Isaac Hull took charge of the naval operations. He sent the *Hornet* back to Malta with dispatches for the commodore and prisoners taken in the assault. But seeing that the conquered bey of Derna was still in the city with some soldiers, he ordered the *Argus* and *Nautilus* to stay off Derna to keep them in check.[96]

The troops from Yusuf who had not arrived in time for the battle now surrounded the town. Eaton and his men secured the fortifications, which they renamed Fort Enterprize, as best they could, but the townspeople did not know who to follow. The former bey had organized an insurgency as well, leading to more trouble.[97] As the troops closed in, Eaton wanted to try a deception like the Old Testament's Gideon against the Mideonites. He requested that Hull send him 100 men from the *Argus* so he could stage a parade of force. He wanted to convince the undecided tribal leaders to join the stronger side—only, his was not the stronger side. So he had to deceive them from a distance by making it look like he had more men than he had.[98]

Eaton was right about the vacillating loyalties of the Arab tribal leaders. The day after one of the sheiks of Derna helped the bey of Derna escape, the sheik returned and pledged his loyalty to Hamet, despite harsh words about Hamet's collusion with Eaton.[99] Unfortunately for the Americans, the bey's escape gave Yusuf's forces the intelligence and incentive they needed to mount an attack. They nearly retook the town on May 13—only a fortunate cannon shot caused them to retreat. On May 16 two sheiks changed sides and joined Eaton, bringing news that Yusuf's camp was in disarray. Disarrayed though they might be, the bashaw's forces had blocked Eaton's access to food from the country. With both sides too weak to mount another aggressive attack, Derna was under siege. Eaton sent off the *Nautilus* in hopes that it would bring back reinforcements soon.[100]

After several more days of posturing on both sides, Eaton was having a hard time keeping the allied factions happy. Strapped for cash and still under siege, Eaton appealed to Hull for help. Hull could only advise that "he must have Patience for a few days" until the *Nautilus* or the *Hornet* returned.[101] At least, Eaton noted on many occasions, Yusuf's troops had similar characteristics to his own: confronted with the prospect of a superior opponent, the leaders of the bashaw's troops had great difficulty getting them to fight. He heard that the assembled tribes "were willing to fight an enemy of their own mode of warfare; but they could not resist the Americans, who fired enormous balls that carried away a man and his camel at once, or rushed on them with bayonets without giving them time to load their muskets."[102]

Peace without Hamet

Even before the news of Derna's fall came, Yusuf Karamanli was putting out feelers for peace. Consul Lear received a letter from Don Gerardo Joseph de Souza, the Spanish consul at Tripoli, "written at the express desire of the Bashaw," offering to charge only $200,000 total for peace and ransom. Though de Souza assured Lear that this offer was only the opening salvo in a negotiation, Lear dismissed it out of hand. He thought that the bashaw would refuse the Americans' terms in order to save face with his fellow Barbary rulers.[103] The Tunisian government tried to inveigle its way into the negotiations, believing that its time to antagonize the United States was near.[104] The dey of Algiers also sent word to the bashaw, ordering him, "You know that the Peace you made first was effected through my mediation; therefore since the Peace first made has ended, you are now going to discuss the Peace with this Consul Lear once more."[105] The American negotiators had already decided not to allow Algiers to be mediators in this discussion, but that did not keep the dey from trying.

Lear felt the time slipping away from the squadron. He had hoped that the navy would be bombarding Tripoli again by this time in the spring, but it seemed unlikely that the squadron would be ready any time soon. Master Commandant Thomas Robinson felt the same. He had finally found a place to build gunboats—Ancona—and was now rushing to complete them. He wrote to James Barron, "Reflect one moment on the Consequences attending an inactive Summer, and how are we to be active with a probability of success without some Boats?"[106]

The frigates of the squadron continued to maintain the blockade off Tripoli, taking several prizes of various origins, including some Tunisian vessels.[107] Some vessels the squadron had sent back for adjudication had already become a source of contention. The Tunisian passports the vessels carried were irregular, but the United States could not afford war with Tunis. Therefore, Consul Lear recommended that Consul Davis give the bey a chance to deny his complicity in sending the vessels to Tripoli. If he did deny it, then the vessels could be returned and further escalation averted.[108]

In Malta, Samuel Barron too felt the time slipping away. Realizing that he might never be well enough to resume command of the squadron, he wrote to Lear that he would likely give up command. With crew enlistments expiring in the fall, the window for action was shrinking rapidly. Three of the frigates were not in sufficient trim to survive another winter in the Mediterranean. Barron was also frustrated by the difficulty in acquiring gunboats from Naples. The reports from Eaton, meant to encourage Barron, had the opposite effect. Barron saw the prospective bashaw's lack of nerve under pressure, that he "has not in himself sufficient energy address & Courage," and therefore "must be considered as no longer a fit subject for our support and Cooperation." Nevertheless, Eaton's successes thus far with Hamet surely must have interested Yusuf in peace. Barron hoped that Lear could capitalize on this instability.[109]

On May 22 Commodore Barron officially transferred command of the squadron to John Rodgers, acknowledging that his health would "greatly diminish & perhaps preclude the probability of my serving my Country at any future Day."[110] On May 26 the *Essex*, bearing Consul Lear, arrived off Tripoli. The *Essex* also brought Samuel Barron's letter relinquishing control of the squadron to John Rodgers. The next day, Captain James Barron hoisted the flag of truce indicating that the Americans wanted to talk.[111] The Americans viewed their negotiating position as very strong, but even at their strongest, they still worked in community. This time, the Spanish consul operated as go-between for the bashaw and Lear.

The arrival of letters from George Davis reminded Rodgers that, even when all his attention was needed against Tripoli, the Americans were not working against a single antagonist. Tunis needed to be dealt with, and soon. "Although it is evident that the Bey of Tunis is afraid of the consequences of a War with the U. States," Rodgers wrote, "yet *at this critical moment*, I conceive it necessary that he should not be neglected." He determined to send one ship to Davis to consult with him as soon as possible about the best strategy.[112] The bey continued to spar with Davis over the captured Tunisian vessels, continuously asserting his right to send ships on official business into Tripoli without capture. To deny Tunis such a right might send it into war with the United States or the Ottoman Porte.[113] It was obvious why the Americans should care about a declaration of war against them, but less obvious why they should care whether Tunis went to war with the grand signior. Perhaps Hamouda was reminding Davis that wars in the Mediterranean could be bad business for everyone, not just for the combatants.

The Mediterranean community was constantly shaped by wars among its members. Even when the United States was not the cause of conflict, it got caught in the middle of conflicts between others. The war with Tripoli to this point had proved how interconnected Mediterranean society was. In order to navigate this web of connections, the navy relied on sources who knew the best ways to get things done unofficially. For instance, in the search for gunpowder in Livorno, Stephen Decatur enlisted the help of the navy agents Degen, Purviance, and Company, who observed that "the Commission for Gun Powder being rather of a delicate nature in the actual political state of this Country, some management would be necessary, to get it executed without drawing the attention of Goverment or rather of the Powers which influences & in a manner directs its measures." This was a subtle way of hinting at the lack of autonomy in the city, which was controlled at the time by the French. Degen and Purviance were able to make an under-the-table agreement with the garrison suppliers at Elba, and sent Decatur there to collect the powder.[114]

Despite the obvious success of the venture, the United States severed its closest connection once Lear began peace talks with Yusuf. In his letters to Eaton, Commodore Barron made it quite clear that the government's dealings with Hamet were at an end. He had achieved the conquest of Derna; he should not expect more. Barron added, "The interests of Sidi Hamet will not be overlooked: it is with Colonel Lear's express sanction that I mention his intention to endeavor at stipulating some Conditions for the unfortunate Exile, provided this can be done without giving up points that are essential, & without any considerable sacrifice of National advantage on our part."[115] In other words, they would hang Hamet out to dry if needed.

Commodore Rodgers agreed. In a letter of May 29, Rodgers assumed that Eaton had evacuated the town under orders from Barron and Lear and was headed back to Syracuse or Malta, but Eaton did not receive the letter ordering his recall until June 1.[116] In his reply to Barron, he argued that his expedition was the reason for the bashaw's sudden pacific leanings. He rightly observed that the navy had done little since Preble's bombardments in August 1804, but the bashaw's interest in peace had started in January 1805, around the time Eaton's mission to Egypt had become widely known. Thus, he was surprised and outraged at the order to leave Hamet just when the mission had succeeded. "I cannot, from any shape in which the subject can be viewed," he wrote, "be persuaded that the manner of serving ourselves of Hamet Bashaw, and abandoning him, can be reconciled to those principles of honor and justice which, I know, actuate the national breast." He further argued that Hamet's lack of character was not such an obstacle, as he had observed the same pusillanimity in the forces of Yusuf. If he pulled out of Derna now, and then Lear's negotiations failed, the Americans would be in a worse position than ever, with nothing to bargain with.

"Could I have apprehended this result of my exertions, certainly no consideration would have prevailed on me to have taken an agency in a tragedy so manifestly fraught with intrigue, so wounding to humane feelings, and, as I must view it, so degrading to our national honor," he told Barron. The tide of sentiment was with Hamet, it seemed to Eaton, and to abandon him now would be not only dishonorable but foolish. For Eaton, though, it was hard to disentangle his sense of personal honor and obligation from the United States' obligation to Hamet, which Barron had made very clear was minimal. Eaton struggled to put Hamet's plight into terms that would be understood by others who did not feel the same attachment to the erstwhile bashaw that he did, but he eventually, grudgingly, realized that the United States had no interest in maintaining his personal honor, if the strategic interests of the country lay elsewhere.

Nonetheless, it was not clear to Eaton that Hamet's expedition was outside the strategic interests of the Americans. Every day Hamet's forces scored another victory of some sort, whether holding off an enemy attack or bringing more chieftains into their number. On June 11 Hamet's forces alone, without the American marine contingent and with little cover from the American ships in the bay, were able to hold off a sustained attack by Yusuf's forces. But when Eaton reported some of Barron and Lear's orders, Hamet admitted that he could not maintain his position without the American navy's assistance. His confidence waned again, and he asked to at least go with the Americans if they made peace with Yusuf.[117]

Despite the fact that Hamet would not take the throne, Eaton's march certainly made a difference in Yusuf's interest for peace. No doubt Yusuf was tired of fighting the Americans, and Eaton's march was an escalation that would make more trouble than Yusuf wanted to deal with. In addition, if Yusuf played the Americans just right, he could use them to eliminate his brother as a threat once and for all—a treaty could effectively cement Yusuf's position as bashaw of Tripoli and force the Americans to get rid of Hamet altogether. The blockades and bombardments of 1804 and 1805 strained the resources of Tripoli, to the point where the Americans were turning out to be too much of a bother and were even restricting Tripoli's ability to extort other nations. Yusuf had not been able to secure the *Philadelphia* and had not received any presents from the United States for four years. In a stalemate, Tripoli was the loser.

Because of all these factors, peace was imminent.[118] On May 29 Consul de Souza brought to Lear a proposal of $130,000 for ransom of the *Philadelphia* captives, with no annuities. Lear countered with a prisoner exchange of all the Tripolitan prisoners the United States held for the *Philadelphia* prisoners. This would be an exchange of about 100 for about 300 men, and Lear was willing to pay $60,000 to make up the difference. Lear had determined not to go on shore to negotiate, which was surprising because it flew in the face of convention, and it also ignored advice William Bainbridge had given repeatedly over the past year: face-to-face meetings were the most likely to accomplish results. But Lear steadfastly refused, instead forcing de Souza to go back and forth between the shore and the *Constitution* for several days.

On June 1 the bashaw allowed Captain Bainbridge to come out to the squadron as a gesture of goodwill. Lear told Bainbridge that he would attempt to have the prisoners released before an official treaty was signed, but the bashaw would not do any further business with de Souza.[119] On June 2, then, the Americans' steadfast friend Nicholas Nissen came out to the *Constitution*, commissioned by the bashaw to negotiate the specifics of the peace treaty. Lear gave Nissen a "sketch" of his stipulations for the treaty. Though Nissen observed that some of the stipulations were more favorable to the Americans than any other comparable treaty he had seen, he took Lear's ideas back to the bashaw. Later that day, Nissen returned to inform Lear that Yusuf had agreed to the articles Lear stipulated, but he had one to add: he wanted the Americans and his brother out of Derna. Lear agreed to these terms if Yusuf would agree to give Hamet's family back to him. Initially, the bashaw would not agree to release Hamet's family, but Lear stood firm and Nissen wore Yusuf down. He insisted on keeping the family for a little while longer but agreed to give them back eventually. In the treaty as sent to Congress, Yusuf agreed to hand them over immediately, but he and Lear actually made a secret agreement giving Yusuf four years to return them.

On June 3 Lear and Yusuf agreed on all the articles of the treaty, and the fort and the *Constitution* exchanged salutes. When Lear went ashore that afternoon, he was met by the officers of the *Philadelphia*, who had been freed. The next day, Lear went ashore again to meet the bashaw. Now that the danger was past, Lear saw him in a different light: "He is a man of a very good presence, manly & dignified, and has not in his appearance so much of the Tyrant as he has been represented to be." The two men complimented each other about their mutual honor and justness. Over the next few days, the treaty articles began to be enforced and the officers of the squadron went ashore "pleasuring in the country."[120] The *Constitution* returned to Malta to collect the Tripolitan prisoners and bring them home. The *Constellation* went to bring the Americans off from Derna. Lear established Dr. John Ridgely, one of the *Philadelphia* prisoners, as naval agent for Tripoli, citing his familiarity with the customs of the court. The past had shown that doctors, who possessed skills that Barbary rulers valued, made good liaisons between Barbary courts and their erstwhile enemies, and Ridgely was already well-liked in the court of Tripoli. The bashaw had also become attached to another captive doctor, Jonathan Cowdery, the surgeon's mate of the *Philadelphia*. Upon his departure from Tripoli, Cowdery recorded, "I bid the Bashaw a final adieu, at which he seemed much affected."[121]

The *Constitution* returned from Malta on June 17. To Lear's chagrin, the 100 Tripolitan prisoners he had expected turned out to number only 48. The other 41 people brought back were enslaved Black people owned by the Tripolitans who had been taken prisoner. In order to skirt the discrepancy, Lear told Yusuf that the enslaved people were Tripolitan subjects, not Tripolitans' property. Lear thought this argument perfectly reasonable, though he was not sure the bashaw completely believed him.

In Lear's view, the United States had bested all the European nations that had dealt with Tripoli in the past, a fact that might not sit well with those nations. "Our peace will be so unusually honorable, that we must not expect it will be fully relished by all the Representatives of the European Nations here, which is already manifested, by the conduct of some which I shall hereafter relate to you," he told Rodgers.[122] Perhaps he referred to a letter he received from Beaussier, requesting that Lear give him the wages due to three sailors of the *Philadelphia*, now free, who Beaussier claimed were French. Lear dismissed his claim, saying that if Beaussier chose to leave the men in slavery for 19 months, rather than redeem them for "the cause of humanity," then Lear certainly would not give their wages to Beaussier, but rather to the men themselves as long as they chose to stay in the American navy.[123] Two of the men deserted to Beaussier, apparently. Rodgers fumed that Beaussier harbored them now "in a manner as equally degrading to yourself, as the tenor of the proceeding is insulting to me."[124]

On June 10 the treaties were officially drawn up. To meet the legal requirements of each country, three copies were made: one in English, one in Turkish, and one in Arabic. Though the Turkish one was the "official" version, supposedly the one drawn up first, scholars later noted that it is obvious that the English version was the primary document, as there are pieces of the Arabic version that make no sense unless collated with the English version, and some pieces are virtually unintelligible. The primacy of the English version backs Lear's claim that the bashaw rested such confidence in Lear that he allowed him to write most of the treaty articles as he pleased. It's not clear why Yusuf suddenly found Lear so trustworthy; perhaps he was just tired of all the bother.[125]

After meeting with the bashaw on June 20, Commodore Rodgers weighed anchor from Tripoli on June 21 along with Colonel Lear. Peace with Tripoli had been restored.

Aftermath

The prisoners from the *Philadelphia* were taken to Syracuse, where navy agent George Dyson had secured for them some land to recuperate on. Dyson said that the land had "open free air, and an excellent Spring of water," but not much development, so the sailors would be sleeping in tents.[126] As much as the navy wanted to give the men time to recuperate, the demands of the service still pressed on them. On June 12 Rodgers instructed that the able-bodied marines from the *Philadelphia* join the crew of the *Constitution* to replace men who had been sent to the hospital.[127] On June 29 Rodgers assembled a court-martial, at Bainbridge's request, to determine whether Bainbridge had been delinquent in his actions during the *Philadelphia*'s capture. James Barron, Hugh G. Campbell, and Stephen Decatur unanimously acquitted Bainbridge.[128]

Once considered the linchpin of operations off Tripoli, the gunboats that had consumed so much American effort to obtain turned out to be unnecessary. By the end of May, Master Commandant Thomas Robinson had finally found a city willing to sell him gunboats. "I cou'd line the Coast of Tripoli with Gun Boats from this place," he wrote after purchasing two boats from Ancona and four from Senigallia. "I am well aware that I am late," he wrote on June 1 to Samuel Barron. He certainly was—on that same day, Lear came to an informal agreement of peace with the bashaw.[129] Eight gunboats had been sent from the United States, but peace was signed before the first of them arrived at Gibraltar on June 5.[130] It took Robinson until July 8 to shepherd his fleet of Italian gunboats to Syracuse.[131]

Nevertheless, there was work left to be done. Commodore Rodgers wrote to James Barron that he should begin transferring the American headquarters back to Malta from Syracuse. Believing the British were going to take Sicily in the next few weeks, Rodgers thought that the disruption of the regime change would "give us more difficulties to contend with" at Syracuse, so he preferred the more stable environment at Malta. He was not yet ready to pull out of the Mediterranean altogether. Tunis still needed to be dealt with, and after Rodgers received dispatches from Consul Simpson at Tangier, he believed he would have to stop at Morocco as well.[132]

Rodgers sent the *Essex* to Syracuse to drop off its sick men in the hospital and collect the Tunisian prisoners in order to take them back to Tunis.[133] He ordered George Cox, now the captain of the *Essex*, not to release the prisoners until talking with Consul Davis, however. He wanted the bey to know that it was not out of guilt over an illegal capture that he was returning the men, but simply because they were an unnecessary bother now that peace with Tripoli had been achieved.[134] But the captures would continue to be a bother. The Neapolitan government registered a protest with the navy about the restitution of the vessels, two of which were Neapolitan prizes to the Tunisian cruiser.[135] Rodgers, however, did not release the actual vessels—only the prisoners were sent back to Tunis.[136]

In Derna, William Eaton did not yet know that peace was signed. On June 5 he told Isaac Hull that he could not leave Derna until he heard official news of the peace negotiation or received explicit instructions from Commodore Rodgers.[137] Before he stepped down, Commodore Barron had sent orders for Eaton's departure, but Rodgers was not at all sure Eaton would obey. "To be sure," he wrote to Lear, "after he [Eaton] has received Commodore Barrons directions to evacuate Derne, a none compliance will make the responsibility his own: nevertheless the consequence will be his Country's."[138] Rodgers dispatched the *Constellation* to Derna to reinforce Eaton's instructions to abandon the city, informing him that the treaty now stipulated his withdrawal.[139] Just to make sure that the treaty was being followed, Yusuf sent a man on board the *Constellation* to observe the proceedings. He would not go on shore at Derna, but he would serve as both proof and guarantee that the treaty was indeed in effect.[140] Lear did throw a bone to Eaton, writing to him that it was his efforts at Derna that had turned the tide toward peace, and that Lear would do what he could for Hamet.[141]

Captain Hugh G. Campbell delivered Lear's messages to Eaton on June 11.[142] Surprisingly, Eaton agreed to come on board the next day.[143] Concerned that Yusuf's troops would fall on Derna before the evacuation was complete, Eaton sent out extra rations and spread a story that the *Constellation* brought reinforcements, not evacuation orders. He also ordered all preparations to be done quickly and secretly. He hoped that fear of the reinforcements would buy enough time to get everyone out. As the last of the Americans and Hamet's retinue boarded the boats for the *Constellation*, the townspeople realized what was happening. They supposedly crowded the shore to beg the Americans to return, but it was too late. The *Constellation* received all its boats back by about 2:00 in the morning. By dawn, all of the Arab chieftains had abandoned the town, along with any townspeople who could flee with them. The bashaw's representative who had traveled on the *Constellation* went ashore with assurances from Yusuf that the townspeople would receive amnesty if they swore renewed allegiance to Yusuf, but "they knew his perfidy too well to suffer themselves to be ensnared by it." Instead, the inhabitants began to fortify the town against the inevitable assault by Yusuf's forces. Eaton had bought them some time, but not much. As the *Constellation* prepared to sail, Eaton wrote,

> In a few minutes more we shall loose sight of this devoted city, which has experienced as strange a reverse in so short a time as ever was recorded in the disasters of war; thrown from proud success and elated prospects into an abys of hopeless wretchedness—Six hours ago the enemy were seeking safety from them by flight—this moment we drop them from ours into the hands of this enemy for no other crime but too much confidence in us! The man whose fortune we have accompanied thus far experiences a reverse as striking—He falls from the most flattering prospects of a Kingdom to beggary!

Eaton requested again that Rodgers deal with Hamet "in such a manner as to acquit our conscience and honor," but he did not want to stay to see the result. As his usefulness to the cause of American peace had clearly come to an end, he requested to return to the United States on the first available warship.[144] The *Constellation*, the *Argus*, and the *Hornet* sailed for Syracuse at noon on June 13.

The appearance of Hamet's entourage in Syracuse caused great alarm in the city. Governor de Gregorio requested that Rodgers put them back on board one of his ships, as the townspeople were "apprehensive of the gravest consequences (from the presence of these men)."[145] Rodgers ordered the entire company, except for Hamet and a few others, back on board the *Constellation*, from which they had only disembarked the previous day, and then gave orders to spread them out across the squadron as necessary.[146] Hamet wrote Eaton a heartfelt letter of gratitude, in which he admitted that his chances of success had been small and that the United States had done everything it could reasonably be expected to do for him: "I ought therefore to say that I am satisfied with all your Nation has done concerning me—I submit to the will of God; and thank the King of America and all his servants for their kind dispositions towards me." His parting request was that Eaton would prevail on Rodgers to send a ship to Tripoli to collect his family and then give him a little money to resettle himself and his family in some faraway country. Thanks to Lear's secret treaty article, this request was denied.[147]

Though Tripoli had been taken care of, the navy's concerns spread further than Tripoli. As more and more of Europe became embroiled in the contest against Napoleon, Americans continued to get caught in the middle. In Spain, R. W. Meade informed Master Commandant Charles Stewart that Americans were being captured by Spanish privateers as they sailed for Gibraltar. Meade suggested that a naval vessel or two off Algeciras and Cadiz would alleviate this problem.[148] But not even American warships were safe from the Spanish. On June 15, four Spanish boats captured Gunboat No. 3 and brought it to Algeciras "without assigning the smallest reason."[149] Though the general intervened and the gunboat was released that day, Gunboat No. 5 was also brought to by Spanish cruisers and delayed before being allowed to proceed.[150]

The British continued to cause problems as well. On its journey from America, Gunboat No. 6, commanded by James Lawrence, had been stopped off Cadiz by an English squadron under Admiral Collingwood. Three members of the crew had been removed by the British after they claimed British citizenship. Though the men were no great loss—Lawrence observed that they had been "very unruly during the passage"—Lawrence felt he needed to fight for the right of American warships to pass unmolested. The three men voluntarily gave evidence that they were indeed British, but Lawrence wanted to hold them under their oath of allegiance to the United States. When Admiral Collingwood refused to give them back, Lawrence tried to surrender his gunboat to the British. His strategy may have been to force the British into an illegal capture, which would then cause them a great deal of time and expense to iron out. Collingworth refused to allow him to surrender the vessel, and Lawrence had to depart without his men because of oncoming weather that the gunboat could not withstand.[151]

John Shaw, commander of the *John Adams* newly arrived at Gibraltar, had more "amiable" sailor exchanges. When two American sailors, one from the *John Adams* and one from Gunboat No. 10, deserted to HMS *Amphitrite*, Captain

Boyle received them and brazenly wrote to Shaw asking that he send over their slops because they had been forced to leave them behind when they deserted. Shaw agreed, as long as Boyle would give him the advance that the sailors had received on their salaries, since the American navy would not pay the salaries of British sailors. He also requested that Boyle return to him Robert Williams, an American that had deserted, including for proof an affidavit that Williams had signed in 1804 certifying his American citizenship.[152]

The Ottoman and Russian governments pressed their grievances with the United States through Sir Alexander Ball at Malta. Rodgers told Ball that he intended to make a ruling on the three Ottoman vessels in question—the *Mastico*, which had been called the *Gheretti* while under Ottoman colors and *Intrepid* under American, plus two additional vessels—but he had received information that a frigate was coming from the United States, and Rodgers hoped that someone else had ruled on their cases and was sending him their decision.[153] When the *John Adams* did not bring him any orders, Rodgers ruled that he would not do anything further about the *Mastico*, having already released its Turkish crew and sent the Tripolitan slaves back to the bashaw of Tripoli. He simply released the other two vessels back to the Ottoman consul, including money to reimburse the cargoes that were sold.[154] He also released the Russian vessels and reimbursed their cargoes.[155]

There was some unfinished business in Messina as well. In January the governor of Messina had written to Captain John H. Dent requesting that he deliver up two of his crew who were accused of murdering a British subject while in the port on January 23. It took until April 13 to track down the men who were supposedly responsible for the crime. One of them, Midshipman Charles Ridgely, offered to give himself up to the Neapolitan government for trial, asserting his complete innocence. The two officers had intervened when they saw a British man being hauled off by a Sicilian gang of men, and thought they had rescued him. If Ridgely had murdered the man, it was in a state of such total inebriation that he did not remember anything about the event or its surroundings, he candidly admitted. The other officer Ridgely was with on the night in question, Midshipman George Reed, likewise had not known of the man's murder until informed by Captain Dent. Despite the testimony of some of the Sicilians, Ridgely did not see any way that he or Reed could possibly be convicted.[156] John Broadbent, naval agent at Messina, hoped that "this misfortune will be of Service to him for the remainder of his days, & that it will make some impression also on the minds of other young Men in the Service, inducing them to guard against the vice of Intoxication, particularly when they are on shore in foreign Countries."[157] Despite some judicial practices that Broadbent found barbaric, he had no doubt that Ridgely would be acquitted, but his opinion of the government of Messina had waned significantly.[158] Both men ultimately were acquitted.

By the end of June, Rodgers was tired of dealing with the threats from Tunis, which continued despite his return of the Tunisian prisoners. He wrote to George Davis, "Least you should again meet with embarrassment, by my not being sufficiently explicit in my communications, I shall in future express myself in such language, as cannot be misunderstood": he would not return the Tunisian vessels.[159] Seemingly buoyed by the success of the Tripolitan operations, Rodgers planned to appear in force off Tunis to remind the bey that the United States would not be bullied. After all, in Eaton's view, the bey was a coward: "You will have no war with Tunis—That Bey finds a better Account in stealing Sheep, than in hunting Tigers."[160]

On July 23 Rodgers had finally taken care of enough of his administrative tasks that he could sail for Tunis with his entire squadron.[161] The gunboats and smaller vessels that had arrived too late for the war with Tripoli at least got a little excitement off Tunis. When the squadron rendezvoused in Tunis Bay on July 30, it totaled 18 vessels: four frigates, three brigs, two schooners, a sloop, and eight gunboats.[162] Hamouda had declared to George Davis that any appearance of American naval force would spark a war. When Rodgers heard this news, he demanded "that your Excellency will have the goodness to inform me whether there has been any mistake in the application of your assertions tending to a declaration of War with the U. States." He gave Hamouda 36 hours to either back off or start a fight.[163]

Davis thought Rodgers had killed the American chances for a reconciliation.[164] He asked for an extension of Rodgers's ultimatum, as the letter did not arrive in court until after the bey had concluded business for the day. Rodgers gave him another day, but he did not back down.[165] Davis requested that Rodgers write to the federal government for advice on this subject, but Rodgers was tired of waiting for orders from America. He informed Davis that he would commence attacks as scheduled unless he received an assurance from Hamouda that he would observe the peace treaty in place. Not trusting Hamouda (or Davis either, apparently), he further demanded that the French and British consuls ratify Hamouda's recommitment to the treaty.[166]

Tobias Lear, on board the *Constitution*, tried diplomatic measures bolstered by the imminent threat of force. On August 5 the bey invited Lear to come ashore to discuss the situation.[167] But Lear declined to come ashore until the bey gave Rodgers the assurance he wanted. Rodgers prepared a statement for the bey to affirm exactly:

WHEREAS the Commander in chief of the Squadron of the U. States of America, now laying in Tunis Bay, has been induced to believe that it was my determination to declare War against the said U. States, in consequence of one of my cruizers and her two prizes having been detained by the aforesaid Squadron in their attempting to enter Tripoli during the late Blockade of that place, or from some other cause, I do hereby solemnly declare that it is not my Intention, and that I will not commence hostilities or declare War against the said U. States so long as the Treaty existing between myself and the said United States shall be faithfully adhered to by them, and not until I shall have made an application to the Goverment of the U. States for redress of any injuries which I may recieve or have recieved from the said United States and have been refused such redress.[168]

He gave the bey until noon on August 9 to affirm this pledge. If Hamouda did not do so, Rodgers told Davis to leave Tunis and come to the squadron so that he would not be injured in the assault.[169] Hamouda did not affirm the pledge. He reached out again to Lear, who agreed to meet him in the morning of August 10.[170] In a letter to the bey, Rodgers reminded him of the immense force anchored off the town, which would be supplemented any day by yet more bomb vessels and gunboats, and suggested that the bey make his pacific intentions clear to Lear when he arrived.[171] Finally, on August 14, Hamouda wrote to Rodgers, "It was never my intention to declare War, against your Nation, nor to begin any hostility if not first provoked on your part." He proposed that the best way to resolve any lingering conflicts was to send an envoy from Tunis to the United States to meet with the president. He also requested that a new American chargé be appointed to Tunis.[172]

Rodgers accepted Hamouda's declaration.[173] It was clear that even if the Tripolitan peace was not exactly the overwhelming victory the United States had looked for, the combined force of the US Navy, along with the increased confidence of the American diplomats charged with keeping the peace, had indeed increased the standing of the United States against potential antagonists such as Tunis.

Rodgers appointed Dr. James Dodge as the new chargé, and George Davis requested to go home on the *Congress*, which would take the Tunisian ambassador to the United States.[174] Rodgers likewise reorganized the crew lists of eight or nine of the vessels in order to send men home whose enlistments had expired.[175] The *John Adams*, the *Franklin*, and the *Constellation* would also return home. But Rodgers and the other half of the squadron would stay in the Mediterranean to make sure the bey kept his word.[176]

Conclusion

The American squadron left Tunis certain that it had showed the bey "more distinctly his own weakness in every sense." Hamouda's ambassador, Suliman Melli Melli, averred that the bey had retreated because he was adhering to the terms of the Tunisian treaty, and not because he was a coward. Commodore John Rodgers believed that Tunis would never make demands for presents or for special treatment regarding prizes again.[1] He was wrong on both counts. In fact, Melli Melli brought demands about both presents and prizes to the US government in person. He arrived in the United States in late 1805 and stayed well into 1806, touring around the country in the care of James Leander Cathcart, who had returned to the United States in 1804.

Melli Melli wrote periodically to James Madison and Thomas Jefferson with his complaints. He emphasized that their rejection of his demands actually excluded them from the Mediterranean community, as "no peace between the United States of America & the Regency of Tunis can be ever permanent, until the Government of said States, conform to the custom practised by other christian powers of the same magnitude, & occasionally make presents of military stores to the Regency of Tunis."[2] It was clear that Melli Melli still rated the United States as a secondary power.

Despite Rodgers's claim, Melli Melli departed from Boston to Tunis in August 1806 with an entire boatload of presents for the bey. Even the ship, along with its guns, was a gift to the bey. But Melli Melli left a few people behind: they had deserted to New York and were apparently running up huge tabs at taverns all across the city.[3] The United States still had not achieved the peace without payment that it had hoped for. Though Algiers was the only nation the United States was still paying annual presents to, the rulers of Tunis and Morocco expected presents "occasionally," which was much more often than the United States wished to provide them.

The American squadron was still in the Mediterranean, since Rodgers believed that its presence contributed materially to the nation's peace with the Barbary states. However, unlike when the Americans had first arrived, the political alignment of the Mediterranean had coalesced into the great fight between the two major powers: Great Britain and France.[4] This realignment—and subjugation of some of the smaller powers—left the United States once again on the outside, since it would not take sides in the fight. In fact, Americans vociferously maintained their neutrality, despite what Captain Isaac Chauncey called in 1807 "base treatment received from a people that we are at peace with and profess a wish to continue so."[5]

The people Chauncey referred to were not North African, but British. He told the secretary of state that the British were now impeding another key commercial route for the young American commercial fleet: the route to China. They were still impressing sailors off commercial vessels. Within three weeks of Chauncey's letter, the situation with the British got much worse. In June 1807 James Barron surrendered the USS *Chesapeake* to HMS *Leopard* after firing only one shot, allowing the British to board the ship and remove some men who they claimed were British deserters. Barron had been preparing to take command of the small squadron that had been left in the Mediterranean, where the British had repeatedly boarded American naval vessels looking for deserters.[6] But the British harassment of the Americans in the Mediterranean had never come to broadsides.

Under the embargo and non-intercourse act that followed the *Chesapeake-Leopard* affair, the navy focused on the defense of the American coast from 1807 to 1811. The disputes over impressment and the impeding of American trade finally boiled over into war in 1812. Even though many of the officers who had served on frigates in the Mediterranean commanded gunboats after they returned to the United States, their service in the Mediterranean bore fruit in the War of 1812. Veterans of the First Barbary War commanded everything from frigates to gunboats to purpose-built lake vessels. Some whose Mediterranean experience had not been glorious got another chance, such as William Bainbridge, who commanded the USS *Constitution* in its victory over HMS *Java*.

The consuls of the Mediterranean too were affected by the war. The new consul to Tripoli, who left the United States to take his post in November 1812, was captured on his way to Tripoli by a British squadron along with six other

American vessels off Cadiz. While in Cadiz, he received news that the Algerians had sent cruisers into the Atlantic looking for Americans.[7] In 1813 the American consul to Tunis, Mordecai Noah, was captured by a British warship while he was taking a circuitous route to the European continent to avoid capture by Algiers.[8] When the tribute payments delivered in 1812 had once again been deficient, the dey had declared the peace treaty defunct, believing (rightly) that the Americans were too busy fighting against the British to pay much attention to Algiers.[9] In fact, the British had convinced the dey to be their ally, offering protection to Algiers if the Algerians would harass the Americans.[10]

It might have felt to the consuls like 1812 and 1813 were gearing up for a repeat of 1801. American shipping was hamstrung by dangerous waters in the Mediterranean, the navy was off somewhere else fighting a bigger opponent, and the American government was providing little to no support to the consuls. But there were a few differences. The American consular presence was now well-established, even if some of the consuls were new. Though the navy had gone away, it had not been dismantled—it would be easy enough to get it back into the Mediterranean. And if peace were signed between Great Britain and the United States, Algiers might be hung out to dry.

Once the war with Britain ended in 1815, the United States turned its attention back to Algiers. This time, instead of sending one lightly armed frigate, the United States sent two large squadrons, commanded by the hero of the First Barbary War, Stephen Decatur, and the former captain of the first naval vessel to Algiers, William Bainbridge. And this time, there would be no protracted war. Less than a month after the first squadron anchored off Algiers, the dey capitulated and reinstituted peace with the United States. Tunis and Tripoli likewise backed off claims they had made against the Americans, seeing how quickly the dey had caved.

William Shaler, the American consul at Algiers, wrote later that the Americans had "stripped the phantom of Barbary importance of its imaginary terrors, and exposed to derision the frauds, by which it has so long been upheld."[11] However, if the United States had done this, it had not done it alone. It was not until the British intervened in Algiers in 1816 that the tributary system was broken for good.[12] Once the Napoleonic wars were ended, the European powers could dedicate time and energy to the North Africans. In fact, the phantom of Barbary importance proved illusory indeed within a few decades when France colonized Algiers in 1830. Though the other three Barbary states were able to hold off longer, they were frequently at war with European nations or fighting off their financial influence. Ultimately, France colonized Tunis in 1881 and Morocco in 1912, and Italy colonized Libya (Tripoli) in 1912 as well.

On its face, the First Barbary War accomplished little. The attitudes of the Barbary rulers changed little, even after Tripoli signed a new peace treaty. Their claims for presents and their outrage over American captures waned only slightly in the aftermath of the war. The United States certainly did not ascend to the status of a great power in the eyes of the British or French. In fact, if anything, the British treated the Americans even worse than before the war. The only part of the community the United States made inroads into was the network of smaller powers including Naples and Denmark, which had each welcomed the United States as one of their own.

However, the situation looks different if viewed on the level of individuals instead of on the level of nations. The young naval officers of the First Barbary War served not only in the War of 1812 but after the war, when the United States began sending its navy out into the world for peacetime commerce protection. Many of the officers who watched as the Americans figured out diplomacy on the fly in the Mediterranean went on to do that kind of diplomacy themselves in the Caribbean and Pacific. The consuls likewise, though they did not all remain in the Mediterranean, helped to establish American commercial interests in the region that have lasted ever since. The needs of the navy, and the rise in American commerce after the war, convinced the State Department to establish more permanent consular posts in places throughout the Mediterranean. Not every individual had a success story, of course. William Eaton was so angry at the US government that he got briefly involved in the Burr conspiracy and died a few years later a bitter and broken man.[13] James Barron, who had served honorably in the Mediterranean, killed Stephen Decatur in 1820 in a duel, egged on by William Bainbridge, whose complicated relationship with Decatur dated back to their Mediterranean service.[14]

The First Barbary War was the end of a few stories—like those of Somers, Caldwell, Decatur, Wadsworth, Dorsey, and Israel, in addition to a few dozen enlisted sailors. But it was the beginning of many others. In the end, as the secretary of the navy had intended, the war did begin to fix a national character and give confidence to merchants, who eventually spread out across the globe.

Introduction

1. The interpretive plaque that resides next to the monument is full of suspect historical claims and some outright falsehoods. If you read all of this book, you may be able to spot some of them. In particular, these six men were by no means the only men killed during the war—each of them died as an officer on a ship or boat that also shipped numerous enlisted sailors. Only James Decatur perished alone; all the others went down with their ships, with the loss of all hands.

2. Denver Brunsman has written eloquently about the difficulties of American impressment and identity: Brunsman, "Subjects vs. Citizens," 557–86.

3. Allison, *The Crescent Obscured*, 4.

4. Thomas Jefferson, "Report on American Trade in the Mediterranean," 28 December 1790, http://rotunda.upress.virginia.edu/founders/TSJN-01-18-02-0139-0004. Hereafter, the digital edition of Jefferson's papers will be referred to as TJ.

5. Rojas, "Insults Unpunished,"165.

6. Rojas, "Insults Unpunished," 166; see also Peskin, "The Lessons of Independence," 299–301.

7. "An Act to Provide a Naval Armament," https://www.loc.gov/item/rbpe.2200050c/.

8. For a detailed explanation of how the United States ended up paying this amount, see Lambert, *The Barbary Wars*, especially ch. 2–3. The United States did not pay out all of this amount in one year, so there was no single year in which 20% of the budget went to the Barbary states.

9. For more on the fight for the navy, see Symonds, *Navalists and Antinavalists*.

10. For more on the United States' trade with the Mediterranean, especially the re-export trade, see Marzagalli, "American Shipping into the Mediterranean during the French Wars," 43–62.

11. George Washington to Lafayette, 15 August 1786, *Founders Online*, NARA, https://founders.archives.gov/documents/Washington/04-04-02-0200.

12. William Eaton to James Madison, 23 August 1802, *Founders Online*, NARA, https://founders.archives.gov/documents/Madison/02-91-02-0463.

13. See, for instance, Seiken, "The Reluctant Warrior," 185–206; Burns, "Washington, Jefferson, and Madison"; Smith, *For the Purposes of Defense*.

14. E.g., Allison, *The Crescent Obscured*; Folayan, "The 'Tripolitan War,'" 615–26; Kitzen, "Money Bags or Cannon Balls," 601–24; Lambert, *The Barbary Wars*; Peskin, *Captives and Countrymen*; Sofka, "The Jeffersonian Idea of National Security," 519–44.

15. I take this idea from Cohen, *History in Three Keys*, 61.

16. Smith, *For the Purposes of Defense*, 2.

Chapter 1 · A Carrier for a Pirate

1. Secretary of State to William Smith, 22 March 1800, *Naval Documents Related to the United States Wars with the Barbary Powers* 1:351 (this collection will hereafter be referred to as BW).

2. Spencer, *Algiers in the Age of the Corsairs*, 58.

3. Lambert, *Seapower States*, 8.

4. Burke, "The Mediterranean of Modernity," 78–79.

5. Tucker, "Piracy of the Eighteenth-Century Mediterranean," 139.

6. Tucker, "Piracy of the Eighteenth-Century Mediterranean," 138.

7. Panzac, *The Barbary Corsairs*, 153.

8. See Rodger, *Command of the Ocean*, 460–63.

9. Log of the USS *George Washington*, 7 September 1800, BW1:370.

10. Richard O'Brien, List of stores wanted for the dey, 25 March 1800, Algiers consular dispatches, NARA.

11. Lambert, *The Barbary Wars*, 87.

12. Lambert, *The Barbary Wars*, 88; BW1:284. Ironically, by the time the *Hassan Bashaw* had arrived in Algiers, Dey Hassan, for whom the ship was ostensibly named, had died and been replaced by Bobba Mustapha.

13. Captain Timothy Newman volunteered for the navy after leaving the *Crescent* in Algiers (BW1:251); he died in 1800. Captain William Maley joined the navy after delivering the *Lelah Eisha*; his naval career was similarly short, but he resigned after a court-martial in which he was accused of cowardice in an action in the Quasi-War with France. It's possible that the captain of the *Hassan Bashaw* also joined the navy—there are two John Smiths who joined the navy between 1799 and 1800—but the commonness of the name makes it difficult to be certain.

14. Richard O'Brien to Secretary of State, January–March 1799, BW1:294.

15. O'Brien to Secretary of State, 19 August 1800, Algiers consular dispatches, NARA.

16. Secretary of the Navy to Israel Whelen, 3 July 1800, BW1:362–63.

17. Secretary of State to O'Brien, 29 July 1800, BW1:365.

18. Invoices for *George Washington* cargo, 24 July 1800, Algiers consular dispatches, NARA.

19. Log of the USS *George Washington*, 18 September 1801, BW1:370; Spencer, *Algiers in the Age of the Corsairs*, 13.

20. Cantor, "A Connecticut Yankee in a Barbary Court," 95–96.

21. William Bainbridge to Secretary of the Navy, 10 October 1800, BW1:378.

22. O'Brien to Secretary of State, 24 September 1800, Algiers consular dispatches, NARA.

23. Samuel Hodgdon to Whelen, 21 July 1800, BW1:363.

24. O'Brien reported to William Bainbridge that the debt owed to the Bacris was between $40,000 and $50,000; he chose to report a much higher number to the secretary of state. O'Brien to Bainbridge, 6 October 1800, BW1:374; cf. O'Brien to Secretary of State, 20 September 1800, BW1:371.

25. Secretary of State to O'Brien, 21 December 1798, BW1:280.

26. Secretary of State to O'Brien, 15 January 1800, BW1:346.

27. James Leander Cathcart to Charles Lee, 18 October 1800, BW1:383.

28. Lambert, *The Barbary Wars*, 94.

29. Eaton to Secretary of State, 23 June 1800, BW1:357–58.

30. Cathcart Protest, BW1:372; Cathcart to Secretary of State, 18 October 1800, BW1:382–84.

31. Cathcart to Secretary of State, 1 November 1800, BW1:394–97.

32. "Marine force of Algiers," 23 October 1800, BW1:371–72.

33. O'Brien to Bainbridge, 9 October 1800, BW1:375–76.

34. Bainbridge to O'Brien, 9 October 1800, BW1:375.

35. O'Brien to William Eaton, 19 October 1800, BW1:385; "Remarks &ca on the Insults and abuses which Great Britain received from the Government of Algiers during a period of eighteen years from 1785 to 1803" (ff. 214–35), BL Add MS 34932, British Library. Though Falcon seems not to have suffered any mortification over this request, the title of the anonymous document that records it seems to indicate that not everyone in Great Britain actually accepted this use of British naval power as standard or acceptable practice.

36. O'Brien to Bainbridge, 9 October 1800, BW1:374.

37. O'Brien to Eaton, 19 October 1800, BW1:385; "Remarks &ca on the Insults and abuses which Great Britain received from the Government of Algiers during a period of eighteen years from 1785 to 1803" (ff. 214–35), BL Add MS 34932, British Library.

38. O'Brien to Bainbridge, 9 October 1800, BW1:375–78.

39. Bainbridge to the Secretary of the Navy, 10 October 1800, BW1:379.

40. Log book of the *George Washington*, 10–12 October 1800, BW1:381.

41. From an officer on board the *George Washington*, 14 October 1800, BW1:381.

42. O'Brien to William Eaton, 19 October 1800, BW1:385.

43. Account of William Brown, 11 December 1800, BW1:387.

44. See Farber, "Millions for Credit," 187–217.

45. Eaton to Secretary of State, 20 December 1800, BW1:403.

46. Bainbridge to Secretary of the Navy, 17 November 1800, BW1:401.

47. "Remarks &ca on the Insults and abuses which Great Britain received from the Government of Algiers during a period of eighteen years from 1785 to 1803" (ff. 214–35), BL Add MS 34932, British Library.

48. Bainbridge to Secretary of the Navy, 17 November 1800, BW1:401.

49. For more on Eaton's antisemitism, see Peskin, "American Exception?," 299–317. There's no reason to think the Bacris would have taken particular interest in humiliating the United States. Rosenstock, "The House of Bacri and Busnach," 348.

50. Jefferson to Madison, 28 August 1801, *Founders Online*, NARA, https://founders.archives.gov/documents/Jefferson/01-35-02-0122.

Chapter 2 · Squadron of Observation

1. Richard O'Brien to William Kirkpatrick, 24 December 1800, *Naval Documents Related to the Quasi-War between the United States and France*, 7:45. (Hereafter this collection will be referred to as QW.)

2. Circular from Cathcart, 3 January 1801, BW1:404–405.

3. James Leander Cathcart to Yusuf Karamanli, 19 February 1801, BW1:420.

4. O'Brien to Henry Pater, 5 April 1801, BW1:427.

5. John Adams to John Marshall, 11 July 1800, *Founders Online*, NARA, https://founders.archives.gov/documents/Adams/99-02-02-4433.

6. Cathcart to Secretary of State, 4 January 1801, BW1:408.

7. Cathcart to Secretary of State, 4 January 1801, BW1:408.

8. Benjamin Stoddert to John Adams, 18 May 1801, *Founders Online*, NARA, https://founders.archives.gov/documents/Adams/99-02-02-4913.

9. James Monroe to James Madison, 23 May 1801, *Founders Online*, NARA, https://founders.archives.gov/documents/Madison/02-01-02-0288.

10. Levi Lincoln to Thomas Jefferson, 16 April 1801, *Founders Online*, NARA, https://founders.archives.gov/documents/Jefferson/01-33-02-0517.

11. Samuel Smith to Thomas Truxtun, 10 April 1801, BW1:429; Truxtun to Smith, 13 April 1801, BW1:432; Smith to Truxtun, 28 April 1801, BW1:439–40.

12. Thomas Boylston Adams to John Quincy Adams, 8 June 1801, *Founders Online*, NARA, https://founders.archives.gov/documents/Adams/99-03-02-0976.

13. Fredriksen, "Dale, Richard (1756–1826), Naval Officer."

14. Maloney, "Barron, James (1769–1851), Naval Officer."

15. Maloney, "Bainbridge, William (1774–1833), Naval Officer."

16. Jefferson to Yusuf Karamanli, 21 May 1801, BW1:470.

17. Samuel Smith to Richard Dale, 20 May 1801, BW1:465–47.

18. Smith to Dale, 20 May 1801, BW1:465.

19. O'Brien to Madison, 24 June 1801, *Founders Online*, NARA, https://founders.archives.gov/documents/Madison/02-01-02-0446.

20. Smith to Dale, 20 May 1801, BW1:465–69.

21. Madison, circular to American consuls in the Mediterranean, 21 May 1801, *Founders Online*, NARA, https://founders.archives.gov/documents/Madison/02-01-02-0271.

22. Madison to O'Brien, 21 May 1801, *Founders Online*, NARA, https://founders.archives.gov/documents/Madison/02-01-02-0274.

23. "An Act Concerning Consuls and Vice-Consuls" (1792), https://www.loc.gov/item/rbpe.21800700/.

24. David Humphreys to Washington, 3 February 1794, *Founders Online*, NARA, http://founders.archives.gov/documents/Washington/05-15-02-0133.

25. Timothy Pickering to Washington, *Founders Online*, NARA, https://founders.archives.gov/documents/Washington/05-19-02-0153.

26. Goodin, *From Captives to Consuls*, 40–42.

27. Cathcart and Newkirk, *The Captives*, 22.

28. Baepler, *White Slaves, African Masters*, 103.

29. Eicher, "To the Shores of Tripoli," 47–48.

30. Allison, *The Crescent Obscured*, 164–65.

31. Cathcart to Secretary of State, 30 March 1803, BW2:379.

32. Cathcart to Secretary of State, 4 January 1801, BW1:408–409.

33. O'Brien to Madison, 16 September 1802, *The Papers of James Madison Digital Edition*, http://rotunda.upress.virginia.edu/founders/JSMN-02-91-02-0493. (This collection will hereafter be referred to as JM.)

34. Eaton to Madison, 19 October 1801, JM, http://rotunda.upress.virginia.edu/founders/JSMN-02-91-02-0182.

35. O'Brien to Madison, 24 June 1801, *Founders Online*, NARA, https://founders
.archives.gov/documents/Madison/02-01-02-0446.

36. William Eaton circular, 23 July 1801, BW1:528; Dale to Smith, 18 August 1801,
BW1:553.

37. Lambert, *War at Sea in the Age of Sail*, 24.

38. Eaton to Madison, 19 October 1801, JM, http://rotunda.upress.virginia.edu
/founders/JSMN-02-91-02-0182.

39. See http://abbymullen.org/projects/Quasi-War/ for a map showing that the navy
concentrated its attentions around key ports of origin for privateers, making many more
captures in small areas than out on the high seas.

40. Eaton to Dale, 24 July 1801, BW1:529.

41. Dale to Samuel Barron, 4 July 1801, BW1:500; Dale to Bainbridge, 4 July 1801,
BW1:500–501.

42. William Turner to unknown, 1 June 1801, BW1:480.

43. Dale to Morris, 28 February 1802, BW2:68–69.

44. Mooney, *Dictionary of American Naval Fighting Ships* (online); Mediterranean
Charts of Stephen Decatur, United States Naval Academy Museum,
USNAM-1922-002-0013.

45. Journal of the *Essex*, 13 October 1801, BW1:598.

46. Cathcart to Eaton, 29 June 1801, BW1:493.

47. Humphreys to Robert Montgomery, 1 December 1793, BW1:56–57.

48. Kitzen, "Money Bags or Cannon Balls," 617.

49. Cathcart to Dale, 17 September 1801, BW1:576; Eaton to Secretary of State, 13
December 1801, BW1:637.

50. Dale to Cederström, 2 February 1802, BW2:46; Dale to Rufus King, 7 February 1802, BW2:54.

51. Alexander Murray to Secretary of the Navy, 7 May 1802, BW2:146.

52. Stein, "Passes and Protection in the Making of a British Mediterranean," 608.

53. Matar, *Europe through Arab Eyes*, 12.

54. Passports could include the name of the master, the ship name, its tonnage, its
guns, its crew complement, its type, and its home port, but the only feature that was
mandatory were the signatures of the president of the United States and the secretary of
state, who had to sign every single passport. If some of the ship's information changed, a
new passport was not issued; rather, changes were noted on the reverse of the passport
and usually validated by a consul. See Mediterranean Passports, 1802–1840, Record
Group 36: Records of the U.S. Customs Service, 1745–1997, NARA.

55. Jefferson, "Opinion on Ship Passports," 3 May 1793, *Founders Online*, NARA,
http://founders.archives.gov/documents/Jefferson/01-25-02-0593.

56. "Treaty of Peace and Amity, Signed at Algiers September 5, 1795," *Avalon Project:
Documents in Law, History, and Diplomacy*, Yale University, https://avalon.law.yale.edu
/18th_century/bar1795t.asp; Stein, "Passes and Protection," 607.

57. An example Algiers-issued passport was good for one year of travel within the
Mediterranean; the passport also protected against molestation by Tunis, Tripoli, or
Morocco. "Passport granted by the Dey of Algiers to an American vessel," 1795, BW1:125.

58. O'Brien to Secretary of State, 25 November 1801, BW1:625.

59. Dale to Nicholas Nissen, 8 August 1801, BW1:537.

60. See Madison's instructions about issuing consular papers in "Circular Letter to American Consuls and Commercial Agents, 1 August 1801," *Founders Online*, NARA, https://founders.archives.gov/documents/Madison/02-02-02-0001.

61. Dale to Eaton, 28 August 1801, BW1:562.

62. Eaton to Dale, 24 July 1801, James L. Cathcart papers, 1785–1817, Library of Congress.

63. Henry Clarke to Eaton, 24 July 1801, James L. Cathcart papers.

64. Dale to Thomas Appleton, 24 November 1801, BW1:624–25.

65. See orders to Sterett, 5 July 1801, BW1:503; orders to Samuel Barron, 9 July 1801, BW1:505–506.

66. Dale to Sterett, 30 July 1801, BW1:534–35.

67. "Naval Victory," 18 November 1801, BW1:538–39.

68. Orders to Sterett, 30 July 1801, BW1:534–35.

69. "Naval Victory," 18 November 1801, BW1:539.

70. *American Citizen* (New York), 17 December 1801. Accessed through America's Historical Imprints.

71. Jefferson, First Annual Message to Congress, 8 December 1801, American Presidency Project, https://www.presidency.ucsb.edu/documents/first-annual-message.

72. Cathcart to Madison, 10 August 1801, JM, http://rotunda.upress.virginia.edu/founders/JSMN-02-91-02-0115.

73. Dale to Yusuf Karamanli, 24 July 1801, BW1:533–34.

74. "News," *Bell's Weekly Messenger*, 30 August 1801, Seventeenth and Eighteenth Century Burney Newspapers Collection, Gale.

75. Humphreys to William Kirkpatrick, 24 October 1801, BW1:602.

76. Circular to U.S. consuls in Europe from Cathcart, 11 September 1801, BW1:573–74.

77. Cathcart to Dale, 13 October 1801, BW1:598.

78. O'Brien to Humphreys, 8 November 1801, BW1:616.

79. Dale does not name the governor in his letter, but it appears to be Major-General Douglas Clephane, who had just taken over for Henry Edward Fox, Lord Holland, in September 1801. Within a year, the British would cede Minorca back to Spain and whatever connection the American navy had with Port Mahon would be lost. Almost no American naval vessels visited Port Mahon again during the war. Gregory, *Minorca, the Illusory Prize*, 97.

80. Dale cited Articles 21 and 24 of the Jay Treaty. Article 24 states: "It shall not be lawful for any Foreign Privateers (not being Subjects or Citizens of either of the said Parties) who have Commissions from any other Prince or State in Enmity with either Nation, to arm their Ships in the Ports of either of the said Parties." *Avalon Project: Documents in Law, History, and Diplomacy*, Yale University, http://avalon.law.yale.edu/18th_century/jay.asp#art21.

81. Dale to governor of Minorca, 19 November 1801, BW1:623.

82. Dale to Appleton, 20 November 1801, BW1:624.

83. Dale to Secretary of the Navy, 18 August 1801, BW1:552.

84. Dale to Sterett, 18 August 1801, BW1:554.

85. Dale to Samuel Barron, 4 July 1801, Richard Dale Papers, Library of Congress.

86. Dale to Bainbridge, 17 July 1801, BW1:515.

87. Dale to Robert Livingston, 9 December 1801, BW1:631.

88. Schroeder, *The Transformation of European Politics*, 223.

89. Dale to Humphreys, 18 October 1801, BW1:600; Dale to Captain John Atonio de Espino, 19 October 1801, BW1:600–601.

90. John Gibson to Willings and Francis, Nicklin and Griffin, and Henry Nixon, 31 July 1801, American State Papers: Documents, Legislative and Executive, of the Congress of the United States, Foreign Relations, 2:442.

91. It is unclear why the governor of San Roque would have jurisdiction in the *American Packet*'s case; in John Gibson's case, the governors of Algeciras and San Roque argued over who would adjudicate. Ibid.

92. Dale to governor of St. Roque, 9 October 1801, BW1:596.

93. Dale to Secretary of the Navy, 26 October 1801, BW1:607–8.

94. Dale to Secretary of the Navy, 26 October 1801, BW1:606–608.

95. See records from 9 July 1802, 18 September 1802, 15 April 1803, and others for a list of the items shipped to the squadron, BW2:197, 276, 392.

96. Abishai Thomas to John Shaw, July 24, 1801, BW1:531.

97. Gavino to Secretary of State, 24 July 1801, BW1:530.

98. Dale to Intendant and Master Builder of Dockyard at Gibraltar, 5 October 1801, BW1:595.

99. Dale to Secretary of the Navy, 18 August 1801, BW1:552–53.

100. Dale to Barron, 25 October 1801, BW1:603.

101. E.g., *Essex* journal, 3 September 1801, 5 September 1801, BW1:569, 570.

102. William Willis to Madison, 28 June 1801, JM, http://rotunda.upress.virginia.edu /founders/JSMN-02-08-02-0597.

103. Dale to Secretary of the Navy, 6 November 1801, BW1:615.

104. For example, Barron to Secretary of the Navy, 10 December 1801, BW1:632; Simpson circular, 25 June 1802, BW2:183–84.

105. Dale to Kirkpatrick, 3 October 1801, BW1:593. He seems to be excluding the *Enterprize*.

106. O'Brien to Madison, 26 September 1801, JM, http://rotunda.upress.virginia.edu /founders/JSMN-02-91-02-0162.

107. Even Harold Langley, who wrote the definitive text on medicine in the early American navy, tends to treat the medical aspects of cruises as separate from commodores' command decisions. Langley, *A History of Medicine in the Early U.S. Navy*.

108. Dale to Eaton, 6 September 1801, BW1:571.

109. *Essex* journal, 10 November 1801, BW1:618.

110. *Essex* journal, 16 November 1801, BW1:621.

111. Dale to Secretary of the Navy, 4 October 1801, BW1:594.

112. Barron to Cathcart, 9 January 1802, BW2:15–16.

113. For more on the yellow fever epidemics in the United States, see Estes and Smith, *A Melancholy Scene of Devastation*; Kornfeld, "Crisis in the Capital," 189–205; Stough, "The Yellow Fever in Philadelphia 1793," 6–13; DeClue and Smith, "Wrestling the 'Pale Faced Messenger," 243–68.

114. McNeill, "Yellow Jack and Geopolitics," 346–47.

115. Humphreys to Secretary of State, 15 February 1799, QW2:360.

116. John Adams to Hamouda Pasha, 15 January 1800, BW1:344.

117. Dols, "The Second Plague Pandemic," 12, 176–78.

118. Testimony of Dr. William Gladstone, "Report from Select Committee on the Doctrine of Contagion in the Plague," 19 March 1819, *Selection of Reports and Papers of the House of Commons: Medical* 35:24.

119. "The History of the Plague," 438.

120. Slack, "The Disappearance of Plague," 474–75.

121. Booker, *Maritime Quarantine*, 258.

122. Booker, *Maritime Quarantine*, 15, 247.

123. Chase-Levenson, *The Yellow Flag*, 29.

124. Martin, *History of the Captivity and Sufferings of Mrs. Maria Martin*, 54. Paul Baepler believes Martin's account is fictional, but he also suggests that the descriptions of Algiers in it are accurate. Baepler, *White Slaves, African Masters*, 11–12.

125. Dale to President of Board of Health at Toulon, 9 December 1801, BW1:630–31. Dale to Secretary of the Navy, 13 December 1801, BW1:633–34.

126. Dale to Livingston, 9 December 1801, BW1:631.

127. O'Brien to Secretary of State, 26 September 1801, BW1:581–82.

Chapter 3 · Quaker Meeting Houses

1. Richard Dale to Stephen Cathalan, 1 January 1802, Richard Dale Papers, Library of Congress.

2. Samuel Barron to James Leander Cathcart, 9 January 1802, BW2:15.

3. Samuel Barron to James Leander Cathcart, 9 January 1802, BW2:15.

4. Dale to Daniel McNeill, 2 February 1802, BW2:44–45.

5. McNeill had probably taken on supplies in L'Orient; doing so was in his orders from the secretary of the navy. Why he then chose to stop at both Gibraltar and Malaga is uncertain. Secretary of the Navy to McNeill, 1 October 1801, BW1:587.

6. Dale to McNeill, 2 February 1802, BW2:44–45.

7. Wadsworth to Eaton, 28 July 1802, BW2:215. Frederick Leiner says that McNeill followed this practice at every port he stopped at. Leiner, *Millions for Defense*, 121.

8. Dale to Secretary of the Navy, 24 January 1802, BW2: 27–28. I assert this based on the many accounts of captains chafing under quarantine restrictions.

9. Much has been written about the cultural productions involving the Barbary states, including Dillon, "Slaves in Algiers," 417. This idea is expanded upon in Matar, *Europe through Arab Eyes*, and Battistini, "Glimpses of the Other before Orientalism," 454–74.

10. Gallatin to Jefferson, 16 August 1802, TJ, http://rotunda.upress.virginia.edu /founders/TSJN-01-38-02-0209; Izard to Mrs. Ralph Izard, 11 October 1803, BW3:127.

11. Cathcart to Dale, 10 August 1801, BW1:545.

12. Shaw to Secretary of the Navy, 2 March 1802, BW2:74.

13. Eaton to Secretary of State, 10 April 1801, BW1:431.

14. Murray to Thomas Bulkeley, 18 May 1802, BW2:155.

15. Dale to Secretary of the Navy, 10 January 1802, BW2:16; Dale to Rufus King, 7 February 1802, BW2:54.

16. Dale to DeButts and Purviance, 13 January 1802, BW2:20.

17. Thomas Truxtun to Secretary of the Navy, 3 March 1802, BW2:76.

18. "List of Officers Retained under the Peace Establishment Act," QW7:135; Secretary of the Navy to Morris, 3 May 1801, QW7:216.

19. Diary of Gouverneur Morris, 22 April 1804, *The Diaries of Gouverneur Morris Digital Edition*, https://rotunda-upress-virginia-edu.mtvernon.idm.oclc.org/founders /GRMS-01-02-02-0006-0004-0022.

20. Murray to John Gavino, 30 April 1802, BW2:140.

21. Cathcart to Secretary of State, 25 August 1802, BW2:250–51.

22. Dearden, *A Nest of Corsairs*, 127.

23. Eaton to Secretary of State, 18 March 1802, BW2:90.

24. Eaton to Secretary of State, 13 December 1801, BW1:637.

25. Eaton to Secretary of State, 18 March 1802, BW2:90–91.

26. Eaton to any American commander, 29 March 1802, James Leander Cathcart Papers, Library of Congress.

27. Eaton to Cathcart, 28 March 1802, James Leander Cathcart Papers.

28. Cathcart to Joseph Pulis, 9 May 1802, Tripoli consular dispatches, NARA, https://catalog.archives.gov/id/211288115.

29. Eaton to McNeill, 24 March 1802, BW2:95.

30. Eaton to Joseph Bounds, 24 March 1802, BW2:95.

31. McNeill to Eaton, 31 March 1802, James Leander Cathcart Papers.

32. "An Act for the protection of the Commerce and Seamen of the United States, against the Tripolitan Cruisers," 6 February 1802, BW2:51.

33. Secretary of the Navy to Morris, 20 March 1802, BW2:92; Secretary of the Navy to Dale, 16 February 1802, BW2:60.

34. Murray to Secretary of the Navy, 1 January 1802, BW2:11.

35. Murray to Eaton, 6 May 1802, BW2:145.

36. *Constellation* journal, 1 April 1802, BW2:102.

37. Entries in the *Constellation* journal: 16 August 1802: Thomas Bird, ordinary seaman (BW2:236); 8 September 1802: Mathias Guise, ordinary seaman (BW2:270); 5 December 1802: Frances Sweeny, marine (BW2:329); 18 December 1802: John Brown, marine (BW2:335).

38. Murray to Morris, 18 September 1802, BW2:277.

39. Murray to Hugh G. Campbell, 21 November 1802, BW2:316.

40. *Constellation* journal, 29 November 1802, BW2:326.

41. Jacob Jones to Murray, unknown date, BW2:299; McKee, *Gentlemanly and Honorable Profession*, 182.

42. Officers of the Continental and U.S. Navy and Marine Corps, 1775–1900; Daniel Carmick to William W. Burrows, 15 October 1802, BW2:293–95.

43. Wadsworth to Eaton, 28 July 1802, BW2:215–16.

44. Murray to Eaton, 6 May 1802, BW2:145.

45. Murray to Secretary of the Navy, 6 May 1802, BW2:146.

46. Eaton to Secretary of State, 8 June 1802, BW2:166.

47. Eaton to Secretary of State, 8 June 1802, BW2:166–67.

48. Murray to Morris, 20 August 1802, BW2:242 (emphasis in original).

49. Eaton to Secretary of State, 9 August 1802, BW2:229 (emphasis in original).

50. Affidavit, 22 August 1802, BW2:247–48.

51. Cathcart to Secretary of State, 25 August 1802, BW2:251–53.

52. Murray to William Kirkpatrick, 30 April 1802, BW2:139–140.

53. Murray to Lord Keith, 5 May 1802, BW2:144.

54. Wadsworth to Nancy Doane, 18 June 1802, BW2:180; journal of Midshipman Henry Wadsworth, Longfellow House archives.

55. Wadsworth journal, 22 February 1803, BW2:387.

56. Wadsworth journal, 15 June 1802, Longfellow House.

57. Morris to Secretary of the Navy, 31 May 1802, BW2:162.

58. Wadsworth journal, 4 July 1802, Longfellow House.

59. Simpson to Secretary of State, 19 March 1802, JM, http://rotunda.upress.virginia .edu/founders/JSMN-02-91-02-0314.

60. Simpson to Secretary of State, 26 June 1802, BW2:186.

61. Simpson to Secretary of State, 3 July 1802, BW2:190.

62. Simpson to Secretary of State, 27 July 1802, BW2:210; Simpson to Secretary of State, 3 August 1802, BW2:220–21. Simpson to Secretary of State, 3 August 1802, JM, https://rotunda.upress.virginia.edu/founders/JSMN-02-91-02-0439.

63. Selawy to Simpson, 6 August 1802, BW2:226.

64. Simpson to Morris, 16 August 1802, BW2:235–36.

65. Richard Valentine Morris, *A Defence of the Conduct of Commodore Morris*, 24–25. (This publication will be referred to hereafter as RVM.)

66. Cathcart to Secretary of State, 4 July 1802, American State Papers: Foreign Relations, 2:462.

67. O'Brien to Secretary of State, 1 February 1802, Algiers consular dispatches, NARA. Secretary of State to Cathcart, 18 April 1802, BW2:126–27.

68. Guiseppe Manucie to Eaton, 6 July 1802, BW2:194.

69. Eaton to Summert & Brown, 9 July 1802, BW2:196.

70. Andrew Morris to Cathcart, 22 July 1802, American State Papers: Foreign Relations, 2:463.

71. Eaton to Any American Commander, 11 July 1802, BW2:201.

72. Cathcart to Secretary of State, 15 July 1802, BW2:204–205.

73. *Constellation* journal, 21 July 1802, BW2:207.

74. Nissen to Cathcart, 22 September 1802, BW2:281–82.

75. O'Brien to Secretary of State, 11 October 1802, BW2:288.

76. Eaton to Secretary of State, 5 August 1802, BW2:224.

77. Cathcart to Secretary of State, 25 January 1803, BW2:349.

78. Nissen to Cathcart, 8 July 1802, BW2:195.

79. Nissen to Eaton, 27 July 1802, BW2:213.

80. Cathcart to Madison, 10 August 1801, JM, http://rotunda.upress.virginia.edu /founders/JSMN-02-91-02-0115.

81. Eaton to Bashaw of Tripoli, 18 September 1802, BW2:279.

82. Eaton to Morris, 16 October 1802, BW2:297–98.

83. Cathcart to Secretary of State, 15 July 1802, BW2:204.

84. Secretary of Navy to Morris, 20 April 1802, BW2:130.

85. Cathcart to O'Brien, 25 November 1802, BW2:322.

86. Secretary of the Navy to Morris, 20 April 1802, BW2:130.

87. Secretary of State to Cathcart, 18 April 1802, BW2:126–27.

88. Eaton to Morris, 16 October 1802, BW2:297–98.

89. Murray to Secretary of the Navy, 30 July 1802, BW2:218.

90. Andrew Morris to Cathcart, 22 July 1802, BW2:176–77 (emphasis in original).

91. Murray to Secretary of the Navy, 5 July 1802, BW2:192–93.

92. Nissen to Eaton, 27 July 1802, BW2:212.

93. Murray to Secretary of the Navy, 30 July 1802, BW2:218; *Constellation* journal, 22 July 1802, BW2:209.

94. Murray to Eaton, 5 September 1802, BW2:266.

95. Murray to Secretary of the Navy, 30 July 1802, BW2:218.

96. Eaton to Secretary of State, 22 October 1802, BW2:306.

97. Eaton to Morris, 16 October 1802, BW2:298.

98. Eaton to Cathcart, 26 April 1802, BW2:134–35.

99. Cathcart to Eaton, 11 June 1802, BW2:171.

100. Eaton to Rufus King, 6 June 1802, BW2:166.

101. Bey of Tunis to Jefferson, 8 September 1802, TJ, http://rotunda.upress.virginia.edu/founders/TSJN-01-38-02-0321.

102. Eaton to Secretary of State, 4 May 1802, BW2:142–43.

103. Eaton to Secretary of State, 4 May 1802, BW2:143.

104. Eaton to Secretary of State, 3 June 1802, Tunis consular dispatches, NARA.

105. Samuel Smith to Jefferson, 9 August 1802, TJ, http://rotunda.upress.virginia.edu/founders/TSJN-01-38-02-0173.

106. *Commercial Advertiser*, 11 August 1802; *National Intelligencer*, 11 August 1802, America's Historical Newspapers, Readex.

107. Albert Gallatin to Jefferson, 16 August 1802, TJ, http://rotunda.upress.virginia.edu/founders/TSJN-01-38-02-0209.

108. McKee, *A Gentlemanly and Honorable Profession*, 191–93.

109. Eaton to Cathcart, 21 May 1802, BW2:158; Eaton to Officer Commanding U.S. Squadron in the Mediterranean, 12 May 1802, BW2:152.

110. Wadsworth to Eaton, 29 May 1802, BW2:161.

111. Secretary of State to Eaton and O'Brien, 20 May 1801, BW1:461.

112. O'Brien to Madison, 26 September 1801, JM, http://rotunda.upress.virginia.edu/founders/JSMN-02-91-02-0162.

113. Dale to McNeill, 18 January 1802, BW2:25.

114. Morris to Rufus King, 25 June 1802, BW2:184.

115. Cathcart to Secretary of State, 15 July 1802, BW2:204–205.

116. Marzagalli, "American Shipping into the Mediterranean during the French Wars," 55.

117. Morris to Yznardi, 3 August 1802, BW2:222–23.

118. Dale to Shaw, 14 November 1801, BW1:619.

119. Shaw to General Acton, 7 January 1802, BW2:14.

120. Shaw to General Acton, 15 January 1802, BW2:22.

121. Eaton to Madison, 7 February 1802, Tunis consular dispatches, NARA.

122. Shaw to Secretary of the Navy, 2 March 1802, BW2:76.

123. Charles Wadsworth to Eaton, 28 July 1802, BW2:215.

124. Morris to Secretary of the Navy, 17 August 1802, BW2:237; Wadsworth journal, 26 August 1802, BW2:263; Cathcart to Secretary of State, 30 March 1803, BW2:380.

125. Morris to Secretary of the Navy, 15 October 1802, BW2:296.

126. Morris to Secretary of the Navy, 30 March 1803, BW2:382–83.

127. Wadsworth journal, 4 November 1802, Longfellow House.

128. Wadsworth journal, 6 April 1803, BW2:388; Resume of ships, BW2:118.

129. Secretary of the Navy to McNeill, 27 October 1802, BW2:307.

130. Symonds, *Navalists and Antinavalists*, 86.

Chapter 4 · *Not an Idle Vessel*

1. Alexander Murray to Richard Valentine Morris, 11 January 1803, BW2:343.

2. Henry Wadsworth journal, 31 January 1803, BW2:356.

3. Richard O'Brien to John Gavino, 2 February 1803, BW2:356–57.

4. O'Brien to John Gavino, 2 February 1803, BW2:357; William Eaton to Secretary of State, 8 February 1803, BW2:359.

5. Eaton to Morris, 26 January 1803, BW2:344–45.

6. James Leander Cathcart to Secretary of State, 25 January 1803, BW3:349.

7. Cathcart to Secretary of State, 28 February 1803, BW2:352. The account of Tunisian negotiations that follows is derived from this source.

8. Windler, "Diplomatic History as a Field for Cultural Analysis," 84.

9. Windler, "Diplomatic History," 87.

10. Windler, "Diplomatic History," 85.

11. Cathcart journal, 13 March 1803, BW2:353–55.

12. Morris to Secretary of the Navy, 30 March 1803, BW2:384.

13. Wadsworth journal, 12 May 1803, BW2:403.

14. *John Adams* journal, 7–8, 9–12 May 1803, BW2:400–401.

15. Simpson to Secretary of State, 24 December 1802, BW2:337–38.

16. Morris to Simpson, 19 May 1803, BW2:408–9.

17. Hadgi Abdel-Wahed Nasar to emperor of Morocco, 2 June 1803, BW2:434.

18. Folayan, "Tripoli and the War with the U.S.A., 1801–5," 267.

19. Simpson to Madison, 9 July 1803, JM, http://rotunda.upress.virginia.edu/founders/JSMN-02-91-02-0769.

20. Simpson to Morris, 20 June 1803, BW2:456.

21. Simpson to Madison, 9 July 1803, JM, http://rotunda.upress.virginia.edu/founders/JSMN-02-91-02-0769.

22. Secretary of the Navy to Morris, 20 April 1802, BW2:130.

23. Secretary of the Navy to Morris, 27 August 1802, BW2:257.

24. Cathcart to Secretary of State, 5 May 1803, BW2:398.

25. Secretary of the Navy to Morris, 4 May 1803, BW2:396.

26. Morris to Simpson, 19 May 1803, BW2:409.

27. Wadsworth journal, 22 May 1803, BW2:416–17.

28. Wadsworth journal, 27 May 1803, BW2:425–26.

29. For a list of the skirmishes between the American navy and the Tripolitans in gunboats and on shore, see Tucker, *Dawn Like Thunder*, 285–323. Tucker's restatement of

all the skirmishes is useful to get a sense of how often the navy interacted with the Tripolitans, but Tucker imbues the skirmishes with much more drama and dash than I find warranted from the texts he is clearly drawing from. For instance, he says one skirmish involves an amphibious assault with hand-to-hand combat on the shore between the Americans and the Tripolitan cavalry. My reading of the text is that Henry Wadsworth climbed onto a rock, claimed it for the United States, and then returned to his boat with his compatriots. Tucker does not use footnotes, and I have not been able to trace any sources that corroborate the more dramatic version.

30. Wadsworth journal, 28 May 1803, BW2:427.

31. Wadsworth journal, 29 May 1803, BW2:427–28.

32. Nicholas Nissen to Cathcart, 4 June 1803, BW2:439.

33. Wadsworth journal, 29 May 1803, BW2:429.

34. *John Adams* journal, 6–7 June 1803, BW2:442.

35. Nissen to Cathcart, 8 June 1803, BW2:447.

36. Wadsworth journal, 9 June 1803, BW2:449.

37. Wadsworth journal, 15 June 1803, BW2:453–54.

38. John Rodgers to Morris, 30 June 1803, BW2:465–66.

39. John Rodgers to Morris, 30 June 1803, BW2:465–66.

40. Cathcart to Secretary of State, 24 July 1803, BW2:496.

41. Cathcart to Madison, 20 June 1803, JM, http://rotunda.upress.virginia.edu/founders/JSMN 02 91 02 0738. The Morrisina referred to here is actually Morrisania, the family home of the Morris family in the Bronx.

42. Nissen to Cathcart, 4 June 1803, BW2:439–40.

43. Eaton to Madison, 21 January 1803, JM, http://rotunda.upress.virginia.edu/founders/JSMN-02-91-02-0584.

44. Morris to Secretary of the Navy, 15 October 1802, BW2:296.

45. Simpson to Morris, 17 June 1802, BW2:182.

46. Nissen to Cathcart, 4 June 1803, BW2:439–40.

47. Richard Dale to Eaton, 19 August 1801, BW1:556.

48. Wadsworth journal, 22 July 1803, BW2:495.

49. Cathcart to Morris, 15 August 1803, BW2:512–13.

50. Simpson to Secretary of State, 15 August 1803, BW2:514; Simpson to Secretary of State, 28 July 1803, BW2:500.

51. Simpson to Secretary of State, 15 August 1803, BW2:514; Simpson to Secretary of State, 28 July 1803, BW2:500.

52. See Grainger, *The Amiens Truce*, 178–209.

53. RVM, 96.

54. It seems likely that this was William Loughton Smith, a well-regarded diplomat, former minister plenipotentiary to Portugal, and head of an aborted mission to make a treaty with the Ottoman Porte in 1799. "October Meeting 1917," 27.

55. Wadsworth journal, 27 August 1803, BW2:521–22.

56. Cathcart to Madison, 25 July 1803, JM, http://rotunda.upress.virginia.edu/founders/JSMN-02-91-02-0785.

57. Cathcart to Secretary of State, 30 August 1803, BW2:524.

58. Morris to Daguize, 25 August 1803, BW2:517–18.

59. Morris to Cathcart, 15 August 1803, BW2:511–12.

60. Cathcart to Secretary of State, 8 September 1803, BW3:4–6; see also Cathcart to the Bey of Tunis, 8 September 1803, BW3:25, where Cathcart alleges that Davis's job was only and ever to sign passports and nothing else. Edward Preble later reinstated Davis with full authority as chargé d'affaires.

61. Bainbridge to Simpson, 29 August 1803, BW2:518–19.

62. Gavino to Joseph Yznardi, 1 September 1803, BW3:1.

63. Bainbridge to Simpson, 1 September 1803, BW3:3.

64. Bainbridge to Simpson, BW3:3; Simpson to Bainbridge, 3 September 1803, BW3:9–10.

65. Simpson to Bainbridge, 3 September 1803, BW3:9–11.

66. Emperor of Morocco to Simpson, 9 September 1803, BW3:25.

67. Emperor of Morocco to consuls, 11 September 1803, BW3:26–27.

68. Trigge to Gavino, 6 September 1803, BW3:22.

69. Lear to Secretary of State, 13 September 1803, BW3:82.

70. Gavino to Trigge, 6 September 1803, BW3:22.

71. Preble's life has been documented in great detail in McKee, *Edward Preble*.

72. Somers to Secretary of the Navy, 31 July 1803, BW2:502.

73. Somers to William Jonas Keen, 11 September 1803, BW3:27–28.

74. Secretary of the Navy to Somers, 7 June 1803, BW2:443.

75. Somers to William Jonas Keen, 11 September 1803, BW3:27–28.

76. Wadsworth journal, 12 September 1803, BW3:30.

77. Jefferson to Philip Mazzei, 18 July 1804, *Founders Online*, NARA, https://founders .archives.gov/documents/Jefferson/01-44-02-0094. As Thomas Sheppard has noted, the court of inquiry stopped short of recommending Morris's dismissal; however, the secretary of the navy revoked his commission in May 1804, so he did not leave the service voluntarily as Sheppard has claimed. Sheppard, *Commanding Petty Despots*, 90; cf. *Jenks' Portland Gazette*, 6 June 1804, *Chronicling America*.

78. RVM, 11–12.

79. RVM, 18–19.

80. RVM, 44–45.

81. RVM, 63–64.

82. RVM, 65.

83. Estes, *Naval Surgeon*, 125–26.

84. Logbook of *Constitution*, 7 September 1803, BW3:24.

85. Preble to Simpson, 13 September 1803, BW3:31.

86. *Constitution* logbook, 14 September 1803, BW3:45. The ships included the *Philadelphia* (Bainbridge), *New York* (Morris), *John Adams* (Rodgers), *Vixen* (Smith), and *Nautilus* (Somers).

87. Rodgers to Preble, 15 September 1803, BW3:47.

88. Preble to Secretary of the Navy, 18 September 1803, BW3:56–57.

89. Preble to Secretary of the Navy, 18 September 1803, BW3:56–57.

90. Preble to Secretary of the Navy, 18 September 1803, BW3:58.

91. Kirkpatrick to Preble, 18 September 1803, BW3:59.

92. Preble to Somers, 19 September 1803, BW3:63; Preble to Charles Stewart, 19 September 1803, BW3:64.

93. Simpson to Gavino, 19 September 1803, BW3:63.

94. Preble to Secretary of the Navy, 22 September 1803, BW3:70.

95. Selawy to Simpson, 24 September 1803, BW3:74.

96. Preble to Simpson, 25 September 1803, BW3:76.

97. Wadsworth to Nancy Doane, 24 September 1803, BW3:75.

98. Lear to Secretary of State, BW3:85.

99. McKee, *Edward Preble*, 153.

100. Simpson to Preble, 3 October 1803, BW3:97.

101. Circular from Tobias Lear, 3 October 1803, BW3:99–100.

102. Simpson to Preble, 4 October 1803, BW3:103.

103. Simpson to Preble, 7 October 1803, BW3:110.

104. Simpson to Preble, 7 October 1803, BW3:109.

105. *Constitution* logbook, 8 October 1803, BW3:119.

106. Simpson to Preble, 7 October 1803, BW3:111.

107. Simpson to Secretary of State, 8 October 1803, BW3:114–15.

108. Preble to Simpson, 8 October 1803, BW3:119.

109. Simpson to Preble, 11 October 1803, BW3:124.

110. Preble to Rodgers, 12 October 1803, BW3:129; Preble to Isaac Hull, 12 October 1803, BW3:129; Preble to Charles Stewart, 12 October 1803, BW3:129; Preble to Somers, 12 October 1803, BW3:130.

111. *Constitution* logbook, 14 October 1803, BW3:134.

112. Secretary of State to Simpson, 4 and 10 November 1803, BW3:198–99.

113. Stewart to John Gore, 7 October 1803, BW3:112–13.

114. Gore to Stewart, 8 October 1803, BW3:113. Initially, Gore demurred on whether the men were actually on board the *Medusa*. Joseph Tarbell, the commander of the prize crew, led a mission through Gibraltar to trace the men's whereabouts, in fine detective form. He found them, as he had suspected, on the *Medusa*. BW3:133–34.

115. Stewart to Preble, 9 October 1803, BW3:121.

116. Christopher McKee argues that foreign-born seamen represented a majority of sailors shipped from New York in 1801, as well as a majority of the *Philadelphia*'s crew in 1803; most of these foreign-born sailors were British. We can extrapolate from these numbers to assert that most American naval vessels had a similar makeup. McKee, "Foreign Seamen in the United States Navy," 388.

117. Izard to Mrs. Ralph Izard, 11 October 1803, BW3:127.

118. Wadsworth letterbook, 10 November 1803, BW3:212.

119. Preble to Captain Sutton, 19 October 1803, BW3:154–55.

120. Correspondence between Hart and Preble, 20–22 October 1803, BW3:155–159.

121. 10 August 1801, BW1:545–46; 7 August 1802, BW2:227–28. See BW2:68, BW2:116, BW2:150, BW2:247 for examples of cordial relations.

122. Preble logbook, 23 October 1803, BW3:161; Wadsworth letterbook, 13 January 1804, Longfellow House.

123. Wadsworth journal, 10 November 1803, BW3:212.

124. Nissen to Cathcart, 28 September 1803, BW3:92.

125. Bainbridge to Preble, 4 October 1803, BW3:103.

126. Preble to Secretary of the Navy, 18 September 1803, BW3:58–59.

127. Morris to Secretary of the Navy, 26 December 1802, BW2:382.

128. Preble to Secretary of the Navy, 23 October 1803, BW3:161.

129. Preble to Secretary of the Navy, 23 October 1803, BW3:161–62.

130. Mustafa Pasha (Bobba Mustapha) to Thomas Jefferson, 14 October 1803, BW3:132.

131. O'Brien to Secretary of State, 15 October 1803, BW3:134–35.

132. O'Brien to Secretary of State, 15 October 1803, BW3:135–36.

133. Bainbridge to Secretary of the Navy, 1 November 1803, BW3:172.

134. Bainbridge to Preble, 6 November 1803, BW3:173.

135. Bainbridge to Preble, 1 November 1803, BW3:171; Bainbridge to Secretary of the Navy, 1 November 1803, BW3:171–73.

136. Secretary of the Navy to Bainbridge, 23 December 1802, BW2:337.

137. Preble to Hull, 7 November 1803, BW3:205.

138. Preble to Secretary of the Navy, 9 November 1803, BW3:210.

139. Preble to James Monroe, 12 November 1803, BW3:215–16.

140. Preble to Lear, 13 November 1803, BW3:218.

141. Preble diary, 24 November 1803, BW3:175.

142. Cathcart to Preble, 18 November 1803, BW3:228–29.

143. See Dale to Humphreys, 28 October 1801, BW1:611; Eaton to Secretary of State, 8 June 1802, BW2:169; Humphreys, *Miscellaneous Works*, 71.

144. Enthoven, "From the Halls of Montezuma," 120–22.

145. Bainbridge to Preble, 25 November 1803, BW3:175–76.

146. The minister in charge of that mission was William Loughton Smith, who had smoothed over the incident between the *Adams* and the French in August 1803. "October Meeting, 1917," 27.

147. Cathcart to Preble, 17 November 1803, BW3:226.

148. Bainbridge to Preble, 5 December 1803, BW3:253.

149. Bainbridge to Preble, 15 November 1803, BW3:223–24.

150. Preble memorandum book, 28 November 1803, BW3:242.

151. Preble diary, 29 November 1803, BW3:243.

152. Preble to Secretary of the Navy, 10 December 1803, BW3:258.

153. Preble diary, 9 December 1803, BW3:256.

154. Preble to Secretary of the Navy, 10 December 1803, BW3:256.

155. *Constitution* logbook, 29 November 1803, BW3:243–44.

156. Preble to Secretary of the Navy, 10 December 1803, BW3:258.

157. Rosenstock, "The House of Bacri and Busnach," 347.

158. O'Brien to William Smith, 10 January 1801, BW1:411.

159. Lear to Secretary of State, 2 December 1803, BW3:246.

160. Joseph Yznardi to Secretary of State, 10 December 1803, BW3:261.

161. Lear to Davis, 18 December 1803, BW3:278.

162. Lear to Secretary of State, 2 December 1803, BW3:245–49.

163. Lear to Dubois Thainville, 2 December 1803, BW3:249.

164. Lear to Bainbridge, 16 December 1803, BW3:274–75.

165. *Green Mountain Patriot* (Peacham, VT), 1 June 1803, America's Historical Newspapers; Lear to Davis, 17 December 1803, BW3:277.

166. Lear to Trigge, 3 December 1803, BW3:250.

167. Preble to Secretary of the Navy, 10 December 1803, BW3:257.

168. Preble to Nissen, 19 December 1803, BW3:279.

169. Dale to Secretary of the Navy, 1 October 1801, BW1:591.

170. O'Brien to Madison, 11 October 1802, JM, http://rotunda.upress.virginia.edu
/founders/JSMN-02-91-02-0513.

171. Preble to Pulis, 28 December 1803, BW3:300.

Chapter 5 · A Secret Expedition

1. Charles Pinckney to Tobias Lear, 18 January 1804, BW3:348–49.

2. Charles G. Koenig to M. Wallen, 28 February 1804, BW3:461–62.

3. Talleyrand to Robert Livingston, 17 January 1804, BW3:335–36.

4. Harris to Aleksandr R. Vorontsov, 20 January 1804, Trask et al., *The United States and Russia*, 391.

5. Vorontsov to Harris, 25 January 1804, Trask et al., *The United States and Russia*, 392.

6. Russia's foreign minister, Adam Czartoryski, was responsible for the empire's shift from pro-France to anti-Bonaparte over the span of 1801 to 1803, according to W. H. Zawadzki. Zawadzki, "Prince Adam Czartoryski and Napoleonic France," 245–46.

7. Mikaberidze, *The Napoleonic Wars*, 116.

8. Harris to Madison, 17 November 1803, JM, http://rotunda.upress.virginia.edu
/founders/JSMN-02-06-02-0062.

9. Robert Livingston to Pierre D'Oubril, 26 March 1804, Trask et al., *The United States and Russia*, 398–99.

10. Cathcart to Bainbridge, 23 January 1804, BW3:353–54.

11. John Johnson to William W. Burrows, 24 January 1804, BW3:357.

12. Preble to Prime Minister of the Bashaw of Tripoli, 4 January 1804, BW3:312–13.

13. Preble diary, 28 January 1804, BW3:371.

14. *Constitution* logbook, 28 January 1804, BW3:371.

15. Preble to General Brune, 4 March 1804, BW3:469.

16. Preble to General Brune, 4 March 1804, BW3:470; Preble diary, 10 March 1804, BW3:485.

17. Preble to Captain Pasha, 7 March 1804, BW3:480–81.

18. White, *Piracy and Law in the Ottoman*, 105.

19. The Russian ship was the *Madonna di Catapoliani*, of which much more will be said later.

20. Bainbridge to Preble, 18 January 1804, BW3:346–47.

21. Bainbridge to Preble, 17 February 1804, BW3:431.

22. Bainbridge to Preble, 18 February 1804, BW3:432.

23. Preble to Lear, 31 January 1804, BW3:378–79.

24. Preble to Secretary of the Navy, 3 February 1804, BW3:384.

25. Preble memo book, 3 February 1804, BW3:388.

26. *Constitution* logbook, 3 February 1804, BW3:388.

27. DeKrafft journal, 3 February 1804, BW3:389.

28. For a more detailed description of the action on the *Philadelphia*, see Toll, *Six Frigates*, 207–210.

29. McKee, *Edward Preble*, 197; "Statement concerning the destruction of the Frigate *Philadelphia*," BW3:423.

30. Decatur to Preble, 17 February 1804, BW3:414–15.

31. Stewart to Preble, 19 February 1804, BW3:415. For more on the burning of the *Philadelphia*, see Leiner, *Prisoners of the Bashaw*, 122–23.

32. Declaration concerning the *Mastico*, 2 February 1804, BW3:181.

33. McKee, *Edward Preble*, 196.

34. McKee records that Catalano wanted to board before Decatur was ready to do so; McKee, *Edward Preble*, 197. In addition, Catalano later gave a deposition that he thought the *Philadelphia*, with his help as a pilot, could have been raised and retaken rather than destroyed. No one else shared his opinion on this matter at the time; "Certificate of Salvatore Catalano," BW3:421.

35. Izard to Mrs. Izard, 20 February 1804, BW3:417.

36. Nicholas Nissen reported on their condition to his counterpart in Marseilles, 29 February 1804, BW3:421–22. See also Leiner, *Prisoners of the Bashaw*, 132.

37. Leiner, *Prisoners of the Bashaw*, 132.

38. Nissen to Preble, 20 February 1804, BW3:446–47.

39. Secretary of the Navy to Preble, 22 May 1804, BW3:427.

40. Resolution of 28 November 1804, BW3:428.

41. Davis to Lear, 9 March 1804, BW3:483.

42. Preble to Secretary of the Navy, 19 February 1804, BW3:439.

43. Lear to Madison, 7 May 1804, JM, http://rotunda.upress.virginia.edu/founders/JSMN-02-07-02-0176.

44. Lear to Preble, 23 March 1804, BW3:516–17.

45. Dghies to Preble, 26 March 1804, BW3:527.

46. Preble to Dghies, 27 March 1804, BW3:535–36.

47. Preble to Beaussier, 27 March 1804, BW3:535.

48. See Leiner, *Prisoners of the Bashaw*, 130.

49. Beaussier to Preble, 28 March 1804, BW3:543–44.

50. Villettes to Preble, 13 January 1804, BW3:328; Preble to Villettes, BW3:333.

51. Schembri to Preble, 16 February–22 March 1804, BW3:511–13.

52. Preble to Schembri, 19 September 1804, BW3:513; Preble to Higgins, 23 February 1803, BW3:452.

53. Gregory, *Malta, Britain, and the European Powers*, 202, 208.

54. Preble to Alexander Ball, 24 February 1804, BW3:454–55.

55. Preble to Secretary of the Navy, 19 April 1804, BW4:41–43. The previous account of the *Santissimo Crocifesso* comes from this source.

56. Preble diary, 7 June 1804, BW4:163.

57. Stewart to Preble, 22 March 1804, BW3:511.

58. P. d'Karpow to Preble, 18 May 1804, BW4:107.

59. Talleyrand to Livingston, 30 January 1804, BW3:372.

60. Petrie, *Prize Game*, 107.

61. Secretary of the Navy to Preble, 4 February 1804, BW3:389.

62. Preble to John Smith, 3 February 1804, BW3:387–88.

63. N. de Manzo to John S. M. Matthieu, 3 May 1804, BW4:83.

64. Preble to Secretary of the Navy, 19 April 1804, BW4:40.

65. Matthieu to Preble, 5 May 1804, BW4:86.

66. Drew, *The Law of Maritime Blockade*, 2.

67. D'Karpow to Preble, 18 May 1804, BW4:107.

68. Cobbett, *Leading Cases and Opinions on International Law*, x.

69. Davis to Preble, 18 May 1804, BW4:109–110 (emphasis in original).

70. Preble diary, 22 April 1804, BW4:53.

71. Gregorio to Preble, 21 April 1804, BW4:47.

72. Preble diary, 22 April 1804, BW4:53.

73. Mrs. F. Leckie to Preble, 21 April 1804, BW4:46.

74. Preble to Mrs. F. Leckie, 21 April 1804, BW4:46–47.

75. Baker, *Written on the Water*, 193–95.

76. Preble memorandum book, 22 April 1804, BW4:52.

77. Preble to Gregorio, 23 April 1804, BW4:56.

78. Anderson to Charles Stewart, 31 May 1804, BW4:136.

79. Preble to Harris, 26 May 1804, Trask et al., *The United States and Russia*, 403. See also Preble to M. D'Italinsky, 6 June 1804, BW4:159.

80. DeKrafft journal, 18 March 1804, BW3:502–3.

81. Preble to Secretary of the Navy, 19 April 1804, BW4:41.

82. DeKrafft journal, 20 March 1804, BW3:508.

83. Preble to Secretary of the Navy, 20 January 1804, BW3:350.

84. Leiner, *Prisoners of the Bashaw*, 146.

85. Schembri to Preble, 22 March 1804? (probably a later date; 22 March relates to the capture of the *Madonna di Catapoliani*), BW3:511–13.

86. Some scholars believe that Schembri and Preble did have some kind of arrangement. Among the scholars who think that Preble had given Schembri some encouragement, at least, are McKee, *Edward Preble*, 188; Tucker, *Stephen Decatur*, 44; and Reid, *Intrepid Sailors*, 116.

87. Preble to Schembri, 19 September 1804, BW3:513–14.

88. Leiner, *Prisoners of the Bashaw*, 146.

89. O'Brien to Tobias Lear, 24 April 1804, BW4:60.

90. Farquhar to Preble, 11 April 1804, BW4:19–20.

91. Beaussier to Preble, 28 March 1804, BW3:543.

92. Preble diary, 28 March 1804, BW3:544–45.

93. Preble to Lear, 2 May 1804, BW4:82.

94. *Constitution* logbook, 18 April 1804, BW4:37.

95. *Constitution* logbook, 24 April 1804, BW4:61.

96. *Constitution* logbook, 25 April 1804, BW4:66.

97. *Constitution* logbook, 18 April 1804, BW4:37; Charles Morris journal, BW4:512.

98. Seamen of the USS *Enterprize* to Preble, 5 April 1804, BW4:11.

99. Jefferson to Hamouda, 27 January 1804, BW3:361–62.

100. Jefferson to Abraham Baldwin, 10 February 1802, TJ, http://rotunda.upress .virginia.edu/ founders/TSJN-01-36-02-0361.

101. American State Papers, Claims, 1:292–94.

102. Madison to Charles Pinckney, 21 April 1804, BW3:343.

103. Davis to Madison, 13 September 1803, Tunis consular dispatches, NARA.

104. Preble diary, 1 April 1804, BW4:1.

105. *Constitution* logbook, 4 April 1804, BW4:7; Preble to Davis, 4 April 1804, BW4:6.

106. Preble to Bey of Tunis, 5 April 1804, BW4:10.

107. Preble to Davis, 6 April 1804, BW4:13.

108. DeKrafft journal, 8 April 1804, BW4:16.

109. Preble to Davis, 6 April 1804, Tunis consular dispatches, NARA.

110. Preble to O'Brien, 31 January 1804, BW3:380. Goodin notes that O'Brien did not return to the United States until 1805 (despite desperately wanting to) because of the births of his children; in the meantime, he seemed willing to help the navy. Goodin, *Captives to Consuls*, 101–102.

111. Cathcart to Preble, 17 April 1804, BW4:32–33.

112. O'Brien to Lear, 24 April 1804, BW4:59.

113. O'Brien to Davis, 25 April 1804, BW4:65–66.

114. O'Brien to Davis, 1 May 1804, BW4:80.

115. Davis and O'Brien, "Remarks on the Affairs of the US at Tunis," 29 April 1804, BW4:73–74.

116. Preble to Secretary of the Navy, 14 March 1804, BW3:491.

117. Davis to Madison, 26 March 1804, JM, http://rotunda.upress.virginia.edu /founders/JSMN-02-06-02-0583.

118. Decatur to Preble, 15 March 1804, BW3:492.

119. Simpson to Preble, 22 February 1804, BW3:450–51.

120. Preble to Secretary of the Navy, 11 March 1804, BW3:485.

121. Simpson to Secretary of State, 28 February 1804, BW3:460–61.

122. Emperor of Morocco to Simpson, 18 March 1804, BW3:498.

123. Preble to Decatur, 20 February 1804, BW3:446; Decatur to Preble, 30 March 1804, BW3:546–47.

124. Preble to Broadbent, 20 February 1804, BW3:446.

125. Preble to Secretary of the Navy, 11 March 1804, BW3:486.

126. Jefferson, Message to Congress, 20 March 1804, BW3:506–7.

127. Secretary of the Navy to John Cassin, 21 March 1804, BW3:509.

128. Preble's diary, 21 January 1804, BW3:351.

129. Preble to Davis, 17 January 1804, BW3:341.

130. Preble to Secretary of the Navy, 3 February 1804, BW3:385–86.

131. Higgins to Preble, 9 February 1804, BW3:400.

132. Preble to Lear, 31 January 1804, BW3:378–79.

133. Cathcart to Cathalan, 3 February 1804, BW3:383.

134. Cathalan to Livingston, 13 February 1804, BW3:406.

135. Cathcart to Preble, 27 February 1804, BW3:458–59.

136. Cathcart to Preble, 19 February 1804, BW3:435–37.

137. Preble to Cathcart, 19 February 1804, BW3:437.

138. Abraham Gibbs to Preble, 21 February 1804, BW3:448. It's not certain that Gibbs had an actual commission from the United States to serve as consul, but he seems to have taken on some consular duties. He received an official commission in 1805. Smith, *America's Diplomats*, 84.

139. Cathcart to Sir John Acton, 5 March 1804, BW3:476.

140. Broadbent to Preble, 6 March 1804, BW3:478.

141. Acton to Cathcart, 27 March 1804, BW3:538.

142. Preble to Cathcart, 19 February 1804, BW3:437.

143. Cathcart to Madison, 29 November 1802, JM, http://rotunda.upress.virginia.edu /founders/JSMN-02-91-02-0551.

144. Folayan, "Tripoli and the War with the U.S.A.," 263.

145. Richard Farquhar to Jefferson, 15 November 1803, BW3:222.

146. Pulis to Preble, 26 November 1803, BW3:236.

147. Salvatore Busuttil to commanding officer of the squadron, 4 January 1804, BW3:314. The letter enclosed was probably from 20 November 1802, Richard Valentine Morris to the agent of Hamet Karamanli, BW2:317.

148. Pulis to Madison, 20 January 1804, JM, http://rotunda.upress.virginia.edu /founders/JSMN-02-06-02–0338.

149. Busuttil to Preble, 22 January 1804, BW3:352.

150. Farquhar to Preble, 1 February 1804, BW3:380.

151. Pulis to Preble, 10 February 1804, BW3:401.

152. Beaussier to Preble, 28 March 1804, BW3:544; Enthoven, "From the Halls of Montezuma," 123.

153. Preble to Secretary of the Navy, 11 March 1804, BW3:486.

154. Bauer, "Republicans of Letters," 149.

155. Preble to Secretary of the Navy, 11 March 1804, BW3:487.

156. Gavino to Secretary of State, 22 March 1804, BW3:515.

157. Preble diary, 15 March 1804, BW3:493.

158. Wadsworth to Nancy Doane, 17 March 1804, BW3:495.

159. McDonogh to Preble, 19 March 1804, BW3:504–5. The United States' relationship with McDonogh changed frequently.

160. Preble to Livingston, 18 March 1804, BW3:498.

161. Preble to Livingston, 18 March 1804, BW3:499.

162. Barnes to Madison, 28 March 1804, JM, http://rotunda.upress.virginia.edu /founders/JSMN-02-06-02-0591. Preble to Barnes, 18 March 1804, BW3:500; Preble to Secretary of State, 3 June 1804, BW4:145.

163. Preble to Cathcart, 18 March 1804, BW3:501.

164. Cathcart to Preble, 17 April 1804, BW4:31–33.

165. Enthoven, "From the Halls of Montezuma," 125.

Chapter 6 · A Considerable Force

1. Davis to Bainbridge, 27 May 1804, BW4:122 (emphasis in original).

2. Preble to Beaussier, 12 June 1804, BW4:180–81.

3. Beaussier to Preble, 13 June 1804, BW4:184.

4. Preble to Secretary of the Navy, 14 June 1804, BW4:188.

5. Bainbridge to Davis, 15 June 1804, BW4:195.

6. Bainbridge to Preble, 8 July 1804, BW4:258.

7. Beaussier to Preble, 6 July 1804, BW4:251.

8. Bainbridge to Davis, 17 June 1804, BW4:199–200.

9. Leiner, *Prisoners of the Bashaw*, 151.

10. Preble to Secretary of the Navy, 14 June 1804, BW4:190.

11. Davis to Don Joseph Noguera, 22 June 1804, BW4:216–17.

12. Noguera to Preble, 24 June 1804, BW4:224.

13. Preble to Noguera, 18 July 1804, BW4:275.

14. Simpson to Samuel Barron, 1 August 1804, BW4:329.

15. Preble diary, 13 May 1804, BW4:98.

16. Tucker, *The Jeffersonian Gunboat Navy*, 14; *Constitution* log, 29 May 1804, BW4:128–29.

17. Preble to Cathcart, 15 May 1804, BW4:102.

18. Secretary of the Navy to Preble, 22 May 1804, BW4:114–15.

19. Preble to Livingston, 26 May 1804, BW4:121; Preble to John Broadbent, 28 May 1804, BW4:126.

20. Preble diary, 1 June 1804, BW4:142.

21. Preble to Cathcart, 28 May 1804, BW4:126.

22. Preble to Davis, 20 June 1804, BW4:210; James Wells to Preble, 20 June 1804, BW4:210.

23. Wadsworth to unknown, 28 June 1804, BW4:234.

24. Wadsworth to unknown, 28 June 1804, BW4:234.

25. Stewart to Preble, 8 July 1804, BW4:254.

26. Preble to commanders, 12 July 1804, BW4:267–68.

27. *Constitution* logbook, 12 July 1804, BW4:269.

28. Preble diary, 16 July 1804, BW4:272–73.

29. *Constitution* logbook, 17 July 1804, BW4:274.

30. Preble diary, 17 March 1804, BW4:274.

31. Preble diary, 21 July 1804, BW4:284.

32. Preble to Secretary of the Navy, 26 Julyff. 1804, BW4:294. The general outlines of the events described during this assault on Tripoli are all taken from this same letter.

33. Preble to Beaussier, 4 August 1804, BW4:363; Preble to Secretary of the Navy, n.d., BW4:298.

34. *Constitution* logbook, 5 August 1804, BW4:365–66.

35. Beaussier to Preble, 6 August 1804, BW4:369.

36. Preble diary, 7 August 1804, BW4:376.

37. Secretary of the Navy to Preble, 22 May 1804, BW4:114–15; Preble to Secretary of the Navy, 26 Julyff. 1804, BW4:301.

38. Preble to Beaussier, 9 August 1804, BW4:389.

39. Beaussier to Preble, 10 August 1804, BW4:393.

40. Letter from Noadiah Morris, 7 September 1804, BW4:356. Morris had switched from being the chaplain on the *Constitution* to being the purser in December 1803.

41. Preble to William Higgins, 15 August 1804, BW4:417–18; e.g., 19 August 1804, BW4:433.

42. Preble diary, 16 August 1804, BW4:420.

43. *Constitution* logbook, 31 August 1804, BW4:493.

44. *Constitution* logbook, 31 August 1804, BW4:493; John Darby journal, 1 September 1804, BW4:498; *Constitution* logbook, 2 September 1804, BW4:499.

45. Preble to Secretary of the Navy, 26 Julyff. 1804, BW4:306; Wadsworth journal, undated 1804, Longfellow House.

46. Preble to Schomberg, 20 August 1804, BW4:437.

47. Preble to Decatur, 6 September 1804, BW4:522.

48. Preble to Acton, 6 September 1804, BW4:523.

49. Beaussier to Preble, 29 August 1804, BW4:481–82.

50. *Constitution* logbook, 10 September 1804, BW5:14.

51. Preble to Secretary of the Navy, 26 Julyff. 1804, BW4:307; Barron to Preble, 11 September 1804, BW5:15.

52. Letter from Morris, 7 September 1804, BW4:358.

53. Darby journal, 9 August 1804, BW4:391.

54. Letter from Morris, 7 September 1804, BW4:358.

55. Darby journal, 7 August 1804, BW4:385.

56. Davis to Preble, 21 August 1804, BW4:442.

57. Ball to Preble, 30 August 1804, BW4:488.

58. Rodgers to Secretary of the Navy, 12 August 1804, BW4:403.

59. Yznardi to Preble, 31 August 1804, BW4:491.

60. Barron to Rodgers, 14 August 1804, BW4:414.

61. Rodgers to James Barron, 17 August 1804, BW4:424.

62. Rodgers to Samuel Barron, 27 August 1804, BW4:467–68.

63. Journal of William Eaton, 21 August 1804, BW4:445.

64. Barron to Isaac Hull, 15 September 1804, BW5:20.

65. Preble to Lt. Charles Gordon, 17 September 1804, BW5:30.

66. Preble to Barron, 17 September 1804, BW5:31.

67. Lear to Secretary of State, 3 November 1804, BW5:114.

68. Eaton journal, 27 September 1804, BW5:56.

69. Eaton to Secretary of the Navy, 27 October 1804, BW5:35.

70. *Constitution* logbook, 23 October 1804, BW5:95.

71. *Constitution* logbook, 24–26 October 1804, BW5:97, 98, 101.

72. Darby journal, 7 October 1804, BW5:78.

73. Rodgers to Barron, 27 October 1804, BW5:102–3.

74. Gavino to Secretary of State, 11 November 1804, BW5:135.

75. Newman, "Reading the Bodies of Early American Seafarers," 69.

76. *Argus* journal, 7–8 November 1804, BW5:128–29. Eaton records an outbreak of smallpox on the *Argus*. Eaton journal, 8 November 1804, BW5:129.

77. Note to certificate of John Rodgers, 1 November 1804, BW5:109.

78. Barron to Rodgers, 3 November 1804, BW5:116.

79. Preble to Barron, 24 September 1804, BW5:48–49; Brings, "Navy Medicine Comes Ashore," 267.

80. Barron and Rodgers to Edward Cutbush, 10 November 1804, BW5:133.

81. Chauncey to Secretary of the Navy, 26 February 1805, BW5:119; *John Adams* logbook, 30 December 1804, BW5:228. It is unknown whether the Neapolitan government ever got its anchors back.

82. Preble to Lear, 23 December 1804, BW5:208.

83. Bainbridge to Davis, 14 October 1804, BW5:83.

84. Lear to Secretary of State, 3 November 1804, BW5:114.

85. Barron to Lear, 13 November 1804, BW5:139–40.

86. Loomis journal, 6 December 1804, BW5:176.

87. Loomis journal, 10 December 1804, BW5:181.

88. Lear to Robert Montgomery, 16 December 1804, BW5:196.

89. Rodgers to Charles Stewart, 19 December 1804, BW5:199.

90. Simpson to Rodgers, 24 December 1804, BW5:212.

91. Pinckney to Secretary of State, 12 December 1804, BW5:183–84.

92. Rodgers to Kirkpatrick, 30 December 1804, BW5:227.

93. Jefferson to Judge Tyler, 29 March 1805, BW5:465.

94. Lear to Dyson, 27 December 1804, BW5:221.

95. Rodgers to Jarvis, 1 January 1805, BW5:245.

96. Jarvis to Rodgers, 1 January 1805, BW5:245–46.

97. Rodgers to Jarvis, 1 January 1805, BW5:246.

98. Jarvis to Rodgers, 3 January 1805, BW5:250–51.

99. Rodgers to Jarvis, 4 January 1805, BW5:253–54.

100. Jarvis to Secretary of State, 19 January 1805, BW5:291–92.

101. Gambier to Jarvis, 15 January 1805, BW5:281.

102. Rodgers to Jarvis, 16 January 1805, BW5:282–83.

103. Rodgers to Jarvis, 19 January 1805, BW5:294.

104. Jarvis to Rodgers, 19 January 1805, BW5:294.

105. Rodgers to Jarvis, 20 January 1805, BW5:296; Jarvis to Rodgers, 22 January 1805, BW5:298.

106. Jarvis to Secretary of State, 5 January 1805, BW5:255–57.

107. Anthony Terry to Secretary of State, 5 January 1805, BW5:259; Gavino to Preble, 6 January 1805, BW5:260–61.

108. Barron to Lear, 11 January 1805, BW5:276–77.

109. Davis to Preble, 20 March 1805, BW5:431–32.

110. For a lengthy explanation of the many changes over the course of the early nineteenth century, see Schroeder, *The Transformation of European Politics, 1763–1848*.

111. William Riggin to Secretary of State, 1 January 1805, BW5:247.

112. Thomas Robinson to Secretary of the Navy, 27 January 1805, BW5:309–11.

113. Robinson to Secretary of the Navy, 18 February 1805, BW5:358.

114. Charles Wadsworth to accountant of the navy, 5 January 1805, BW5:260.

115. Chauncey logbook, 6 January 1805, BW5:262.

116. Gavino to Preble, 6 January 1805, BW5:261.

117. Preble to Simpson, 9 January 1805, BW5:269.

118. Lear to Barron, 10 January 1805, BW5:272–73.

119. Yznardi to Admiral John Orde, 27 February 1805, BW5:453.

120. Orde to Yznardi, 11 March 1805, BW5:453–54.

121. Campbell to Secretary of the Navy, 11 April 1805, BW5:502–3; Barron to Lear, 14 January 1805, BW5:277.

122. Barron to Preble, 15 November 1804, BW5:143.

123. Barron to General Acton, 10 January 1805, BW5:270–71.

124. Davis to Barron, 11 January 1805, BW5:274–75.

125. Barron to Nicolo de Manza, 15 January 1805, BW5:278–79; Barron to Levett Harris, 16 January 1805, BW5:283–86.

126. Harris to Barron, 20 March 1805, BW5:428–30.

127. Barron to Ball, 20 March 1805, BW5:430–31.

128. Davis to Preble, 20 March 1805, BW5:431–32.

129. Timothy Mountford to Gavino, 1 February 1805, BW5:325–26.

130. Lear to Lord Nelson, 19 February 1805, BW5:363–64.

131. Lear to Mountford, 30 April 1805, BW5:557–60.

132. Simpson to Barron, 13 February 1805, BW5:345–46.

133. Secretary of the Navy to Stewart, 24 April 1805, BW5:535.

134. Dyson to Preble, 9 February 1805, BW5:341.

135. Charles Morris journal, 11 February 1805, BW5:343.

136. Loomis journal, 11 February 1805, BW5:344.

137. Simpson to Rodgers, 13 February 1805, BW5:347–48.

138. Rodgers to Secretary of the Navy, 16 February 1805, BW5:356–57.

139. Orders from Robert Denison to Rodgers, 21 February 1805; Barron to Dent, 21 February 1805, BW5:365; Barron to Rodgers, 28 February 1805, BW5:377.

140. Samuel Barron to James Barron, 3 March 1805, BW5:386–87.

141. James Barron to Robinson, 21 March 1805, BW5:434.

142. Robinson to James Barron, 3 April 1805, BW5:479.

143. Robinson to Samuel Barron, 13 April 1805, BW5:507.

144. Barron to Robinson, 23 April 1805, BW5:531.

145. Robinson to Secretary of the Navy, 23 April 1805, BW5:531–32.

146. Barron to Rodgers, 28 February 1805, BW5:378.

147. Campbell to Rodgers, 9 March 1805, BW5:401.

148. Rodgers to Campbell, 9 March 1805, BW5:401.

149. Rodgers to Campbell, 12 March 1805, BW5:409.

150. Rodgers to Barron, 19 March 1805, BW5:425–26.

151. Rodgers to Barron, 19 March 1805, BW5:426.

152. Dearden, *A Nest of Corsairs*, 29; Bainbridge to Lear, 27 January 1805, BW5:311–12.

153. Bainbridge to Barron, 16 March 1805, BW5:417.

154. Nissen to Barron, 18 March 1805, BW5:421–23

155. Lear to Bainbridge, 28 March 1805, BW5:461–62.

156. Lear to Don Joseph de Souza; Lear to Nissen; Lear to Beaussier, 28 March 1805, BW5:463–64.

157. Barron to Rodgers, 1 April 1805, BW5:475.

158. Rodgers to Campbell, 5 April 1805, BW5:482–83.

159. Rodgers to Lear, 17 April 1805, BW5:518.

160. Secretary of the Navy to Barron, 23 April 1805, BW5:532.

161. Rodgers to Barron, 25 April 1805, BW5:539.

Chapter 7 · *Rather a Rabble than an Army*

1. Eaton to Secretary of the Navy, 18 September 1804, BW5:33–34.

2. Eaton to Secretary of the Navy, 27 October 1804, BW5:35.

3. Eaton journal, 26 September 1804, BW5:55.

4. Farquhar to Barron, 1 November 1804, BW5:109–110; Busuttil to Barron, 1 November 1804, BW5:110.

5. Lear to Secretary of State, 3 November 1804, BW5:116.

6. Bainbridge to Lear, 11 November 1804, BW5:136.

7. Bainbridge to Davis, 22 November 1804, BW5:155.

8. Barron to Hull, 10 November 1804, BW5:134.

9. Barron to Lear, 13 November 1804, BW5:139.

10. Eaton to Secretary of the Navy, 14 November 1804, BW5:140–41.

11. Eaton to Ball, 16 November 1804, BW5:143.

12. Ball to Eaton, 16 November 1804, BW5:144.

13. Eaton to Secretary of the Navy, 28 November 1804, BW5:166.

14. Eaton journal, 30 November 1804, BW5:169.

15. A resident is a diplomatic official who is a permanent resident of another country, often a colonized one, but with official diplomatic standing for his country of origin. He is less connected to commercial concerns than a consul, but also has more permanency than an envoy. It was a position of indirect rule over a subject nation, including maintaining political ties with other nations and advocating for citizens who got into trouble in the colonies. For a study on how political residents functioned, see Onley, "Britain's Native Agents in Arabia and Persia in the Nineteenth Century," 129–37.

16. Tignor, *Egypt*, 208; Sayyid-Marsot, *A History of Egypt*, 59–64.

17. Eaton to Ball, 13 and 16 December 1804, BW5:190–92.

18. Eaton to John Cotton Smith, 26 December 1804, in Prentiss, *Life of Eaton*, 284–85.

19. Coleridge, "Essay IX," 254–55.

20. Eaton to Hamet, 4 December 1804, BW5:172–73.

21. Eaton journal, 4 December 1805, BW5:173.

22. Eaton journal, 6 and 7 December 1804, BW5:175, 177.

23. Eaton journal, 8 December 1804, BW5:178.

24. Eaton to Secretary of the Navy, 13 December 1804, BW5:188–89.

25. Eaton to Secretary of the Navy, 13 December 1804, BW5:189.

26. Eaton to Hamet, 10 December 1804, BW5:180.

27. Eaton to Secretary of the Navy, 13 December 1804, BW5:189.

28. Eaton to Hull, 19 December 1804, BW5:202.

29. Hull to Eaton, 24 December 1804, BW5:214–15.

30. Eaton to Francisco Mendrici, 13 December 1804; Eaton to Secretary of the Navy, 13 December 1804, BW5:185–86.

31. Hull to Eaton, 27 December 1804, BW5:222.

32. Eaton to Hull, 8 January 1805, BW5:268.

33. Eaton to Hull, 29–31 December 1804, BW5:223–25.

34. Eaton to Hull, 3 January 1805, BW5:251–52.

35. Hull to Eaton, 5 January 1805, BW5:254–55.

36. Hamet Karamanli to Eaton, 3 January 1805, BW5:252.

37. Eaton to Hull, 8 January 1805, BW5:268; Eaton to Hull, 29 January 1805, BW5:319.

38. Hull to Eaton, 11 January 1805, BW5:275.

39. Eaton to Hull, 14 January 1805, BW5:277–78.

40. Hamet Karamanli to Eaton, 15 January 1805, BW5:279.

41. Eaton to Hamet Karamanli, 15 January 1805, BW5:279; Prentiss, *Life of Eaton*, 288.

42. Eaton to Preble, 25 January 1805ff., in Prentiss, *Life of Eaton*, 285–93.

43. Hull to Eaton, 28 January 1805, BW5:317.

44. Hull to Eaton, 29 January 1805, BW5:320.

45. Eaton to Hull, 31 January 1805, BW5:323.

46. Hull to Eaton, 5 February 1805, BW5:333.

47. Eaton to Preble, 25 January 1805ff., in Prentiss, *Life of Eaton*, 285–93.

48. Eaton to Secretary of the Navy, 13 February 1805, BW5:349–50.

49. Viceroy of Cairo to Hamet Karamanli, 8 February 1805, BW5:339–40.

50. Farquhar to Hull, 12 February 1805, BW5:344.

51. Hull to Farquhar, 13 February 1805, BW5:352.

52. Eaton journal, 3 March 1805, BW5:388, 6 April 1805, BW5:487.

53. Eaton to Secretary of the Navy, 13 February 1805, BW5:350–51.

54. Eaton to Barron, 14 February 1805, BW5:353; Hamet to Barron, 15 February 1805, BW5:356.

55. Eaton to Barron, 14 February 1805, BW5:353–54.

56. Convention between the United States of America and his Highness, Hamet, Caramanly, Bashaw of Tripoli, 23 February 1805, BW5:367–69.

57. Convention between the United States of America and his Highness, Hamet, Caramanly, Bashaw of Tripoli, 23 February 1805, BW5:367–69.

58. Eaton journal, 2 March 1805, BW5:384.

59. Eaton to Drovetti, 3 March 1805, BW5:388.

60. Samuel Briggs to Drovetti, 5 March 1805, BW5:390.

61. Eaton to Briggs Brothers, 7 March 1805, BW5:395–96.

62. Eaton journal, 5 March 1805, BW5:391.

63. Briggs Brothers to Eaton, 7 March 1805, BW5:395.

64. Eaton journal, 6 March 1805, BW5:394. For a more granular look at the progress of the expedition, see http://abbymullen.org/projects/barbary/eaton.html. For a more fleshed-out treatment of the expedition, see Reid, *To the Walls of Derne*.

65. Eaton journal, 8 March 1805, BW5:398–99.

66. For a discussion of the political and social conflicts between the city and the hinterland, see McLachlan, "Tripoli and Tripolitania," 285–94.

67. Eaton journal, 20 March 1805, BW5:432–33.

68. Eaton journal, 23 March 1805, BW5:448.

69. Barron to Eaton, 22 March 1805, BW5:438–41 (emphasis in original); Barron to Secretary of the Navy, 6 April 1805, BW5:485–86.

70. Eaton journal, 22 March 1805, BW5:444.

71. Eaton journal, 23 March 1805, BW5:448.

72. Eaton journal, 25 March 1805, BW5:454.

73. Eaton journal, 26 March 1805, BW5:456.

74. Eaton journal, 27 March 1805, BW5:459.

75. Kidd, "Is It Worse to Follow Mahomet," 786; for more on Eaton's antisemitism, see Peskin, "American Exception?," 299–317.

76. Proclamation of William Eaton to the Inhabitants of Tripoli, 29 March 1805, BW5:467–70.

77. Dearden, *A Nest of Corsairs*, 189–90.

78. Eaton journal, 6 April 1805, BW5:487.

79. Eaton journal, 8 April 1805, BW5:490–91.

80. Hull to Eaton, 9 April 1805, BW5:493–94.

81. Eaton journal, 10 April 1805, BW5:498–99; Eaton journal, 12 April 1805, BW5:505–6.

82. Eaton journal, 14 April 1805, BW5:509–10.

83. Bainbridge to Barron, 12 April 1805, BW5:505.

84. Eaton journal, 15–22 April 1805, BW5:512–13.

85. Eaton to Hull, 21 April 1805, BW5:527–28.

86. O'Bannon to Hull, 21 April 1805, BW5:528; George Mann to Hull, 21 April 1805, BW5:528.

87. Hull to Barron, 22 April 1805, BW5:529–30.

88. Eaton journal, 23 April 1805, BW5:533.

89. Eaton journal, 24 April 1805, BW5:538.

90. Hull to John H. Dent, 25 April 1805, BW5:540.

91. Eaton journal, 25 April 1805, BW5:540–41.

92. Eaton to Governor of Derna, 26 April 1805, BW5:542.

93. Dent to Eaton, 26 April 1805, BW5:542.

94. Hull to Barron, 28 April 1805, BW5:547–48.

95. Eaton to Barron, 29 April 1805, BW5:550–53.

96. Hull to Samuel Evans, 30 April 1805, BW5:557; Hull to Barron, 29 April 1805, BW5:555–56.

97. Eaton journal, 8 May 1805, BW6:6.

98. Eaton to Hull, 13 May 1805, BW6:12.

99. Eaton journal, 13 May 1805, BW6:12–13.

100. Eaton to Barron, 15–17 May 1805, BW6:14–15.

101. *Argus* journal, 20 May 1805, BW6:27–28.

102. Eaton to Barron, 2 June 1805, BW6:59.

103. Lear to Rodgers, 1 May 1805, BW6:1.

104. Davis to Lear, 9 May 1805, BW6:7–8.

105. Dey of Algiers to Bashaw of Tripoli, 15 May 1805?, BW6:17–18.

106. Robinson to James Barron, 1 May 1805, BW6:2–3.

107. Morris journal, 11 May 1805, BW6:10; *Constitution* logbook, 10 May 1805, BW6:9.

108. Lear to Davis, 15 May 1805, BW6:16–17.

109. Barron to Lear, 18 May 1805, BW6:22.

110. Barron to Rodgers, 22 May 1805, BW6:32.

111. Morris journal, 27 May 1805, BW6:52.

112. Rodgers to Barron, 28–30 May 1805, BW6:52–53.

113. Davis to Barron, 29 May 1805, BW6:56–57.

114. Degen, Purviance, and Co. to Barron, 29 May 1805, BW6:57.

115. Barron to Eaton, 19 May 1805, BW6:25–26.

116. Rodgers to Barron, 29 May 1805, BW6:56.

117. Eaton to Barron, 29 May–11 June 1805, BW6:58–63.

118. This section on the peace negotiations is taken, unless otherwise indicated, from Lear to Madison, 5 July 1805, *Founders Online*, National Archives, http://founders .archives.gov/documents/Madison/02-10-02-0016.

119. Report of Nicholas Nissen, 10 June 1805, BW6:103–4.

120. Journal of Hezekiah Loomis, 8 June 1805, RG 45, NARA.

121. Lear to Ridgely, 6 June 1805, BW6:93. Cowdery journal, 6 June 1805, BW6:96.

122. Lear to Rodgers, 4 June 1805, BW6:82.

123. Lear to Beaussier, 5 June 1805, BW6:88.

124. Rodgers to Beaussier, 20 June 1805, BW6:128.

125. For a copy of the treaty in Arabic and in English, as well as a discussion of the differences between the two, see Miller, *Treaties and Other International Acts of the United States of America*, 2:531–56.

126. Dyson to Rodgers, 8 June 1805, BW6:100.

127. Rodgers to Thomas W. Hooper, 12 June 1805, BW6:110.

128. Morris journal, 29 June 1805, BW6:144.

129. Robinson to Barron, 1 June 1805, BW6:71.

130. Haraden to Secretary of the Navy, 9 June 1805, BW6:103.

131. Robinson to Rodgers, 12 July 1805, BW6:133–35.

132. Rodgers to James Barron, 2 June 1805, BW6:75; Rodgers to Samuel Barron, 3 June 1805, BW6:78.

133. Rodgers to Lear, 5 June 1805, BW6:87.

134. Rodgers to Cox, 12 June 1805, BW6:112.

135. Robert Denison to Rodgers, 17 June 1805, BW6:123.

136. Davis to Rodgers, 20 June 1805, BW6:128–29.

137. Eaton to Hull, 5 June 1805, BW6:89.

138. Rodgers to Lear, 4 June 1805, BW6:83.

139. Rodgers to Eaton, 6 June 1805, BW6:91.

140. Lear to Rodgers, 6 June 1805, BW6:91.

141. Lear to Eaton, 6 June 1805, BW6:92.

142. Campbell to Eaton, 12 June 1805, BW6:111.

143. Eaton to Campbell, 12 June 1805, BW6:111.

144. Eaton to Rodgers, 13 June 1805, BW6:116–17.

145. De Gregorio to Rodgers, 29 June 1805, BW6:142.

146. Rodgers to Campbell, 29 June 1805, BW6:143.

147. Hamet Karamanli to Eaton, 29 June 1805, BW6:144.

148. R.W. Meade to Stewart, 31 May 1805, BW6:68–69.

149. Joseph J. Maxwell to General Castanio, 15 June 1805, BW6:119.

150. Gavino to Secretary of State, 22 June 1805, BW6:131.

151. Lawrence to Rodgers, 12 June 1805, BW6:112–13.

152. Shaw to Captain C. Boyle, 18 June 1805, BW6:124–25.

153. Rodgers to Ball, 25 June 1805, BW6:137–38.

154. Rodgers to Ball, 15 July 1805, BW6:182–83.

155. Rodgers to Higgins, 17 July 1805, BW6:186.

156. Charles L. Ridgely to Barron, 13 April 1805, BW5:508–9. The Reed that Ridgely speaks of was probably Midshipman George Washington Reed, also an officer on the *Nautilus*. See *Register of Officer Personnel, United States Navy and Marine Corps, and Ships' Data, 1801–1807*, 45; https//catalog.hathitrust.org/Record/001622556.

157. Broadbent to Barron, 17 June 1805, BW6:123.

158. Broadbent to Barron, 4 July 1805, BW6:159.

159. Rodgers to Davis, 29 June 1805, BW6:143.

160. Eaton to Hull, 26 July 1805, BW6:196.

161. *Constitution* logbook, 23 July 1805, BW6:195.

162. Loomis journal, 30 July 1805, BW6:198–99.

163. Rodgers to Hamouda, 2 August 1805, BW6:202.

164. Davis to Rodgers, 3 August 1805, BW6:203–4.

165. Rodgers to Davis, 3 August 1805, BW6:204.

166. Rodgers to Davis, 4 August 1805, BW6:206.

167. Hamouda to Lear, 5 August 1805, BW6:207–8.

168. Rodgers to Davis, 5 August 1805, BW6:208.

169. Rodgers to Davis, 8 August 1805, BW6:212.

170. Lear to Hamouda, 9 August 1805, BW6:222.

171. Rodgers to Hamouda, 11 August 1805, BW6:223.

172. Hamouda to Rodgers, 14 August 1805, BW6:227.
173. Rodgers to Hamouda, 16 August 1805, BW6:233.
174. Davis to Rodgers, 18 August 1805, BW6:236.
175. Rodgers to Lear, 19 August 1805, BW6:236.
176. Rodgers to Secretary of the Navy, 21 August 1805, BW6:240.

Conclusion

1. Rodgers to Secretary of the Navy, 21 August 1805, BW6:240; Suliman Melli Melli to James Madison, 31 December 1805, Tunis consular dispatches, NARA.

2. Melli Melli to James Madison, 18 March 1806, Tunis consular dispatches, NARA. The letters from Melli Melli to Madison seem to have been more like Cathcart's distillation of conversations he had with Melli Melli, rather than a dictation and translation, so even though they are signed by Melli Melli, they have Cathcart's characteristic elegant but overblown style.

3. Cathcart to Secretary of State, 4 August 1806, Tunis consular dispatches, NARA; Cathcart to Secretary of State, 30 August 1806, Tunis consular dispatches, NARA.

4. Rodgers to Secretary of the Navy, 19 March 1806, BW6:396.

5. Chauncey to Secretary of State, 9 June 1807, BW6:532.

6. Secretary of the Navy to James Barron, 12 September 1807, BW6:557.

7. Richard B. Jones to Secretary of State, 13 November 1812, Tripoli consular dispatches, NARA.

8. Mordecai Noah to Secretary of State, 29 July 1813, Tunis consular dispatches, NARA.

9. Richard B. Jones to Secretary of State, 13 November 1812, Tripoli consular dispatches, NARA.

10. Lambert, *Barbary Wars*, 184.

11. Shaler, *Sketches of Algiers*, iii.

12. The best (and one of the only) books about the Second Barbary War is Leiner, *The End of Barbary Terror*.

13. Wright and Macleod, "William Eaton's Relations with Aaron Burr," 523–25.

14. Long, "William Bainbridge and the Barron-Decatur Duel," 1979.

Archival Sources (Manuscript)

British Library, Additional Manuscripts MS34932
Henry Wadsworth Letterbook and Journal, Longfellow House–Washington's Headquarters National Historic Site
Hezekiah Loomis Journal, National Archives and Records Administration
James Leander Cathcart Papers, Library of Congress
Mediterranean Charts of Stephen Decatur, United States Naval Academy Museum Collection
Richard Dale Papers, Library of Congress

Archival Sources (Digitized)

"An Act Concerning Consuls and Vice-Consuls" (1792). Library of Congress Online. https://www.loc.gov/item/2020769578/.
"An Act to Provide a Naval Armament" (1794). Library of Congress Online. https://www.loc.gov/law/help/statutes-at-large/3rd-congress/session-1/c3s1ch12.pdf.
American Presidency Project. University of California, Santa Barbara. https://www.presidency.ucsb.edu/.
American State Papers. Library of Congress. https://memory.loc.gov/ammem/amlaw/lwsp.html.
America's Historical Newspapers. Readex.
Avalon Project: Documents in Law, History, and Diplomacy. Yale Law School, Lillian Goldman Law Library. https://avalon.law.yale.edu/.
Despatches from U.S. Consuls in Algiers, Algeria, 1785–1906. General Records of the Department of State, Record Group 59; National Archives and Records Administration (NARA), online version, https://catalog.archives.gov/id/196006730.
Despatches from U.S. Consuls in Tripoli, Libya, 1796–1885. General Records of the Department of State, Record Group 59; National Archives and Records Administration (NARA), online version, https://catalog.archives.gov/id/196006782.
Despatches from U.S. Consuls in Tunis, Tunisia, 1797–1906. General Records of the Department of State, Record Group 59; National Archives and Records Administration (NARA), online version, https://catalog.archives.gov/id/196006899.
The Diaries of Gouverneur Morris Digital Edition, ed. Melanie Randolph Miller. Charlottesville: University of Virginia Press, Rotunda, 2015.

Founders Online. National Archives and Records Administration (NARA). https://founders.archives.gov.

Mediterranean Passports, 1802–1840. Records of the U.S. Customs Service, Record Group 36; Department of the Treasury, Customs Service, Collection District of New Bedford, Massachusetts. Office of the Collector of Customs. 7/31/1789–1913; National Archives and Records Administration (NARA), online version, https://catalog.archives.gov/id/594976.

The Papers of James Madison Digital Edition, ed. J.C.A. Stagg. Charlottesville: University of Virginia Press, Rotunda, 2010. (Cited in text as JM.)

The Papers of Thomas Jefferson Digital Edition, ed. James P. McClure and J. Jefferson Looney. Charlottesville: University of Virginia Press, Rotunda, 2008–2023. (Cited in text as TJ.)

Seventeenth and Eighteenth Century Burney Collection Newspapers, Gale.

Secondary Sources and Published Primary Sources: If a source was consulted primarily online, I have indicated the digital repository from which it came (e.g., Google Books, JSTOR) at the end of the bibliographic entry.

Allison, Robert J. *The Crescent Obscured: The United States and the Muslim World, 1776–1815*. New York: Oxford University Press, 1995.

Baepler, Paul Michel. *White Slaves, African Masters: An Anthology of American Barbary Captivity Narratives*. Chicago: University of Chicago Press, 1999.

Baker, Samuel. *Written on the Water: British Romanticism and the Maritime Empire of Culture*. Charlottesville: University of Virginia Press, 2010. JSTOR.

Battistini, Robert. "Glimpses of the Other before Orientalism: The Muslim World in Early American Periodicals, 1785–1800." *Early American Studies* 8, no. 2 (April 1, 2010): 446–74. JSTOR.

Bauer, Jean. "Republicans of Letters: The Early American Foreign Service as Information Network, 1775–1825." PhD diss., University of Virginia, 2015. ProQuest Dissertations and Theses.

Booker, John. *Maritime Quarantine: The British Experience, c.1650–1900*. Burlington, VT: Ashgate, 2007.

Brings, Hans A. "Navy Medicine Comes Ashore: Establishing the First Permanent U.S. Naval Hospitals." *Journal of the History of Medicine and Allied Sciences* 41, no. 3 (1986): 257–92. JSTOR.

Brunsman, Denver. "Subjects vs. Citizens: Impressment and Identity in the Anglo-American Atlantic." *Journal of the Early Republic* 30, no. 4 (2010): 557–86. JSTOR.

Burke, Edmund III. "The Mediterranean of Modernity: A Longue Durée Perspective." In *The Making of the Modern Mediterranean: Views from the South*, edited by Judith E. Tucker, 67–94. Berkeley: University of California Press, 2019.

Burns, Sarah. "Washington, Jefferson, and Madison: Early Debates over War Powers." In *The Politics of War Powers*, 79–105. Lawrence: University Press of Kansas, 2019.

Cantor, Milton. "A Connecticut Yankee in a Barbary Court: Joel Barlow's Algerian Letters to His Wife." *William and Mary Quarterly* 19, no. 1 (1962): 86–109. JSTOR.

Cathcart, James Leander, and Jane Bancker Newkirk. *The Captives*. La Porte, IN: Herald Print, 1899. Internet Archive.

Chase-Levenson, Alex. *The Yellow Flag: Quarantine and the British Mediterranean World, 1780–1860*. Cambridge: Cambridge University Press, 2020.

Cobbett, Pitt. *Leading Cases and Opinions on International Law: Collected and Digested from English and Foreign Reports, Official Documents, Parliamentary Papers, and Other Sources. With Notes and Excursus, Containing the Views of the Text Writers on the Topics Referred To, Together with Supplementary Cases, Treaties, and Statutes*. London: Stevens & Haynes, 1892. Google Books.

Cohen, Paul A. *History in Three Keys: The Boxers as Event, Experience, and Myth*. New York: Columbia University Press, 1997.

Coleridge, Samuel Taylor. "Essay IX." In *The Collected Works of Samuel Taylor Coleridge*, Volume 4 (Part I): *The Friend*, 251–62. Princeton, NJ: Princeton University Press, 1969.

Dearden, Seton. *A Nest of Corsairs: The Fighting Karamanlis of Tripoli*. London: J. Murray, 1976.

DeClue, Anita, and Billy G. Smith. "Wrestling the 'Pale Faced Messenger': The Diary of Edward Garrigues during the 1798 Philadelphia Yellow Fever Epidemic." *Pennsylvania History: A Journal of Mid-Atlantic Studies* 65 (1998): 243–68. JSTOR.

Dillon, Elizabeth Maddock. "'Slaves in Algiers': Race, Republican Genealogies, and the Global Stage." *American Literary History* 16, no. 3 (October 1, 2004): 407–36. JSTOR.

Dols, Michael W. "The Second Plague Pandemic and Its Recurrences in the Middle East: 1347–1894." *Journal of the Economic and Social History of the Orient* 22, no. 2 (May 1, 1979). 162–89. JSTOR.

Drew, Phillip. *The Law of Maritime Blockade: Past, Present, and Future*. Oxford: Oxford University Press, 2018.

Eicher, Peter D. "To the Shores of Tripoli: James Cathcart, William Eaton, and the First Barbary War." In *Raising the Flag: America's First Envoys in Faraway Lands*, 34–71. Lincoln: University of Nebraska Press, 2018.

Enthoven, Victor. "'From the Halls of Montezuma, to the Shores of Tripoli': Antoine Zuchet and the First Barbary War, 1801–1805." In *Rough Waters: American Involvement with the Mediterranean in the Eighteenth and Nineteenth Centuries*, edited by Silvia Marzagalli, James R. Sofka, and John J. McCusker, 117–34. St. Johns, Newfoundland: International Maritime Economic History Association, 2010.

Estes, J. Worth. *Naval Surgeon: Life and Death at Sea in the Age of Sail*. Canton, MA: Science History Publications, 1998.

Estes, J. Worth, and Billy G. Smith. *A Melancholy Scene of Devastation: The Public Response to the 1793 Philadelphia Yellow Fever Epidemic*. Canton, MA: Science History Publications, 1997.

Farber, Hannah. "Millions for Credit: Peace with Algiers and the Establishment of America's Commercial Reputation Overseas, 1795–96." *Journal of the Early Republic* 34, no. 2 (2014): 187–217. JSTOR.

Folayan, Kola. "Tripoli and the War with the U.S.A., 1801–5." *Journal of African History* 13, no. 2 (1972): 261–70. JSTOR.

Folayan, Kola. "The 'Tripolitan War': A Reconsideration of the Causes." *Africa: Rivista Trimestrale Di Studi e Documentazione Dell'Istituto Italiano per l'Africa e l'Oriente* 27, no. 1 (1972): 615–26. JSTOR.

Fredriksen, John C. "Dale, Richard (1756–1826), Naval Officer." In *American National Biography Online*. Vol. 1. Oxford University Press, February 2000.

Goodin, Brett. *From Captives to Consuls: Three Sailors in Barbary and Their Self-Making across the Early American Republic, 1770–1840*. Baltimore: Johns Hopkins University Press, 2020.

Grainger, John D. *The Amiens Truce: Britain and Bonaparte 1801–1803*. Martlesham, UK: Boydell & Brewer, 2004.

Gregory, Desmond. *Malta, Britain, and the European Powers, 1793–1815*. Vancouver: Fairleigh Dickinson University Press, 1996.

Gregory, Desmond. *Minorca, the Illusory Prize: A History of the British Occupations of Minorca Between 1708 and 1802*. Vancouver: Fairleigh Dickinson University Press, 1990.

"The History of the Plague." In *The Spirit of the English Magazines*, vol. 9, September 1821. Boston: Munroe and Francis, 1821. Google Books.

Humphreys, David. *The Miscellaneous Works of David Humphreys, Late Minister Plenipotentiary . . . : To the Court of Madrid*. New York: T. and J. Swords, 1804. Google Books.

Kidd, Thomas S. "'Is It Worse to Follow Mahomet than the Devil?' Early American Uses of Islam." *Church History* 72, no. 4 (December 1, 2003): 766–90. JSTOR.

Kitzen, Michael. "Money Bags or Cannon Balls: The Origins of the Tripolitan War, 1795–1801." *Journal of the Early Republic* 16, no. 4 (Winter 1996): 601–24. JSTOR.

Kornfeld, Eve. "Crisis in the Capital: The Cultural Significance of Philadelphia's Great Yellow Fever Epidemic." *Pennsylvania History* 51, no. 3 (July 1, 1984): 189–205. JSTOR.

Lambert, Andrew. *Seapower States: Maritime Culture, Continental Empires and the Conflict That Made the Modern World*. New Haven, CT: Yale University Press, 2018.

Lambert, Andrew. *War at Sea in the Age of Sail, 1650–1850*. Washington, DC: Smithsonian, 2005.

Lambert, Frank. *The Barbary Wars: American Independence in the Atlantic World*. New York: Hill & Wang, 2005.

Langley, Harold D. *A History of Medicine in the Early U.S. Navy*. Baltimore: Johns Hopkins University Press, 1995.

Leiner, Frederick C. *The End of Barbary Terror: America's 1815 War against the Pirates of North Africa*. New York: Oxford University Press, 2006.

Leiner, Frederick C. *Millions for Defense: The Subscription Warships of 1798*. Annapolis: Naval Institute Press, 2000.

Leiner, Frederick C. *Prisoners of the Bashaw: The Nineteen-Month Captivity of American Sailors in Tripoli, 1803–1805*. Yardley, PA: Westholme Publishing, 2022.

Long, David F. "William Bainbridge and the Barron-Decatur Duel: Mere Participant or Active Plotter?" *Pennsylvania Magazine of History and Biography* 103, no. 1 (January 1, 1979): 34–52. JSTOR.

Maloney, Linda M. "Bainbridge, William (1774–1833), Naval Officer." In *American National Biography Online*. Vol. 1. Oxford University Press, February 2000.

Maloney, Linda M. "Barron, James (1769–1851), Naval Officer." In *American National Biography Online*. Vol. 1. Oxford University Press, February 2000.

Martin, Maria. *History of the Captivity and Sufferings of Mrs. Maria Martin: Who Was Six Years a Slave in Algiers, Two of Which She Was Confined in a Dark and Dismal Dungeon, Loaded with Irons for Refusing to Comply with the Brutal Request of a Turkish Officer*. Printed for W. Crary, 1807. Google Books.

Marzagalli, Silvia. "American Shipping into the Mediterranean during the French Wars: A First Approach." In *Rough Waters: American Involvement with the Mediterranean in the Eighteenth and Nineteenth Centuries*, edited by Silvia Marzagalli, James R. Sofka, and John J. McCusker, 43–62. St. Johns, Newfoundland: International Maritime Economic History Association, 2010.

Matar, Nabil. *Europe through Arab Eyes, 1578–1727.* New York: Columbia University Press, 2008.

McKee, Christopher. *Edward Preble: A Naval Biography, 1761–1807.* Annapolis: Naval Institute Press, 1996.

McKee, Christopher. "Foreign Seamen in the United States Navy: A Census of 1808." *William and Mary Quarterly* 42, no. 3 (July 1, 1985): 383–93. JSTOR.

McKee, Christopher. *A Gentlemanly and Honorable Profession: The Creation of the U.S. Naval Officer Corps, 1794–1815.* Annapolis: Naval Institute Press, 1991.

McLachlan, K. S. "Tripoli and Tripolitania: Conflict and Cohesion during the Period of the Barbary Corsairs (1551–1850)." *Transactions of the Institute of British Geographers* 3, no. 3 (January 1, 1978): 285–94. JSTOR.

McNeill, J. R. "Yellow Jack and Geopolitics: Environment, Epidemics, and the Struggles for Empire in the American Tropics, 1640–1830." *Review (Fernand Braudel Center)* 27, no. 4 (January 1, 2004): 343–64.

Mikaberidze, Alexander. *The Napoleonic Wars: A Global History.* New York: Oxford University Press, 2020.

Miller, Hunter, ed. *Treaties and Other International Acts of the United States of America.* Vol. 2. Washington, DC: US Government Printing Office, 1931. HathiTrust.

Mooney, James L., ed. *Dictionary of American Naval Fighting Ships.* Washington, DC: Naval Historical Center, 1991.

Morris, Richard Valentine. *A Defence of the Conduct of Commodore Morris during His Command in the Mediterranean.* New York: Printed for J. Riley and Co., 1804. (Cited in text as RVM.)

Naval Documents Related to the Quasi-War between the United States and France. 7 vols. Washington, DC: US Government Printing Office, 1935. American Naval Records Society. (Cited in text as QW.)

Naval Documents Related to the United States Wars with the Barbary Powers. 6 vols. Washington, DC: US Government Printing Office, 1939. American Naval Records Society. (Cited in text as BW.)

Newman, Simon P. "Reading the Bodies of Early American Seafarers." *William and Mary Quarterly* 55, no. 1 (1998): 59–82. JSTOR.

"October Meeting, 1917. A Membership of Fifty Years; Recent Congressional Legislation; Journal of William Loughton Smith, 1790–1791." *Proceedings of the Massachusetts Historical Society* 51 (1917): 1–88. JSTOR.

Onley, James. "Britain's Native Agents in Arabia and Persia in the Nineteenth Century." *Comparative Studies of South Asia, Africa and the Middle East* 24, no. 1 (April 6, 2005): 129–37. JSTOR.

Panzac, Daniel. *The Barbary Corsairs: The End of a Legend, 1800–1820.* Leiden, the Netherlands: Brill, 2005.

Peskin, Lawrence A. "American Exception? William Eaton and Early National Antisemitism." *American Jewish History* 100, no. 3 (2016): 299–317. JSTOR.

Peskin, Lawrence A. *Captives and Countrymen: Barbary Slavery and the American Public, 1785–1816*. Baltimore: Johns Hopkins University Press, 2009.

Peskin, Lawrence A. "The Lessons of Independence: How the Algerian Crisis Shaped Early American Identity." *Diplomatic History* 28, no. 3 (2004): 297–319. JSTOR.

Petrie, Donald A. *The Prize Game: Lawful Looting on the High Seas in the Days of Fighting Sail*. New York: Berkley, 2001.

Prentiss, Charles. *The Life of the Late Gen. William Eaton: Several Years an Officer in the United States' Army, Consul at the Regency of Tunis on the Coast of Barbary, and Commander of the Christian and Other Forces That Marched from Egypt Through the Desert of Barca, in 1805 . . . Principally Collected from His Correspondence and Other Manuscripts*. West Brookfield, MA: E. Merriam & Co., 1813. Google Books.

Register of Officer Personnel, United States Navy and Marine Corps, and Ships' Data, 1801–1807. Office of Naval Records and Library, 1934. American Naval Records Society.

Reid, Chipp. *Intrepid Sailors: The Legacy of Preble's Boys and the Tripoli Campaign*. Annapolis: Naval Institute Press, 2012.

Reid, Chipp. *To the Walls of Derne: William Eaton, the Tripoli Coup, and the End of the First Barbary War*. Annapolis: Naval Institute Press, 2017.

"Report from Select Committee on the Contagious Fever in London." In *Selection of Reports and Papers of the House of Commons: Medical*, 35:1–52, 1836. Google Books.

Rodger, N. A. M. *The Command of the Ocean: A Naval History of Britain, 1649–1815*. New York: W. W. Norton, 2005.

Rojas, Martha Elena. "'Insults Unpunished': Barbary Captives, American Slaves, and the Negotiation of Liberty." *Early American Studies* (fall 2003): 159–86. JSTOR.

Rosenstock, Morton. "The House of Bacri and Busnach: A Chapter from Algeria's Commercial History." *Jewish Social Studies* 14, no. 4 (October 1, 1952): 343–64. JSTOR.

Sayyid-Marsot, Afaf Lutfi. *A History of Egypt: From the Arab Conquest to the Present*, 2nd ed. Cambridge: Cambridge University Press, 2007.

Schroeder, Paul W. *The Transformation of European Politics, 1763–1848*. Oxford: Clarendon Press, 1994.

Seiken, Jeff. "The Reluctant Warrior: Thomas Jefferson and the Tripolitan War, 1801–1805." In *Rough Waters: American Involvement with the Mediterranean in the Eighteenth and Nineteenth Centuries*, edited by Silvia Marzagalli, James R. Sofka, and John McCusker, 185–206. Liverpool: Liverpool University Press, 2010.

Shaler, William. *Sketches of Algiers, Political, Historical, and Civil: Containing an Account of the Geography, Population, Government, Revenues, Commerce, Agriculture, Arts, Civil Institutions, Tribes, Manners, Languages, and Recent Political History of That Country*. Boston: Cummings & Hilliard, 1826. Google Books.

Sheppard, Thomas. *Commanding Petty Despots: The American Navy in the New Republic*. Annapolis: Naval Institute Press, 2022.

Slack, Paul. "The Disappearance of Plague: An Alternative View." *Economic History Review* 34, no. 3 (August 1, 1981): 469–76. JSTOR.

Smith, Gene A. *For the Purposes of Defense: The Politics of the Jeffersonian Gunboat Program*. Cranbury, NJ: Associated University Presses, 1995.

Smith, Walter Burges. *America's Diplomats and Consuls of 1776–1865: A Geographic and Biographic Directory of the Foreign Service from the Declaration of Independence to the*

End of the Civil War. Center for the Study of Foreign Affairs, Foreign Service Institute, US Department of State, 1986. Google Books.

Sofka, James R. "The Jeffersonian Idea of National Security: Commerce, the Atlantic Balance of Power, and the Barbary War, 1786–1805." *Diplomatic History* 21, no. 4 (October 1, 1997): 519–44. JSTOR.

Spencer, William. *Algiers in the Age of the Corsairs*. Norman: University of Oklahoma Press, 1976.

Stein, Tristan. "Passes and Protection in the Making of a British Mediterranean." *Journal of British Studies* 54, no. 3 (2015): 602–31. JSTOR.

Stough, Mulford. "The Yellow Fever in Philadelphia 1793." *Pennsylvania History* 6, no. 1 (January 1, 1939): 6–13. JSTOR.

Symonds, Craig L. *Navalists and Antinavalists: The Naval Policy Debate in the United States, 1785–1827*. Newark: University of Delaware Press, 1980.

Tignor, Robert L. *Egypt: A Short History*. Princeton, NJ: Princeton University Press, 2010.

Toll, Ian W. *Six Frigates: The Epic History of the Founding of the U.S. Navy*. New York: W. W. Norton, 2006.

Trask, David F., Nina N. Bashkina, Nikolai H. Bolhovitinov, John H. Brown, J. Dane Hartgrove, Ivan I. Kudriatsev, Natalia B. Kuznetsova, et al., eds. *The United States and Russia: The Beginning of Relations, 1765–1815*. Washington, DC: US Department of State, 1980. HathiTrust.

Tucker, Glenn. *Dawn Like Thunder: The Barbary Wars and the Birth of the U.S. Navy*. Indianapolis: Bobbs-Merrill, 1963.

Tucker, Judith E. "Piracy of the Eighteenth-Century Mediterranean: Navigating Laws and Legal Practices." In *The Making of the Modern Mediterranean: Views from the South*, edited by Judith E. Tucker, 123–48. Berkeley: University of California Press, 2019.

Tucker, Spencer. *The Jeffersonian Gunboat Navy*. Columbia: University of South Carolina Press, 1993.

Tucker, Spencer. *Stephen Decatur: A Life Most Bold and Daring*. Annapolis: Naval Institute Press, 2005.

White, Joshua M. *Piracy and Law in the Ottoman Mediterranean*. Stanford, CA: Stanford University Press, 2018.

Windler, Christian. "Diplomatic History as a Field for Cultural Analysis: Muslim-Christian Relations in Tunis, 1700–1840." *Historical Journal* 44, no. 1 (2001): 79–106. JSTOR.

Wright, Louis B., and Julia H. Macleod. "William Eaton's Relations with Aaron Burr." *Mississippi Valley Historical Review* 31, no. 4 (1945): 523–36. JSTOR.

Zawadzki, W. H. "Prince Adam Czartoryski and Napoleonic France, 1801–1805: A Study in Political Attitudes." *Historical Journal* 18, no. 2 (1975): 245–77. JSTOR.